DATE DUE

Political Campaigns and Political Advertising

Political Campaigns and Political Advertising

A Media Literacy Guide

Frank W. Baker

Foreword by David Considine

GREENWOOD PRESS
An Imprint of ABC-CLIO, LLC

A B C · C L I O

Santa Barbara, California • Denver, Colorado • Oxford, England

Library of Congress Cataloging-in-Publication Data

Baker, Frank W.
    Political campaigns and political advertising : a media literacy guide / Frank W. Baker ;
    foreword by David Considine.
        p. cm.
    Includes bibliographical references and index.
    ISBN: 978–0–313–34755–9 (hard copy : alk. paper) — ISBN: 978–0–313–34756–6 (ebook)
1. Political campaigns—United States. 2. Advertising, Political—United States. 3. Media literacy—United
States. 4. United States—Politics and government—21st century. I. Title.
JK2281.B33 2009
324.70973—dc22   2008032942

13 12 11 10 09   1 2 3 4 5

This book is also available on the World Wide Web as an eBook.
Visit www.abc-clio.com for details.

ABC-CLIO, LLC
130 Cremona Drive, P.O. Box 1911
Santa Barbara, California 93116-1911

This book is printed on acid-free paper ∞

Manufactured in the United States of America

Every reasonable effort has been made to trace the owners of copyrighted materials in this book, but in some
instances this has proven impossible. The author and publisher will be glad to receive information leading to
more complete acknowledgments in subsequent printings of the book and in the meantime extend their
apologies for any omissions.

Contents

Foreword

So who won? Your guy? The other guy? Some guy? Not your gal? Who cares? What difference does it make? They'll be gone in four or eight years, right? I mean, like, how much harm can one person do? And let's be real here, we all know politics is just so BORING! Ya think? Maybe the real question is not WHO won, but HOW . . . not WHO lost, but WHY—and then, perhaps, it's not so boring. I mean, what does the word even mean?

Boring? Compared to what? To Ludacris, to Paris, or to Britney? They all ended up as part of the 2008 presidential campaign. Part coronation, part celebration, political conventions these days pull out all the bells and whistles necessary to gain and maintain the attention of the audience, whose attention span may well have been diminished over the years by constant exposure to flickering screens. So the Democrats in Denver gave us performers Sheryl Crow, Stevie Wonder, and will.i.am, the hip-hop artist whose tribute to Democratic presidential nominee Barack Obama, "Yes We Can," generated millions of hits on YouTube. And oh, yes, we got fireworks, just like in the Summer Olympic Games in Beijing, China —not to mention the location of the convention finale in Mile High Stadium. More like a symphony than a speech, gushed one commentator, while others noted that Obama's speech owed something to media creator Aaron Sorkin and his fictitious presidents in television's *The West Wing* and the motion picture *The American President.* That's entertainment!

So what about you? Would you rather read a page of print or look at a screen? If you're in your late teens or early twenties and you're reading this book, there may be something radically wrong. So turn off your iPod, you multitasker you, and pay attention.

This is a book about politics, about democracy, citizenship, and literacy. It's full of words. Some of you might think it's full of it (you know what I mean). . . . Either way, it's a book, and its pages are full of words . . . and there's some folks out there who are sure your generation doesn't like to read. Some would argue that you actually have difficulty reading . . . that you prefer to look at pictures. So do I, but are the images that confront us on our laptops, iPods, cell phones, and TVs images that inform and engage us? Or are they weapons of mass distraction that really prevent us from understanding, perhaps even caring about, the wider world around us? Do they hurt or help us to develop what the National Council for the Social Studies refers to as "civic competence?"

Is the ability to seek information from Google or Yahoo enough in this day and age, or do we really need critical viewing, thinking, and listening skills to evaluate and analyze the information we find and that sometimes finds us? Have your teachers and schools provided you with opportunities to apply critical criteria for evaluating broadcast news, political ads, film, TV, and other media, or has most of your school work been based on reading printed pages? Are you so wired, connected, and tuned in at home that sometimes you open the classroom door and hear yourself saying, "like, this place is so yesterday?"

Here's one of the problems you're facing. While two-thirds of secondary school students want to be able to use mobile devices like laptops and cell phones as part of their regular schoolwork, only 15 percent of your school administrators support this idea (according to Project Tomorrow's 2007 Speak Up Survey). There's a generational difference between you, not simply a difference in years but a difference in the way you perceive emerging and converging technologies. For many young people, these tools represent creativity, freedom, personal expression, continuous social networking. Candidate Obama was quick to recognize your interest in these technologies, announcing his choice of vice presidential candidate to his supporters via text message. With 80,000 people packed into Denver's Mile High Stadium and a TV viewing audience larger than the one that watched the opening ceremony of the Olympic Games, Obama's campaign called on the audience to text-message the organization—building a data bank for the fall campaign. Mobile technologies have become a significant part of the political process, and your generation wants them to be part of the educational process, too.

Unfortunately, many adults who make decisions about you view these tools as potential problems that need to be controlled and regulated, which, of course, means controlling and regulating you. Don't you find it curious that a school system that claims to nurture responsible citizenship functions so often as a custodial institution? As James Coleman said of the students in our nation's schools in his 1973 report "Youth: Transition to Adulthood" (also known as the "Coleman Report"), "we deny them responsibility and they become irresponsible." Of course, schools do all of that while claiming to protect you.

I suspect most of you don't believe you need protecting. But don't be so sure. The Pew Internet and American Life Project studies how Americans interact with emerging technologies. Director Lee Ranie has looked at the data regarding your age group and says that you are "not all tech savvy"; that you are "often uncaring" about your own privacy; that someone should "model media literacy [for you] before someone gets into real trouble." So you know how to download, and some of you have amazing hand-eye coordination, but is hands-on the same as heads-on? Want to sample a heads-off moment that received hits from around the world? Visit YouTube and search "Miss Teen USA 2007-South Carolina Answers a Question." Now there's an example of geographical illiteracy for you!

So, are you mad yet? PO'd to the max; ready to drop this book into the nearest trash can? Maybe you've started to wonder, "Who the heck is this guy and where does he get off talking down to me like this?" I hope some of you have gotten to that point. It's a good point. In this day and age, it's crucial to ask questions about all the messages you receive. That means not just comprehending the text (in this book we'll use the word *text* to refer to a page in a magazine, an advertisement, a photograph, a song, or a Web site.) They are all types of media texts, and this book will help you analyze and evaluate the types of texts you are surrounded by daily in the constant glow and flow of information and popular culture.

But understanding media messages—whether in print, image, or multimedia combinations of words, visuals, and sounds—requires more than simply reading or recognizing the content of the messages. It requires understanding the context in which these texts are created and consumed—the way these media messages can influence us, often without our knowledge. If you think that's an exaggeration, just cast your mind back to childhood. Did you ever see a toy advertised on TV that looked so incredible you just begged your parents to get it for you? So they paid $29.95, and when you finally got the thing out of the box—well, you know the story: what a letdown! That dumb toy wasn't anything like it seemed to be on TV. Seeing is not always believing. It's not always true that what you see is what you get. The real question is whether you "get" (I mean, understand) what you see. Think about Dorothy in *The Wizard of Oz* and the discovery she and Toto made about the so-called great and powerful wizard. Or think about the character Neo in *The Matrix* and the lessons he had to learn to distinguish illusion from reality. That's part of the process we call media literacy, and it usually consists of a series of questions. My mate Frank, the author of this book, explores that questioning process with you.

One good starting point is to always begin with a series of questions. WHERE is that message coming from? WHO is sending me that message? WHAT do I know about that individual, industry, or institution that might help me accept or reject what they have to say? Those questions were certainly useful during the 2008 presidential election when *The New Yorker* magazine (July 21, 2008) featured a cartoon on its cover depicting Barack and Michelle Obama in Muslim clothing, in the White House Oval Office, with a portrait of Osama bin Laden hanging on the wall and an American flag burning in the fireplace. The Obama campaign called the image "tasteless and offensive." *Newsweek*'s Jonathan Alter called the image "indisputably harmful." Back at *The New Yorker,* criticism was dismissed as a failure to recognize the satirical nature of the cover. Anyone who understood the liberal nature of the publication would never have believed they intended the cartoon to be taken seriously. But there's a gap between intent, content, and impact. Take the image off the circulation stands, where readers familiar with the magazine's perspective would understand it, move that same image onto conservative news and talk shows (whose readers and viewers are not *The New Yorker*'s target audience), and suddenly the cover reinforces all the suspicions and rumors about Obama that had been circulating on the Internet.

But let's get back to me, one of my favorite subjects (but, of course, not yours). So here you are reading the foreword of this book (unless you skipped to the beginning, which is where the important stuff starts, right?). So far, some of you may not be happy with what I have to say. So other than just blowing my ideas off, dissing everything I have said so far or have yet to say, how might you try to get a handle on my credibility as a source?

So, other than my name, David Considine, what things might help you understand my point of view or perspective so you can understand it and evaluate it? Age is often a good clue. Watch a national network news broadcast (ABC, CBS, and NBC) on almost any evening, and your age group will be largely invisible. Most of the anchors and the reporters do not focus their stories around your age group. They might talk *about you* but they don't talk *to you*. You're not the target audience. I could tell you who the target audience is, but I'll make you think for a moment. Ready? OK, so if I told you most of the commercials during network news are for Beano, bladder control, Preparation H, arthritis medicine, pain killers, and a bunch of chemicals promising relief, security, protection, or prevention in one form or another—who do you think is watching network news?

Yep, folks like me. Baby Boomers, those born between 1946–1964, and even older folks. Now, in my case, that means a 58-year-old guy is writing this to readers whom I fully expect to be some 35 or 40 years younger than I am. Like most people my age, I have accumulated a certain amount of knowledge over the years—I'm not going to claim that it's wisdom—I'll leave that to others. And there are plenty of others. I have spent a lot of time over the years talking in schools and libraries and civic groups and at professional conferences. I've also spent a lot of time listening. It makes a school presentation much more interesting if I get to hear from you, too: if the session is about dialogue, not monologue. I suspect you like that, too, because it makes it interactive and that's one of the things we know your generation is into, whether it's playing video games or instant messaging. By the way, while I come from the Baby Boomer generation, your age group, those born after 1982, are referred to variously as Millennials, the Google Generation, or Generation M (for *media,* or *multitaskers*).

Over the years, I've had the privilege of making presentations throughout the United States as well as in Canada and Mexico. I've conducted a lot of presentations for the Discovery Channel and even for the White House Office of National Drug Control Policy, which is kinda interesting, because I'm not even an American. That's two strikes against me, right; 50-something and foreign, to boot!

Well, like, how foreign am I? Hmmm, I've been here for more than 30 years, but I am not one of you. My son is, my grandchildren are, but I'm a holdout from . . . no, on second thought, I won't tell you. Let's see if I can get you to think for a moment. (I know: that's twice in two pages!) A few paragraphs ago, I referred to the author of this book as my *mate* Frank. I could have been formal and called him my *colleague,* or informal and called him my *buddy.* But in my country, my culture, we use the word *mate.* SO, what country am I from?

If you said Australia, you got it right. So quickly now, right off the top of your head, what images or ideas come to mind when you think of Australia? If you're like most of the audiences I talk to, you went fairly quickly to kangaroos and koalas (hopefully, none of you called them bears). And if you had a good dose of Steve Irwin (aka the *Animal Planet*'s Croc Hunter) while growing up, you might also have imagined spiders and snakes. Crikey!

If you've never been to Australia you have had no direct, firsthand, or immediate experience of the place or people. But you've still got some ideas, some impressions, fragments of information about the place, that may or may not be accurate. The media mediate, and when we have no firsthand experience, those media messages tend to take on greater influence because we have nothing, really, to compare them to. Just recently I had the mother of a nine-year-old girl tell me that her daughter had announced one night that Australia was "not inhabited by human beings!"

My grandkids, Ellen and Wyett, know better. They live in Colorado and get to study Australia in second grade. If you were a student here in North Carolina, you'd have to wait: Australia is studied in seventh grade. But school is not the only place where we learn. It may be the most formal, but we learn all the time, often without knowing it. Our brain just takes it in and absorbs it, layering one image or idea on top of another. So watch enough wildlife programs and you're sure to believe Australia is full of deadly and dangerous reptiles and spiders. The problem with this perception is not that it is untrue, simply that it is unrepresentative. In other words, while it is true to say that there are some deadly snakes in Australia, it is completely untrue to suggest most Australians live in fear of snakes or have regular encounters with them. Surrounded by so many different media messages, thoughtful, competent consumers and citizens need to be able to distinguish fact from falsehood, balance from bias, and information from innuendo.

Which gets us back to you. People are talking. Your ears should be burning. So what are they saying? Some good. Some bad. The messages we are getting about you are mixed. The Intercollegiate Studies Institute has said that the results of a civics survey of college freshmen and seniors suggests a crisis of citizenship and a young generation that does not understand what America stands for. The year 2008 saw the publication of the book *The Dumbest Generation: How the Digital Age Stupefies Young Americans and Jeopardizes our Future.* Another book, *Binge: What Your College Students Won't Tell You,* documented an ethical erosion among students, particularly when it came to cheating—which is on the rise, thanks in no small part to modern technology that makes plagiarism as easy as the point and click of a mouse. Surveyed anonymously and later engaged in open discussion about this subject, my own university students tend to substantiate these claims, explaining that plagiarism happens most of the time because they don't have enough time. One hears the same statement being made by the New Jersey high school students featured in the 2008 *Frontline* (PBS) broadcast "Growing

Up Online." And in the summer of 2008, the publication *Government Technology* featured a cover story about your generation called "The Millennials Are Coming." In part, the article expressed concerns that young people who are entering government agencies have the technical skills but not the ethics to use IT (informational technology) wisely and not breach security practices or policies.

On the other hand, the authors of *Millennials Rising: The Next Great Generation* characterize you as "more affluent, better educated, more ethnically diverse," manifesting "a wide range of positive social habits . . . including a new focus on teamwork, achievement, modesty and good conduct." Way to go! While prior younger generations have often made political noise, they have not developed the habit of showing up on election day. This year, voters in their teens and twenties made a difference for Senator Barack Obama in several primaries, prompting *Time Magazine*'s (2/11/08) cover story "Why Young Voters Care Again." In the disputed 2000 presidential election, decided by court intervention and a handful of votes, only 13 percent of 18- to 29-year-olds reported paying close attention. In 2008 that figure had increased to 71 percent, thanks in no small part to the politicians' use of media and technology to talk to your needs and concerns. The Obama campaign, for example, specifically targeted your age group—especially evangelical and Catholic youth through what they called Young People of Faith.

So what do you think? How do you make sense of the two quite different depictions of YOU that I have discussed? If you've been paying attention, I hope some of you found yourself asking these questions: WHO wrote these reports? WHAT did they leave out? What more do I need to know? HOW might this influence schools and teachers in the way they respond to us? IS this portrait of modern youth the whole picture or just part of the picture? Good questions! Unfortunately, too many young people do not question the sources of information readily available at their fingertips through modern search engines. Researchers who have studied how your age group deals with online searches have concluded that you are in fact a "cut & paste generation" that spends little time evaluating information for accuracy or authority.

As such, it leaves you—and many of us adults as well—susceptible, perhaps even vulnerable, to those who know a lot more or who can push our buttons with tools and techniques most of us have never heard of. In the world of advertising, for example, that might mean the use of VALS (values and lifestyles), psychographics, PRIZMS (Potential Rating Index by ZIP Market System), eyescanners, T-scopes, analog machines, and neuromarketing, all carefully utilized to research us and to exploit the physiology of the human eye, directing our eyes to a page or a screen and then using colors, words, and images to reach and influence us on an emotional and psychological level that we are often completely unaware of.

That's why former Vice President Al Gore, writing in *An Inconvenient Truth* (2006) warns that "our democracy is in danger of being hollowed out" . . . by "a new generation of media Machiavellis." Software like Photoshop has made it easier to manipulate images, to mislead, or worse. And it's not just young people who are susceptible to these high-tech tricks. In the summer of 2008, prestigious newspapers and media outlets in this country and abroad featured a photograph of four missiles being launched by Iran. The images were distributed by the respected international news service Agence France-Presse, and many Western news outlets accepted the legitimacy of the image based on the source. However, the French news agency was not the origin of the image: the photograph originated from the Sepah News, the media organization of Iran's Revolutionary Guard—in other words, an agency with propaganda goals. What was subsequently discovered was that the image had been doctored—Photoshopped, as they say. In reality, three—not four—missiles were launched. So what's the difference, you say? Obviously, one missile. More importantly, the gate-keeping role of the media, the process of determining what stories are or are not in play, has become compromised by commercial pressures, an increasing reliance on image-driven stories, and the potential these new technologies offer to those who would deceive us.

That's where this book comes in. It is an important book, a timely book that offers you readers the skills, strategies, and ideas to help you recognize, read—and yes, even resist—potentially biased, distorted, or inaccurate media messages about political campaigns. No matter how book-bright you may be, no matter how strong your GPA might be, unless you have had some education about mass media, including its form, content, language, ideology, structure, and organization, you probably will be unaware of just how pervasive and persuasive modern media can be.

That's one reason why groups such as the Partnership for 21st Century Skills has identified media literacy as a competency all citizens need. But the United States is behind much of the Western world when it comes to not only articulating this in state and national curriculum standards but also meaningfully implementing it and integrating it throughout the curriculum. Decades ago, Australia, Canada, the United Kingdom, New Zealand, and other nations introduced media literacy (sometimes called media studies or media education) to the public school curriculum.

It's important to note that the goals of media literacy include promoting critical thinking skills and developing healthy skepticism—not cynicism. Pick a single story or event in the news and try to analyze and evaluate not only that incident but also the way the media covered the story, the reason for this type of coverage, the things the media left out, and alternative ways of covering the story.

A good way to get a feel for this process is to check out the National Public Radio (NPR) program *On the Media*. It airs weekends, but you can access it online at http://www.onthemedia.org/. You can download segments of the broadcast, which usually run for no longer than six or seven minutes. Find a story that interests you and consider the key questions the broadcast raises about the coverage and its potential impact. Do this two or three times and you'll begin to discover, when it comes to modern media, there really is more to it than meets either the eye or the ear—whether addressing the Olympic Games in China, the 2008 presidential election, the killings at Virginia Tech University, or a major natural disaster such as Hurricane Katrina.

It's also important to understand that media literacy involves much more than reading other people's media messages. Literacy is not just the ability to read; it's also the ability to write. Same thing goes for media literacy—it involves creating, not just consuming or comprehending, media messages. And your generation is already doing that. Every study points to the fact that people your age are making movies, videos, music, photos—which you post and share with friends, some of whom you have only ever met online. Sadly, many of you tend to engage in those types of activities at home rather than at school. Wouldn't school be cool if you could use those skills and social networks as part of your learning process?

The National School Boards Association thinks it would. They believe you need to be given those opportunities and said so in their position paper "Creating and Connecting" (2007). So if your school has equipment and facilities but won't let you engage in these types of creative activities, maybe you could develop a dialogue or a debate or a petition to try and get the school administration to recognize creative approaches to media and technology across the curriculum. How you go about this is important. It's actually an exercise in democracy, but you will be more successful if you engage rather than enrage, and if you request rather than demand. And don't try too much too quickly. Think about change as evolutionary, not just revolutionary, so policies and practices might happen gradually and incrementally. Maybe the thing to do is to start with a pilot program as a test case to demonstrate that you are responsible enough to have some policies relaxed, changed, or eliminated.

This is a cooperative venture, and you need to work together with all the different constituencies involved—what we call stakeholders. That is how communities function to bring about change, and that is where democracy is not just learned, but lived.

I learned about democracy in two profoundly different ways. At school I was taught about British and Australian parliamentary traditions. I had a natural interest in that, since my grandfather served as a Labor member of Parliament. My father was an active union member, and I learned that workers united together could improve conditions and wages, sometimes through legal arbitration and sometimes through strikes and other industrial action. In Australia industrial action was not limited to blue-collar unions but was something professional organizations and associations, including schoolteachers, routinely engaged in—and they still do.

My schools also taught me that, despite the lip service they paid to democracy in the curriculum, in reality I had few rights. They imposed school uniforms on us and punished variations or deviations from the dress code. Not content to regulate our clothing, they also wanted to regulate our appearance—in particular the length of our hair. While girls were constantly regulated in terms of the length of their skirts, we boys were monitored for the length of our hair. The idea that a principal or teacher would line boys up in a row and actually measure the distance from their shirt collars to their hair or check the length of a fringe seems preposterous today, but it happened. I was actually demoted, moved back two grade levels because I would not cut my hair. Then I was told I had to wear a bow in it. Then, to become more confrontational, I dyed it. I was what the administration in the 1960s termed a "hair rebel." Later, when I became a teacher, I supported the hair rebels of the 1970s. A generation of 20-something teachers who had resisted and resented what schools had done to them just a few years earlier, we were able to abolish school uniforms.

These may not be issues that you value today, but when I talk with people your age, I am surprised to discover how negatively many of you say you feel about politics. That is, of course, until I actually bring the discussion down to the micro or local level, to issues that have meaning for you. Invariably those issues revolve around a sense of fairness, equality, and justice. At times they are the issues and incidents that attract national attention, such as the case of the so-called Jena Six in Louisiana. If long hair was an issue for boys of my generation, then for many young men and boys today, the issue is sagging jeans. In fact some towns have actually passed ordinances and imposed fines on young men who wear their pants so low that they expose underwear. The claim is that such a fashion statement is indecent and constitutes a public threat. While many young people regard this as an attack on hip hop and their freedom of expression, the town elders passing such regulations get away with it because they have the power.

From my point of view, incidents like this can become useful catalysts and conversation starters for exploring our rights, roles, and responsibilities. The same holds true for cell phones, iPods, and other technologies. If you're in a public place where other people can hear your conversation, is it private or public? Can you use the same language in a public place that you would use behind closed doors, including the doors of your car? And speaking of cars—if you do use a cell phone while driving, should you be subjected to higher insurance rates than drivers who are not distracted by cell phones while driving?

One state legislature actually debated imposing fines on pedestrians who used iPods, since they constituted a potential hazard for drivers. Now I, for one, fully support that approach, but then again, I come from a country that regulates the use of cell phones in automobiles. Maybe Australia's history as a penal colony explains Australians' willingness to accept more restrictions or regulations in our lives. It might also mean that Australia strikes a better balance between rights and responsibilities. I have always suspected that Americans are much quicker to assert their rights than to exercise their responsibilities—after all, most of the time, barely 50 percent of eligible voters actually cast a vote.

In my homeland voter turnout on election day—especially for federal parliamentary elections—is in the high 90-percent range. So how come? Are we better citizens? Is it because our elections are held on Saturday, when more people have the day off, compared with your country, which votes on Tuesday? Perhaps. But it might have something to do with the fact that it's illegal not to vote. Australia makes voting compulsory, and if you don't show up at the polling booth to have your name crossed off the roll, we fine you! How's that . . . a compulsory democracy! Would you like to see that system used in this country? What would be the benefits, and what would you see as the disadvantages?

I, for one, never resented being required to vote. It was a rite of passage that I eagerly awaited. In those days you had to be 21 to cast a vote. My first vote was cast on December 2, 1972. It brought down a government that had been in power 23 years. Of course, it wasn't my vote alone, but thousands, millions of Australians—many of whom had given up on the idea of change. The next day, Gough Whitlam, our new Labor Prime Minister moved quickly to get conscientious objectors who had resisted the Vietnam War released from jail. After an election, change comes quickly in my homeland. In November 2007, Australia had another election. Faced with the choice between a new, untested leader or continuing the conservative course of Prime Minister John Howard, the electorate shrugged off the risk and went for change. They got it: our first woman Deputy Prime Minister, the first woman Governor General, and a formal national apology to our indigenous people from Prime Minister Kevin Rudd and the new Labor government.

As I write this, America faces a historic election. Whichever party wins, the face of the new administration that takes office in January 2009 will be a face strikingly different from the administrations that have gone before: either we will have our first African American president or our first woman vice president. If your candidate prevailed, congratulations. If your candidate lost, don't give up hope or retreat. If your candidate was *None of the Above,* don't *wait for* the right candidate to come along—*work for it.* If you stay home and tune out, we all lose. Democracy cannot become a spectator sport with you in the bleachers. In his party nomination acceptance speech, Senator Obama located you in the process. "This election," he said, "has never been about me, it's about you." His campaign rival, now his campaign supporter, Senator Hillary Rodham Clinton, told the convention delegates the same thing: "It comes down to you." And so it does. For the health of this democracy, we need your caring, your commitment, your creativity, and your communication skills. This book and the ideas in it will serve you well in your role as informed responsible citizens.

I wish you well.

David M. Considine
Appalachian State University
Boone, North Carolina
September 2008

Acknowledgments

Writing this book was one of the hardest things I have ever done. I truly enjoyed the research part; it was the writing that I found difficult. This book started out as an outline delivered to the folks at Greenwood Press, who had their librarian/consultant team review it and provide feedback. To them, I first say, thanks.

The book grew out of a Web site I developed some years ago: The Role of The Media In Politics (http://www.frankwbaker.com/media_politics). At the time I created the site, I was most interested in the 30-second political advertisement. While working for the South Carolina Educational Television network, I even took advantage of their distance learning capabilities and taught a one-hour course on political media and persuasion for high school students. To the folks at SC-ETV, I thank you.

I regularly presented on this topic at the South Carolina Council for the Social Studies annual teachers' conference. My workshops were always well attended and that just told me that teachers really wanted and needed this kind of information. (Teachers also told me that this topic just wasn't adequately covered in their textbooks.) Thanks to SCCSS.

In 2006, Time Warner Cable-Ohio invited me to be their keynoter at the Columbus Metropolitan Club. To my pleasure, teachers were also in the audience that day. I talked about the importance of critical thinking and viewing in an election year. Thanks to TWC and its national organization, Cable in the Classroom.

I also need to thank the many media educators who I have admired and who have taught me so much. Canadians John Pungente, Chris Worsnop, and Barry Duncan are well-respected leaders in the field, as are Neil Andersen and Mike Gange. The work of Barrie McMahon in Australia and Geoff Lealand in New

Zealand cannot be overlooked. And in the United Kingdom, Len Masterman, David Buckingham, and all of the wonderful professionals who are part of the British Film Institute have provided tremendous models for how media education should and could be done in the United States. Lastly, my colleagues in America have given me much guidance and support: David Considine (Appalachian State University), Cyndy Scheibe and Chris Sperry (Project Look Sharp), Marieli Rowe (National Telemedia Council), Robert Kubey (Rutgers University), and Elizabeth Thoman (Center for Media Literacy).

Thanks also to my editor Sandy Towers for her unending devotion to this project and providing guidance, suggestions, and recommendations—all of which made the book so much better.

Finally, I must acknowledge my family: my sons Bryan and Josh, my step-daughter Paige, and my tremendously supportive wife, Melanie. To her I say: you deserve so much credit—for putting up with my long hours in the library, my used-book purchases, and my time away from you. I hope you think it was worth it.

Frank W. Baker
March 2008

Timeline: A History of the Media and Politics

1913   Woodrow Wilson becomes the first president to hold regular news conferences in the White House. Reporters gather in the East Room.

1924   For the first time, the presidential election is reported on radio.

1928   Radio plays a role in the presidential election for the first time. Both candidates buy radio ads. Herbert Hoover defeats Alfred E. Smith.

1930s   Franklin Delano Roosevelt becomes the first American president to make extensive use of radio as a means of direct communication with the voters.

1932   Twenty million American homes have radio.

1933   FDR broadcasts the first of what become known as his "fireside chats."

1934   Communications Act of 1934 requires broadcasters to allow political candidates "equal air time."

1939   FDR becomes the first president to appear on television.

1940   AT&T transmits the 1940 Republican convention from Philadelphia to New York. There it is televised to a few hundred receivers from RCA's experimental station.

1942   Thirty million American homes have radio.

1948   TV networks broadcast their first live reports (June 21). Fewer than 500,000 TV sets exist in America. Harry Truman campaigns cross-country on a "whistle stop" tour.

1949   Federal Communications Commission adopts the "Fairness Doctrine."

1950   Ninety million radio sets and 10 million TV sets are in use in U.S. homes.

1951   AT&T completes construction of the first transcontinental broadband communications network. President Harry Truman's September 4 address to the Japan Peace Treaty Conference is the first live transcontinental television broadcast.

1952   Nineteen million American homes have TV sets. The Republican Party's "Eisenhower Answers America" airs; it is considered the first presidential campaign TV commercial. Vice-presidential candidate Richard Nixon uses a nationally televised address (the "Checkers Speech") to defend himself against corruption charges.

1953   Dwight D. Eisenhower's first inauguration is the first to be covered live on television. Senator John F. Kennedy and Mrs. Kennedy, newly married, are interviewed live by Edward R. Murrow on the CBS series *Person to Person.*

1954   Regular color TV broadcasts begin.

1955   Eisenhower holds the first televised presidential press conference (January 19). Actor and future U.S. President Ronald Reagan becomes host of *General Electric Theater,* a long-running CBS series (1953–1961) in which many well-known television and Broadway stars appear.

1956   Candidate Adlai E. Stevenson tries out TV in his second presidential run.

1958   Videotape delivers color.

1960   Televised Kennedy-Nixon presidential campaign debates show TV's power. Theodore White publishes *The Making of the President, 1960.*

1962   Bell Labs's Telstar 1 satellite transmits image across the Atlantic Ocean.

1963   Television covers the assassination of John F. Kennedy, the swearing-in of Vice President Lyndon B. Johnson as president, and, in live footage, the murder of suspect Lee Harvey Oswald.

1964   Top advertising agency Doyle Dane Bernbach produces historic Daisy Ad campaign for LBJ. (See "The Daisy Spot," Chapter 2.)

1965   Most TV broadcasts are in color.

1966   Innovative ads for Governor Nelson A. Rockefeller are credited with swaying the New York governor's race.

1968   Joe McGinniss publishes *The Selling of the President,* profiling the marketing of Richard M. Nixon's candidacy. Nixon creates the White House's Office of Communication. Nixon makes a cameo appearance on NBC's *Laugh In* variety program.

1973   Unprecedented gavel-to-gavel coverage on the major TV networks of the first session of the Congressional Watergate hearings (May 17 to August 7).

1980   Jimmy Carter's election campaign ads stress hardworking leadership.

1984   Reagan perfects nostalgic, soft-sell approach in political commercials.

1987   Half of all U.S. homes with TV have cable. The Fairness Doctrine is repealed.

1988   George H. W. Bush's election campaign ads attack opponent Michael Dukakis; "Willie Horton" ad airs.

1992   Independent candidate Ross Perot uses "infomercial" approach in presidential campaign. Political parties and candidates begin to use the Internet. Candidate Bill Clinton dons sunglasses and plays the sax on the late-night TV *Arsenio Hall Show.*

1994	Morphing becomes a popular technique in political commercials.
1996	Clinton perfects "compassion" ads.
1998	Unprecedented spending on ads in the California governor's race provokes a negative reaction from the electorate. "Issue ads" produced by interest groups influence elections.
2002	Congress passes McCain-Feingold campaign finance reform law.
2003	In 5–4 vote, the U.S. Supreme Court upholds McCain-Feingold campaign finance reform law.
2004	The dynamic of the presidential election campaign is changed by ads run by the "527" interest group, Swift Boat Veterans for Truth, challenging Democratic candidate Senator John Kerry's Vietnam War record. GOP and Democratic parties allow select groups of bloggers to report live from their conventions.
2007	U.S. Supreme Court lifts restrictions on "issue ads" placed by special interest groups, declaring a section of the McCain-Feingold campaign finance reform law unconstitutional. Republican and Democratic candidates raise millions via online donations. YouTube.com and CNN solicit video-submitted questions for presidential candidates to respond to during televised debates. MySpace.com and YouTube.com devote space to presidential candidates' media messages.
2008	An estimated 38 million people watched both Senator John McCain and Senator Barack Obama's political convention acceptance speeches; 56.5 million people watched the third (and final) McCain/Obama presidential debate; and 78.6 million people watched the prime time election coverage on TV, the night of November 4, 2008.

Introduction

An enlightened citizenry is indispensable for the proper functioning of a republic.
—Thomas Jefferson

The Jeffersonian ideal of an informed electorate necessitates media literacy education. . . . With the incredible rise of the internet and the unedited nature of many web sites, students need more than ever to learn how to assess the validity and credibility of the information to which they are exposed.
—Robert Kubey, Director,
Center for Media Studies, Rutgers University

We created the first fully advertised presidency in U.S. history.
—Dick Morris, media consultant to
President Bill Clinton

Without an understanding of media grammars, we cannot hope to achieve a contemporary awareness of the world in which we live.
—Marshall McLuhan

Who did you support in the election for president of the United States? How did you decide who to support or vote for? Where did you get the information you needed about the candidates and the issues? Was TV the main source of your information? How about blogs, or Comedy Central's *The Daily Show with Jon Stewart,* or newspapers and magazines? What deciding factors were most important to you in choosing the right person for the job?

The election of the president of the United States is a tremendously important event. Every four years, a large campaign machine resumes (some say it never quits!). But this machine does not run on gas; it runs on money. Money is used primarily to buy media time in order to get a candidate's message in front of a large target audience—those people who are the most likely to go to the polls on election day. And the machine employs hundreds of people, all with their own specialties.

One of a candidate's key players is the media adviser/consultant. As the experts in charge of their candidate's media messages, consultants spend many hours making sure the message seen by potential voters looks and sounds both persuasive and appealing.

Today, the image is considered as important as the words delivered by politicians, if not more so. Controlling the message is the marching order for politicians and their consultants. Increasingly, that message is visual. But most Americans don't understand how to comprehend visual messages. Teaching the "language of media" is not in the curriculum of most American schools. But it should be. Visually elaborate and carefully orchestrated campaign events and political advertising are now constructed to appeal to our emotions, not our intellect.

This is a book about presidential campaigns and advertising. It is also about the powerful role money plays in today's elections. And it is about media literacy.

Contemporary advertising, in some form or another, has been around for more than 150 years, but it is only in the past 50 years that television has become the central player in communicating candidates' messages. Why? Television reaches a large audience, all of whom are watching at the same time. (The 2009 Super Bowl football game was seen on television by an estimated 98 million American viewers.) Even with the growing popular appeal of watching television programs on the Internet, broadcast TV remains the medium of choice for candidates.

Money is central in campaign advertising. For the 2008 election cycle, according to the ad tracking company PQ, political advertising on broadcast or cable TV, radio, newspapers, magazines, the Internet, and other outlets was expected to soar to $4.5 billion, an all-time high.[1] Candidates must raise millions of dollars to run their campaigns and purchase advertising time on radio and TV stations and cable networks. When it comes to reaching the voters via TV, the candidates' consultants have become experts at placing ads during specific programs in order to reach key target audiences (for example, women ages 24–44). Who wins when candidates purchase ad time? The media! Increasingly though, the Internet has become a powerful communication tool used by all politicians. One prediction had it that online political advertising would total only $20 million in 2008.[2] Still the Web is popular with candidates: at the start of the 2008 presidential election cycle, every candidate's Web site offered voters an opportunity to contribute online.

Media literacy is a phrase foreign to many people. Most of us have never been taught how to "read the media," to understand how images and sound are manipulated to achieve desired results. In the 21st century, being media literate means understanding not only how a message is constructed, but also who its target audience is, who benefits from it, and who makes money from it. To be media literate is to understand the process behind the making of the message and to have the capability to see through the "spin" techniques used to persuade or influence us.

Asking questions is at the heart of media literacy. So throughout this text, the reader will be asked to consider some critical thinking questions and be asked to apply them to campaign media messages. The goal is to help you to become enlightened, more educated, and wiser voters—and healthier skeptics.

Future voters must be knowledgeable about not only who is running for president of the United States, but also how candidates use the media to get and keep voter attention. Learning how to deconstruct the slick, sophisticated political campaign media messages is an important and life-long skill.

Eighty-one percent of Americans say they get most of their information from television.[3] But while many of us still rely on television as our primary source of information, television has its limitations, not the least of which is time. The three national network TV newscasts (ABC, CBS, and NBC) are still 30 minutes in length, but when one takes commercial time into account, there are really only 22 minutes of actual news. On any given night during a presidential race, a reporter may have about two minutes to tell the story. Of that two minutes, a news consumer may actually hear from the candidate for less than 10 seconds.

During the 2007–2008 campaign cycle, the media and public's apparently insatiable appetite for celebrity news (for example, about Paris Hilton, Britney Spears, Lindsay Lohan, and so on) competed for attention with legitimate information about the Iraq War, the immigration debate, and the race for the White House, among other issues.

Another major criticism of the media during election campaigns is that it focuses too much on the "horse race." Media researchers have continually discovered that the mainstream media report "who's first in the polls" and "who's raised the most money" instead of concentrating on exploring in-depth those issues most important to American voters, such as health care, education, and the economy.

In the 21st century, the challenge for those seeking real news and information about the candidates and their positions is where to find accurate, reliable information. For all of us, the rise of blogs, wikis, and other digital media resources, for example, create an ever-stronger need for dependable information and media literacy.

In this book, the reader will be challenged to think critically about politics and the media. A list of media literacy concepts and critical thinking questions are scattered throughout the text. Relevant quotes from experts, politicians, and the media are used to emphasize issues. After reading the text, and considering the role of media in politics, will you believe that media literacy is important and vital in the 21st century?

A democratic civilization will save itself only if it makes the language of the image into a stimulus for critical reflection—not an invitation for hypnosis.

—Umberto Eco, Italian philosopher and author

Candidates must have razzle-dazzle. Boring is the fatal label. Programs and concepts that cannot be collapsed into a slogan or a thirty second sound bite go largely unheard and unremembered, for what the modern campaign offers in length, it lacks in depth.

—Hedrick Smith, political reporter and columnist

Many people will watch videos and use traditional media like TV to acquire political information about the candidates, but they also are going to the Internet and using social networking sites to see who people they know support. The information gleaned from their social networks may be the information they find most credible and persuasive.

—Dr. Paul Haridakis, associate professor of
Communication Studies at Kent State University

NOTES

1. "Political Spending Expected to Soar in 2008 Election Cycle," *Editor & Publisher,* http://www.editorandpublisher.com/eandp/news/article_display.jsp?vnu_content_id=100 3681885 (accessed December 6, 2007).

2. Katy Bachman, "Candidates Favor Old Media," *Adweek,* January 23, 2008, http://www.adweek.com/aw/national/article_display.jsp?vnu_content_id=1003700427.

3. Pew Internet and American Life Project, "How Americans Used the Internet after the Terror Attack," http://www.pewinternet.org/pdfs/PIP_Terror_Report.pdf.

1

Media Literacy: Understanding the Meaning behind the Messages

Media education is both essential to the exercising of our democratic rights and a necessary safeguard against the worst excesses of media manipulation for political purposes.

—Len Masterman, *Teaching Media* (1985)

At the heart of media literacy is the principle of inquiry.

—Elizabeth Thoman, Center for Media Literacy (1999)

Media literacy has considerable potential as long as it involves an explanation of how the media system actually works, and leads people to want to work toward a better system.

—Robert W. McChesney (1999)

Every day, experts say, we come in contact with between 1,000 and 3,000 media messages, including advertising. From the moment we wake up in the morning until we go to sleep at night, we will have been exposed to media messages on the radio, TV, Internet, cell phones, on clothes we wear, on the roads we drive, even at school. There is almost nowhere we can go anymore to escape advertising.

Advertising continues to invade every possible space: everything from a pregnant woman selling ad space on her stomach to product placements in films . . . if you can dream it, advertisers are probably thinking right now about how they can use it to get our attention.

In essence, we are all target markets for some product or service. When we were in elementary school, the toy advertising market was interested in us; when we were in middle school, the clothing and fad industries were interested in us; and

Almost any newsstand offers a dizzying array of magazines purveying everything from lengthy news analysis to celebrity gossip. (Courtesy of Frank W. Baker)

in high school, we were the target for MP3 players, blue jeans, shoes, video games, cell phones; college . . . the sky is the limit.

Think about the hundreds of different magazines at your local bookstore or newsstand: there are titles for men, women, teens, and children; for hunters, photographers, artists, writers, film enthusiasts, coin collectors, and many, many more. They cover topics such as news, fashion, music, sports, decorating, entertainment, leisure, and business. Each publication is aimed at a specific demographic: people the publishers know are interested. Each magazine has its own niche audience (and enough advertisers who keep it in print).

What do you know about advertising? Perhaps you have learned about some of the common techniques of persuasion:

Technique:	What it says:	Examples:
Bandwagon	Everybody is doing it—why not you?	Everybody is getting the new and improved teeth whitening toothpaste.
Everyday people (aka "plain folks")	People like you shop here; shouldn't you?	Join your neighbor at the new Wal-Mart.
Testimonials	Famous personalities use a product or service; you connect with this person, product, or idea.	Tiger Woods loves to drive a Buick.
Fear	There is some potential risk to you if you don't heed this message.	A car crash is shown in a "buckle your seatbelt" campaign.

You might have even had a school or college assignment in which you were required to create or produce an ad using these persuasive techniques in some form of media technology.

What you were doing involved what we now call "media literacy." To use advertising as the example: if you studied techniques of persuasion, you were most likely involved in analyzing or learning how to deconstruct (take apart) or "read" ads. If you created your own ad, you experimented with creating and producing it.

MEDIA LITERACY = ANALYSIS + PRODUCTION

Analysis

To analyze a media message, one must break it down, or deconstruct it, to study its component parts in order to understand how it was constructed. Newspapers and magazines, for example, rely on words, photographs, and other graphic images. So understanding print media involves analyzing words and images. Television and motion pictures—the moving images—involve visual and aural techniques. The Internet combines the elements of both print and nonprint media.

Many of us have never been trained to analyze an advertisement, television program, movie, or Web page. Media studies, as the subject is called in some colleges and universities, helps students appreciate the importance of media analysis techniques. Understanding these techniques is part of knowing how to "read the media" and how to appreciate the "languages of media." In this text, the reader is provided guidance on how to analyze campaign photos, campaign events, and political advertisements.

Production

Producing media involves hands-on creation of media messages. Producing media might mean writing a news story or blog, creating your own podcast, or simply making your own photograph or video. Experts know that when students are given the opportunity to create media, it allows them to comprehend and appreciate more fully the messages they come in contact with every day. Today, more schools *are* acquiring the tools which allow young people to become media makers themselves. We know that young people not only like to create media, but also like to see their productions shared with their peers. This fact alone explains the explosion in popularity of user-generated Web sites such as YouTube and Flickr, among many others. "Digital storytelling" (using digital tools to tell stories) has also become popular in schools because it links traditional narrative storytelling with the use of visual and media production.

MEDIA LITERACY IN THE UNITED STATES AND CANADA

Because media literacy is relatively new in the United States, many media educators have looked to Canada for guidance, for example, where media education, as it is also called, has been mandated in most of the provinces since the 1970s. Millions of students in Canada, the United Kingdom, and Australia, to name a few countries, have already received media education through formal instruction in school.

In Canada, media literacy has been defined as follows:

develop(ing) an informed and critical understanding of the nature of mass media, the techniques used by them, and the impact of these techniques. More specifically, [media literacy education] aims to increase the students' understanding and enjoyment of how the media work, how they produce meaning, how they are organized, and how they construct reality. Media literacy also aims to provide students with the ability to create media products.[1]

In U.S. schools, teaching media literacy has slowly caught on with more and more educators. A 1999 survey found "elements of media literacy" in almost every state's K–12 educational teaching standards, in the curricular standards for English and Language Arts, Social Studies/History, and Health.[2] In fact, media literacy is now regarded as one of the important 21st-century skills young people should learn in order to become attractive to employers in our global society.[3]

STARTING POINT FOR APPLYING MEDIA LITERACY TO MEDIA MESSAGES

In order to understand how media work, you need a framework: a lens through which to study and comprehend the process. One popular framework was produced and promoted by the Center for Media Literacy. Its "core concepts" and "key questions," derived from earlier ideas developed in the United Kingdom, Australia, and Canada, have been adopted and followed throughout North America.

Media Literacy's Core Concepts

1. All media messages are constructed.
2. Media messages are constructed using a creative language with its own set of rules.
3. Different people experience the same media message differently.
4. Media have embedded values and points of view.
5. Most media messages are organized to gain profit and/or power.[4]

Let's apply these core concepts to political media messages:

Core concepts:	Application to media and politics:
1. All media messages are constructed.	A media message doesn't just happen: somebody creates it. From the morning newspaper to the evening news to the Web site to the political event or ad, all are constructions. Each medium employs a gatekeeper whose job it is to decide what is used and what is not. Photographers by necessity use a viewfinder to frame images; political campaign advisers control the photographer's position in order to ensure that the best images of the candidate are captured; TV news people shoot and then edit footage of campaign events. News producers select which stories and images are used and which are not.

2. Media messages are constructed using a creative language with its own set of rules.	Radio depends on sound; TV depends on pictures; newspaper depends on print and images; the Internet utilizes many media. Filmmakers oftentimes use visual symbolism. When designing a message, a producer strongly considers the characteristics of the medium—which of its techniques are most effective, all designed to influence those who consume it.
3. Different people experience the same media message differently.	While you may think or feel one way after seeing or/hearing a media message, another person (e.g., of a different age, gender, or ethnicity) probably sees and understands the same message completely differently. This is because we all have various frames of reference, backgrounds, experiences, and education.
4. Media have embedded values and points of view.	Because all media messages are constructed, choices have to be made. These choices inevitably reflect the values, attitudes and points of view of those doing the constructing. Political campaign strategists decide how their candidate will be portrayed by attempting to control as many elements of the presentation as possible. They want you, the viewer, to feel good about their candidate so that you will vote for him or her.
5. Most media messages are organized to gain profit and/or power.	All media—and media messages—are designed to make money: pure and simple. If it doesn't make money, it disappears. Money drives the political process, too, since candidates must raise millions to purchase advertising time on radio and television. By examining who funds campaigns and the media messages they produce, we also begin to understand how the media profits during the campaign for the presidency.

Every medium uses a variety of techniques designed to evoke some kind of unconscious response from us, the viewers. The colors, the music, the layout, the editing, the selection of actors and their clothes and expressions—all should be considered when we examine and deconstruct media messages. Together these are generally known as the "languages of media." When a political advertisement is created, an enormous amount of time, energy (and money) is spent considering how the audience will react to the package as a whole.

MEDIA LITERACY AND CRITICAL THINKING

Media literacy also involves understanding not only how a message was made, but also who made it, for what purpose, using which techniques, to achieve what desired outcomes. Media literacy, then, is concerned, among other things, with encouraging us to ask questions about media messages: a healthy skepticism, asking the right questions and knowing where to get the answers, is an important step to becoming media literate.

So what is media literacy? It is a set of critical thinking and viewing skills one applies to media messages. Media are institutions that employ hundreds of people who are specialists in different tasks. Think about a newspaper for a moment. How does it get constructed? Every day, reporters are assigned to cover and write stories. Photographers take companion photographs. Editors refine stories, letters, and photos. Someone is responsible for selling ad space. Someone else must design the paper and lay out its pages or screens. Others are in charge of printing and delivering the paper. You get the idea. But do you know who owns your newspaper? How might that affect its coverage of events? How much does the newspaper company charge for advertising? What stories or editorials does the paper leave out, and why? Where can you go to read information that you can't find locally? These are also important questions to ask as a media literate citizen.

Over time, media educators have created a list of critical thinking questions that can be applied to any text, whether it's a photograph, news story, commercial, or political campaign message.

Media Literacy's Key Questions

1. Who created this message?
2. What techniques are used by the creator to attract attention?
3. How might different people understand this message differently than I do?
4. What lifestyles, values, points of view are represented in, or omitted from, this message?
5. Why was this message sent?[5]

Here are the key questions as applied to political media messages:

Key (critical thinking) questions:	Applications to media and politics:
1. Who created this message?	This question goes to *authorship:* who is responsible for writing, producing, or paying for this message? For example, can you determine from watching an ad who put it together? The message may be for the candidate or a cause, but do you really know *who* created it? In political campaigns, highly skilled consultants are usually the ones behind creating the messages. Increasingly, independent groups also raise millions of dollars to create issue advocacy ads.
2. What techniques are used by the creator to attract attention?	This question gets to the specific *method* used by producers to make a message attractive and believable. For a political event, it might be music or use of banners and colors. For a political advertisement, it is persuasive language (words), images, and sounds.
3. How might different people understand this message differently than I do?	This question is aimed at *audience:* who is reading, listening and/or watching; what do they know or not know about the topic, person, or event? An older person probably interprets a message differently from someone from Generation M. As we will see, many candidates first decide who (in terms of age, gender, political persuasion) they are trying to reach and tailor the message for them. Then they purchase ad time or ad space

on those TV shows, radio stations, or Web sites where they know their audience will be watching, listening, reading, or surfing.

4. What lifestyles, values, points of view are represented in, or omitted from, this message?	This question is aimed at the *content:* since most news stories on television are under two minutes and most political ads are just 30 seconds long, each cannot avoid omitting very important information. So you might ask yourself: What am I not being told or shown, and why? Where can I locate more information that is nonpartisan or unbiased? Remember, advertisers make their products look their best for their commercials—and so do the political media consultants, except that their "product" is their candidate.
5. Why was this message sent?	This question goes to *purpose.* Most media consultants will agree that political messages are designed to persuade you to feel good about their candidate or feel negatively toward the opposing candidate. Is the message designed to get you to think more positively or more negatively about a candidate or cause? Is the message intended to cast doubt on conventional thinking? Might the message instill fear? Does the message try to sway you to take some action—make a phone call, or log onto a Web site, or send a contribution? Obviously the candidate gleans some benefit when his or her message is broadcast to millions of people: we might all hear the same message at the same time. Voters also benefit from the information conveyed in the messages. Since we know that media exist to make money, it is logical to conclude that when politicians buy time on TV, cable, or radio, or ad space on Web sites, it is those media and technology companies that benefit the most.

OTHER QUESTIONS TO CONSIDER

Canadian media educator Chris Worsnop has helped teachers and students alike to learn to question media messages. Using the following chart[6] apply these other questions to political campaign media messages (note that the word *text* below applies to both print and nonprint media messages):

Media image:	Questions to ask:
Industry	Who's in charge? What do they want of me, and why? What else do they want? HOW DO I KNOW?
Product	What kind of text is this? Are conventions followed or broken? How is this message constructed? HOW DO I KNOW?
Audience	Who is this intended for? What assumptions does the text make about the audience? Who am I supposed to be in relation to this text? HOW DO I KNOW?

Values	How real is this text? How/where do I find the meaning? What values are presented? What is the commercial message? What is the ideology of this text? What social/artistic/political messages does the text contain? HOW DO I KNOW?
Predisposition	Do I agree with (assent to) this text's message? Do I disagree with (resist) this text's message? Do I argue/negotiate with the message of this text? HOW DO I KNOW?
Perception	How does the text fit my personal values/beliefs/ideology? How does the text relate to my personal needs/hopes/fears/experiences? HOW DO I KNOW?
Skills	What skills do I need to apply to this text? How do I deconstruct/reconstruct this text? What new skills does this text demand of me? HOW DO I KNOW?
Receiver	What does all this mean in the end? HOW DO I KNOW?

Source: Chris M. Worsnop. Adapted by the author from *Screening Images: Ideas for Media Education,* 2nd ed., Wright Communications, 1999.

The Annenberg Public Policy Center (home of FactCheck.org) offers students these "Tools of the Trade" to consider:[7]

A Process for Avoiding Deception

1. *Keep an open mind.* Most of us have biases, and we can easily fool ourselves if we don't make a conscious effort to keep our minds open to new information. Psychologists have shown over and over again that humans naturally tend to accept any information that supports what they already believe, even if the information isn't very reliable. And humans also naturally tend to reject information that conflicts with those beliefs, even if the information is solid. These predilections are powerful. Unless we make an active effort to listen to all sides, we can become trapped into believing something that isn't so, and won't even know it.

2. *Ask the right questions.* Don't accept claims at face value; test them by asking a few questions. Who is speaking, and where are they getting their information? How can I validate what they're saying? What facts would prove this claim wrong? Does the evidence presented really back up what's being said? If an ad says a product is "better," for instance, what does that mean? Better than what?

3. *Cross-check.* Don't rely on one source or one study, but look to see what others say. When two or three reliable sources independently report the same facts or conclusions, you can be more confident of them. But when two independent sources contradict each other, you know you need to dig more deeply to discover who's right.

4. *Consider the source.* Not all sources are equal. As any *CSI* viewer knows, sometimes physical evidence is a better source than an eyewitness, whose memory can play tricks. And an eyewitness is more credible than somebody telling a story they heard from somebody else. By the same token, an Internet Web site that offers primary source material is more trustworthy than one that publishes information gained second- or third-hand. For example, official vote totals posted by a county clerk or state

election board are more authoritative than election returns reported by a political blog or even a newspaper, which can be out of date or mistaken.

5. *Weigh the evidence.* Know the difference between random anecdotes and real scientific data from controlled studies. Know how to avoid common errors of reasoning, such as assuming that one thing causes another simply because the two happen one after the other. Does a rooster's crowing cause the sun to rise? Only a rooster would think so.

Media literacy empowers people to be both critical thinkers and creative producers of an increasingly wide range of messages using image, language, and sound. It is the skillful application of literacy skills to media and technology messages. As communication technologies transform society, they impact our understanding of ourselves, our communities, and our diverse cultures, making media literacy an essential life-skill for the 21st century.
—The Alliance for a Media Literate America

Candidates must have razzle-dazzle. Boring is the fatal label. Programs and concepts that cannot be collapsed into a slogan or a thirty second sound bite go largely unheard and unremembered, for what the modern campaign offers in length, it lacks in depth.
—Dick Morris, media consultant to President Bill Clinton

NOTES

1. *Media Literacy Resource Guide* (Ontario Ministry of Education, 1997).

2. Robert Kubey and Frank Baker, "Has Media Education Found a Curricular Foothold?" *Education Week,* October 27, 1999.

3. Partnership for 21st-Century Skills.

4. Center for Media Literacy.

5. Ibid.

6. Chris M. Worsnop. Adapted by the author from *Screening Images: Ideas for Media Education,* 2nd ed., Wright Communications, 1999.

7. Annenberg Public Policy Center, http://www.factchecked.org/ToolsOfTheTrade.aspx.

2

Propaganda and Spin: The Power of the Image over the Word

I think the American people will be shocked by such contempt for their intelligence. This isn't Ivory Soap versus Palmolive.

—Presidential candidate Adlai E. Stevenson, reacting to the use of TV ads in campaigns (1952)

It was TV more than anything that turned the tide.

—President-elect John F. Kennedy

Politics will eventually be replaced by imagery. The politician will be only too happy to abdicate in favor of his image, because the image will be much more powerful than he could ever be.

—Marshall McLuhan

Television images penetrate and then shape public consciousness.

—Media scholar Neil Postman

Picture news will always be show business because the brain does not have to translate the information.

—James B. Twitchell, *Carnival Culture* (1992)

CREATING AND CONTROLLING THE IMAGE

"Image is everything." It might surprise you that the speaker is tennis player Andre Agassi. The same phrase has also been uttered for decades by advertisers and political media consultants.

Media Literacy Core Concept:

All media messages are constructed.

Media Literacy Key Questions:

What techniques are used by the creator to attract attention?

What lifestyles, values, points of view are represented in, or omitted from, this message?

If you can control the image that Americans see every day in their morning newspapers, and every night on the evening news, then you manipulate everything they see, read, hear, and understand. Yesterday it was called propaganda; today, it's called "spin."

It's no accident that many of those who call themselves "media consultants," and who work on presidential campaigns, have come directly from the advertising, broadcasting, public relations, and marketing industries. There, they learned the tricks of the trade: a certain color creates the right mood; a specific camera angle makes the subject look strong and powerful; good lighting evokes the right impression. When the right words are combined with the right images and sounds, you have a winning combination—an event or ad that promises to sell. And it can sell dish detergent as well as the latest candidate. It doesn't matter—the techniques of persuasion are identical.

Despite their apparently informal tone, staged events such as this January 2004 conference of women who own small businesses, held at the Commerce Department in Washington, D.C., were carefully managed to exploit Pres. George W. Bush's easy rapport with relatively small, selected audiences. (AP Photo/Ron Edmonds)

According to *Washington Post* White House reporter Mike Allen, the White House under President George W. Bush put a premium on the visual image. Allen says there are people in the White House's communications department whose expertise is lighting, backdrops, and set design.[1]

From the moment TV became prevalent in American homes, it transformed the family and the living room. The television became what some called the "new fireplace," a place for the family to gather around. So-called TV dinners, frozen entrees, were created in the 1960s so that families could eat and watch at the same time.

1952: EISENHOWER VS. STEVENSON

Eisenhower Commercial

"Eisenhower answers America"

"I paid twenty-four dollars for these groceries—look, for this little"

"A few years ago those same groceries cost you ten dollars, now twenty-four, next year thirty—that's what will happen unless we have a change"

Dwight D. Eisenhower was the first American president to draw on modern advertising techniques to "sell" his message. Famed ad man Rosser Reeves created the "Eisenhower Answers America" television "spot" campaign for the 1952 presidential election. *Source:* Edwin Diamond and Stephen Bates, *The Spot: The Rise of Political Advertising on Television,* 3rd ed. (Cambridge, Mass.: MIT Press, 1992) 130–131. (Images courtesy of the Wisconsin Center for Film and Theater Research, Wisconsin Historical Society)

Radio soon drifted into second place as millions of people bought televisions, and programming entered what has become known as the "Golden Age," with well-crafted dramas from some of the finest American writers.

One of the earliest uses of an advertising agency in a presidential race was in 1936, when Hill Blackett (of Blackett-Sample-Hummert) worked as a media adviser for Republican candidate Alfred Landon. The agency helped the candidate to purchase radio time for Landon's speeches.[2]

Ad man Rosser Reeves, who had worked for New York agency Ted Bates & Co., spearheaded Dwight Eisenhower's 1952 campaign for president. Ike had campaigned as the "man from Abilene," and Reeves helped create a commercial that showed Eisenhower as the everyman.

Watch Ike ads: http://www.pbs.org/30secondcandidate/from_idea_to_ad/ collection/31.html.

THE DAISY SPOT: BROADCAST ONCE—SEEN MANY TIMES

Ad executive Tony Schwartz, working with the Doyle Dane Bernbach (DDB) ad agency, helped create the famous "Daisy" spot for incumbent President Lyndon B. Johnson's 1964 campaign against Republican challenger Barry Goldwater.

The ad showed a little girl picking the petals off a daisy as she counts down from 10. As she does, the camera slowly zooms into her eye, which dissolves into a nuclear bomb detonation. Johnson's words are heard at the end of the ad.

Ad Transcript

"These are the stakes. To make a world in which all of God's children can live or to go into the dark. We must either love each other . . . or we must die." A voice over announcer closes: "Vote for President Johnson on November 3rd. The stakes are too high to stay home."

Writing in his classic text *The Responsive Chord* (1973), Schwartz noted that the Daisy spot never mentioned Goldwater by name: "Someone unfamiliar with the political climate in 1964 and viewing the spot today will not perceive any allusion at all to Goldwater. Then why did it bring such a reaction in 1964? Well, Senator Goldwater had stated previously that he supported the use of tactical atomic weapons. The commercial evoked a deep feeling in many people that Goldwater might actually use nuclear weapons. This mistrust was not in the Daisy spot. It was in the people who viewed the commercial. The stimuli of the film and sound evoked these feelings and allowed people to express what they inherently believed."[3]

Even though the Daisy ad aired only once, it generated lots of press. The *New York Times* newspaper, as well as the ABC and CBS television networks and *TIME Magazine* all did stories about it. "The hubhub helped reinforce

Stills from the 1964 presidential campaign television spot "Peace, Little Girl," also known as the "Daisy Spot." (Courtesy of the Lyndon Baines Johnson Presidential Library and Museum and the Democratic National Committee)

the trigger-happy association pinned on Goldwater—and to imply that a vote for Johnson was a vote against escalation in Vietnam."[4]

Starting with the Nixon campaign of 1968, candidates and their advisers became extremely adept not only at creating powerful political ads but also in the elaborate staging of media events. Nixon hired H. R. Haldeman, a former ad executive, to help manage TV coverage of his successful 1968 presidential campaign.[5]

One president in particular was a master at using the medium of television to his advantage.

RONALD REAGAN: THE GREAT COMMUNICATOR

Reagan was a great communicator because he was a great storyteller.
—Garry Wills, *Reagan's America: Innocents at Home* (1987)

Not many people realize that Ronald Reagan had a lifetime of being both in the public spotlight and in broadcasting long before he was elected president in 1981. He honed his skills while working in radio early in his career; he was a film actor in the 1940s and 1950s; he hosted *GE Theater,* a weekly television drama series (1955–1958). He wrote and narrated a series of radio commentaries. And

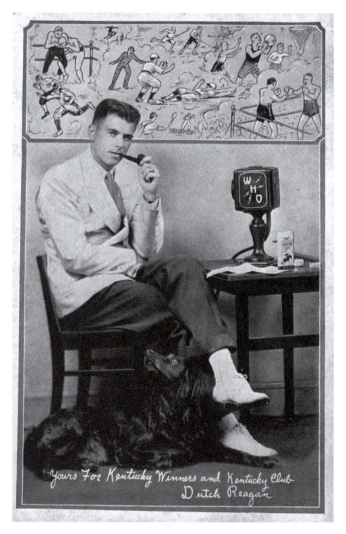

Ronald "Dutch" Reagan as a young radio sportscaster at WHO Radio in Des Moines, Iowa, in 1932–1933. Used to answer fan mail, this postcard showed the future president, a nonsmoker, promoting the brands of his show's sponsors. (AP Photo)

he became a popular speaker for Republican causes, giving a nationally televised address in support of Barry Goldwater's failed presidential bid.

From his early identification with Roosevelt and his professional training came the Great Communicator. Reagan's idea of a President was of a leader who could rally the country to a cause with the power of his voice and use public opinion as a catalyst for change. His communicative skill was a principal source of his effectiveness as President, but it rested on stronger foundations than mere mastery of television.

Believability was the key. Reagan was not believable because he was the Great Communicator; he was the Great Communicator because he was believable.[6]

As governor of California, Reagan surrounded himself with highly qualified aides, including Ed Meese, James Baker, and Michael Deaver, a former public relations executive. The "ruling troika," as Reagan biographer Edmund Morris called them, followed Reagan all the way to the White House.

Deaver had a gift for understanding the visual rhetoric of television. It was Deaver who orchestrated and choreographed every public appearance by Ronald Reagan. Deaver knew Reagan's strengths (as both actor and orator) and crafted press events to take advantage of both.

In an interview with Cable News Network reporter Frank Sesno, Deaver explained how the setting for a White House press conference was represented to make the chief executive look strong and powerful:

DEAVER: You didn't have to do anything with Reagan. I mean, he looked presidential. I always thought of my job (a) as lighting him well and (b) filling up the space around him so that the visual that the public saw in every way we could would tell the story of that particular action, whatever it was.

SESNO (on camera):   This photo over here, this red carpet, it's not an accident.

DEAVER: No. That was the background that we used for the press conferences, and there was a reason for it. But you see, the whole visual there is formality and power, high ceilings, pillars, crystal chandeliers, red carpet. It's a place of importance. It's obviously the White House, and important things happen there. That's what it says.[7]

CBS White House correspondent Lesley Stahl summed up what made Reagan a great communicator: "Being an actor was part of his secret. No president was ever that at ease before the cameras, and cowboys are always at ease. He came across on television as natural, easy in his laugh and his walk. Without once raising his voice, Ronald Reagan sold the country on his dreams and illusions, and he sold himself as a strong leader. The CBS pollster Kathy Frankovic told me that much of Reagan's popularity derived from his aura of consistency. This was something he worked at communicating. Even when he didn't stick to his guns, he said he did! Reagan raised taxes over and over, but each time he would insist he was a tax cutter and persuaded everyone he was. Now, that's communicating!"[8] Yet Stahl herself experienced the White House's media manipulation.

How One News Report Backfired

In October 1984, in the midst of Reagan's reelection campaign, Stahl and her producer produced a lengthy report for the *CBS Evening News with Dan Rather*

Pres. Ronald Reagan, the "Great Communicator," brought to politics a professional understanding of how to control his image in the media, based on his years of experience in radio, television, and film. (Courtesy of the Ronald Reagan Presidential Library)

about how the White House used television and images of Ronald Reagan to deflect much of the criticism of the president, who, in fact, had been known for cutting many social programs. The report said:

How does Ronald Reagan use television? Brilliantly. He's been criticized as the rich man's president, but the TV pictures say it isn't so.

The images showed Reagan picnicking with ordinary folks; later he was surrounded by black kids, farmers, and then flag-waving supporters. The report continued:

At 73, Mr. Reagan could have an age problem, but the TV pictures say it isn't so.

Now the images showed Reagan pumping iron, tossing a football. The report went on:

The orchestration of television coverage absorbs the White House. Their goal? To emphasize the president's greatest asset, which his aides say is his personality. They provide pictures of him looking like a leader . . . confident, with his Marlboro Man walk . . . a good family man.

Then, Stahl admits, the report turned critical:

Mr. Reagan tries to counter the memory of an unpopular issue with a carefully chosen backdrop that actually contradicts the president's policy. Look at the handicapped Olympics, or the opening ceremony of an old-age home. No hint that he tried to cut the budgets for the disabled or for federally subsidized housing for the elderly.

Once again, the CBS News report showed Reagan at campaign events with throngs of fans waving American flags.

Since the report was obviously critical of the president, Stahl worried publicly that the White House would punish her by limiting her access to the chief executive. Sure enough, just after the piece aired on the network, the White House called the CBS Newsroom. Dick Darman, one of the White House's communications officials, spoke to Stahl: "What a great story! We loved it." To which Stahl replied: "Why are you so happy? Didn't you hear what I said?" Darman told her: "No one heard what you said . . . you guys in televisionland haven't figured it out . . . when the pictures are powerful and emotional, they override if not completely drown out the sound."[9]

Please Follow the Chalk Marks, Mr. President: Scripting Reagan

Donald Regan served as President Reagan's Treasury Secretary from 1981 until 1985. In his book *For The Record,* Regan explained the depth of image creation during his boss's term:

Every moment of every public appearance was scheduled, every word was scripted, every place where Reagan was expected to stand was chalked with toe marks. The president was always being prepared for a performance, and this had the inevitable effect of preserving him from confrontation and the genuine interplay of opinion, question, and argument that form the basis of decision.[10]

Today, the White House has a Communications Office, comprised of ex-broadcast news producers and photographers. Who better to help you get the best image of the president than those who used to work in the news business? Today, White House communications experts routinely confer with network TV news, making sure their cameras have the best view of the chief executive.

THE DEMOCRATS DO IT, TOO

It's not just the Republicans who understand image manipulation. Josh King was the White House Director of Production for Presidential Events during President Bill Clinton's administration. Some have dubbed King "the father of the modern backdrop," because of his ability to alter the setting and background of news images.[11]

King says his primary interests are "the optics and the theatrics." In other words, how he can control how the president is photographed (by the news media), how events are staged, and what audiences see (in person and via television). "The (Clinton) White House analyzed the picture structure of television stories: almost every TV story began with a wide shot to set the scene (Clinton comes to

Chicago), a medium shot to show who Clinton was with on-stage (Mayor Daley is standing next to him on the podium), a cut-away shot to show the audience (people applauding, laughing, cheering), and then the tight shot of Clinton's face during the speech (the president actually speaks the words). The White House analysis showed that the tight shot lasted the longest, since the viewers had to hear what Clinton was saying. So it was the most important shot."[12]

King figured out that he could always place some visual, usually a banner, to the left or right of the president's head. And so the modern TV news image began to be manipulated with banners such as "Stronger American Families" and "Stronger American Communities." Watch any news coverage today of the chief executive out on the road at some speaking engagement, and you will see it.

As the photo of President Clinton promoting his programs on the road demonstrates, a specially designed backdrop was strategically placed behind him, ensuring that news photographers, all positioned in the identical location, would include the visual in their camera frames.

Former Clinton aide Dick Morris, writing in his *The New Prince,* underlines the importance of a focused message that the politician can use to "translate the

At an event in Philadelphia in April 1999, Pres. Bill Clinton speaks on behalf of health care reform, framed by a large banner proclaiming a "real" Patient's Bill of Rights. By the Clinton years, both catchy program names and the use of graphic backdrops had become commonplace. (AP Photo/ Rusty Kennedy)

public's grief into the system's issues." The next step is "media play" for the message. "It is the one-paragraph sound-bite on which the story lives or dies." Visuals are also key. "In handling television, bear in mind that the medium cannot help itself. It needs pretty pictures," he writes. "Backdrops matter. The candidate should stand in front of an assemblage of American flags or a bevy of uniformed police with medals."[13] Sex can't hurt either. In the fall of 1990, as President George H. W. Bush exhorted a televised rally in Minnesota to support the looming Gulf War, a row of cheerleaders kicked their legs in the background.

DIGITAL ALTERATION OF IMAGES

With today's digital photo alteration tools, it is easier for photographers to alter images. There are plenty of stories about this throughout photojournalism. Even the national news photographer's association has established a code of ethics about when it is and is not proper for a photographer to change an image.

More troubling is the practice of altering images or sound in political advertising.

A favorite photo trick is digitally sewing a celebrity's head onto another's body. In August 2007, the Republican Party of Kentucky printed a campaign brochure with a fake photo of the Democratic candidate for governor, Steve Beshear, looking sleazy in a casino. The image was labeled "not an actual photo" and was designed to mock the candidate's stance on gambling. But the picture also demonstrates two clear signs of a stitched photo: an unnatural tilt of the head and an awkward seam where the head meets the collarbone.[14]

An analysis of spots from 1952 to 1992 found 15 percent had "some ethically questionable use of technology." A later study found even more manipulations:

- news conferences that were never held
- debates that never took place
- use of audio or video tricks to stereotype or ridicule an opponent[15]

Sometimes, when an image is altered (or cropped) and published, it can be misleading. *TIME Magazine* found itself in this situation during the Clinton administration.

The media critics of the *Columbia Journalism Review* criticized *TIME:* "Filling up the space behind its April 4 cover line, 'DEEP WATER: How the President's Men Tried to Hinder the Whitewater Investigation,' was a photo purporting to capture the White House in the throes of Whitewater despair—Clinton clutching head in hands, [aide George] Stephanopoulos staring stonily into the abyss. In fact, as an angry administration soon made clear, the photo had nothing whatsoever to do with Whitewater and was, in fact, a relic from the past, having been taken last November at a meeting in which the president and aides were wrestling with problems in scheduling the president's time. The warped defense of *TIME* spokesman Robert Pondiscio, as quoted in the *Washington Post:* 'I don't think the readers of *TIME* expect the cover photo is going to be a representation of that event.' "[16]

Cover of the April 4, 1994, *TIME Magazine*. (White House Photo/*TIME Magazine*)

More Questions to Consider

- What role does TV play in communicating politicians' messages?
- How do campaigns control news coverage of events?
- How does the White House control news images and coverage?
- What do you need to know in order to better understand media spin?
- Where might you go to find more information about edited news events?

NOTES

1. Mike Allen, White House reporter, the *Washington Post* quoted in *Campaign Essentials,* a year-long series produced by New York Times Television for Discovery Times Channel, 2004.

2. John McDonough, *The Advertising Age Encyclopedia of Advertising,* vol. 3 (2003), 1248.

3. Tony Schwartz, *The Responsive Chord* (Garden City, NY: Anchor Press, 1973), 93.

4. Erik Barnouw, *The Image Empire,* vol. 3 of *A History of Broadcasting in the United States* (1970; repr., New York: Oxford University Press, 1977).

5. Ben Fritz et al. *All the President's Spin: George W. Bush, the Media, and the Truth* (New York: Simon & Schuster, 2004).

6. Lou Cannon, *Reagan* (New York: Putnam, 1982).

7. http://transcripts.cnn.com/TRANSCRIPTS/0102/18/cgs.00.html.

8. "The Great Communicator," in *Ronald Reagan Remembered: CBS News,* ed. Ian Jackman (New York: Simon & Schuster, 2004), 57–58.

9. Lesley Stahl, *Reporting Live* (New York: Simon & Schuster, 1999), 209–11. Michael Deaver reportedly told the CBS reporter "Lesley, when you're showing four-and-a-half minutes of great pictures of Ronald Reagan, no one listens to what you say" (*All The President's Spin,* 14).

10. Donald T. Regan, *For the Record* (San Diego: Harcourt Brace Jovanovich, 1988), 248, as quoted in http://hypertextbook.com/eworld/present.shtml.

11. dailynightly.msnbc.com/2006/01/flat_tuesday.html.

12. Roger Simon, *Show Time: The American Political Circus and the Race for The White House* (New York: Times Books, 1998), xv–xvii.

13. Dick Morris, *The New Prince: Machiavelli Updated for the Twenty-First Century* (Los Angeles: Renaissance Books, 1999), 124.

14. "Digital Detectives Discern Photoshop Fakery," *Christian Science Monitor,* August 28, 2007, http://www.csmonitor.com/2007/0829/p13s02-stct.html?page=2.

15. Dennis W. Johnson, *No Place for Amateurs: How Political Consultants Are Reshaping American Democracy* (New York: Routledge, 2001), 136.

16. *CJR* (May/June 1994), http://backissues.cjrarchives.org/year/94/3/d_l.asp.

3

The Media Experts

Pay no attention to that man behind the curtain!
> —The Wizard of Oz image manipulator,
> *The Wizard of Oz* (film, 1939)

Political issues and politicians are regularly subjected to the cosmetic sorcery of image managers, providing the public with a telegenic commodity.
> —Stuart Ewen, *All Consuming Images:*
> *The Politics of Style in Contemporary Culture* (1988)

Since you're the ones who are selling the soap, I thought you'd like to see the bar.
> —Ronald Reagan, upon sticking his head into the room of
> advertising executives crafting his famous
> "Morning in America" spot (1984)

As the White House has become more and more of a stage for television, those who are within the White House want to become the stage managers.
> —David Gergen, former Assistant to the
> President for Communications

If you have to hire a roomful of consultants to tell you what you believe, maybe you shouldn't be president.
> —Mike Huckabee, Republican presidential candidate and
> former Arkansas governor

CONSULTANTS, THE PEOPLE CRAFTING THE IMAGES

One of the most important people in a presidential candidate's campaign is the political consultant. Today, the consultant is a "jack-of-all-trades." What does a

> **Media Literacy Core Concept:**
> *Media have embedded values and points of view.*
>
> **Media Literacy Key Questions:**
> *Who created this message?*
> *What techniques are used by the creator to attract attention?*

consultant do? The consultant is "part of a team of advisers that includes a pollster, a direct mail expert and the full time campaign staff, including a campaign manager, fund-raiser and press secretary. In these ensemble campaigns, the political consultant's role is to write and produce television commercials. But since TV ads are the most prominent part of any campaign, that gives consultants huge influence over the shape and direction of a campaign."[1]

Not so surprisingly, many political consultants came to their jobs from advertising and broadcasting, where they learned the "tricks of the trade." Political consultants, who may also be experts in the media, know just about everything concerning the voters they are trying to reach. For the most part, they know what Web pages we view, what we eat and drink, what kind of car we drive, and what TV shows we watch. How do they know all of this? It's all part of the intensive demographic research they conduct.

Today, that consultant must also be an expert in using new and emerging media and technology (e.g., cell phones, blogs, and streaming video) as other tools designed to reach and engage voters. Political science professor Larry Sabato calls the consultants "gods of the political wars,"[2] noting that not only has the technology changed, but also that campaigning is a yearly endeavor amounting to a multibillion-dollar enterprise.

A *Boston Globe* newspaper analysis of the Federal Election Commission reports filed by the 2008 presidential candidates revealed an alarming increase in consultants and their work, which includes such things as managing Web sites, staging trips and events, managing the media, and, of course, fundraising.[3]

One of the consultants' tools is called "behavioral target marketing." Successful campaigns now know how to target the message to key demographic niches such as so-called "Soccer Moms" and "NASCAR Dads." In the 2004 (presidential) campaign, Karl Rove (political strategist for George Bush) used zip code data to identify local swing voters in the most contested "battleground states," for instance, and then used direct mail and cable to reach them. More recently, with the advent of the Internet, advisors have a deeper trough of information in which to work with, including (Web) sites (people) visited, petitions, polls, or types of magazines—and within those publications, specific articles they've read.[4]

Targeting the TV Shows You Like to Watch

The depth of information used by political consultants is astounding. Since television is the medium most people still pay attention to, consultants take advantage of accessible audience ratings and demographic details.[5] For example, they can now decipher voter income, education levels, jobs, ethnicity, and voting habits when deciding where to broadcast their ads. Consultants also know if a specific program is more likely to be viewed by Republicans, Democrats, or Independent voters. So it is possible to target a message, for example, to men aged 35–55 who have voted in the past.

Thinking Like a Political Media Consultant

If you had developed a new product to sell to young people aged 18–26, and you were trying to decide how to reach them, you might ask yourself these important questions:

- What does my target audience read? (newspapers, magazines, blogs)
- What Web sites do they frequent?
- To which social networking Web sites do they belong?
- What TV shows or music do they watch/download or listen to?
- What kinds of movies do they prefer? (drama, comedy, thrillers, horror, science fiction)
- How often do they rent video or download movies?
- What are their favorite video games?

Once you have a picture of their media/technology habits, you can best create the campaign and target and purchase ad space or time in order to capture their attention.

Controlling the Images

Ok, so you are in charge of the candidate. You have a lot of decisions to make:

- What color dress or tie will your candidate wear today?
- What is the "message of the day" you hope to communicate?
- Have you contacted TV, radio, newspapers, bloggers to cover the event?
- Where will the TV cameras and photographers be positioned?
- What's in the background? (for example, ordinary people, dignitaries, billboard, political signs)

THE SELLING OF THE PRESIDENT

In 1968 Richard Nixon knew that in 1960 television had hurt his chances against John Kennedy. The televised debates of 1960, which were seen by millions, reflected something Kennedy had, but Nixon did not have: the right image. So if he was going to be elected this time, he had better look good on TV. Among the first steps Nixon took was to hire advertising and television experts. H. R. Haldeman joined the campaign, bringing with him 20 years of experience as an advertising executive with the large J. Walter Thompson ad firm. As Nixon's chief-of-staff, Haldeman told his boss that television could be used to bypass reporters, many of whom were hostile to Nixon. Television, Haldeman argued, allowed you to go directly to the people.[6]

One of the experts Nixon hired was Roger Ailes. In 1968 Ailes was the executive producer of the popular nationwide talk show *The Mike Douglas Show.* When candidate Nixon was invited to be a guest on the show, Ailes took time to talk to him about politics and the medium of television. Ailes made a strong impression on the future president when the two discussed television's role in elections: "I told him TV wasn't a gimmick . . . that nobody would ever be elected to major office again without presenting himself reasonably well on TV."[7] Ailes's work in entertainment television was short-lived: Nixon was so impressed that he hired him to be one of his new media advisers.

Ailes, along with Nixon's media team, decided to show off their man's strengths. They created a series of televised town-hall-type gatherings, in which Nixon was surrounded by hand-picked residents asking questions. Chicago was the first of 10 markets to broadcast the program. Other programs originated from Massachusetts to Texas. The team said the shows would "make it seem to home viewers that enthusiasm for his candidacy was all but uncontrollable." Added Ailes, "This is an electronic election, the first there's ever been. TV has the power now." The television expert, hoping to improve on each broadcast, compiled meticulous notes following each appearance. After one such taping, Ailes wrote: "Try slightly whiter makeup on upper eyelids." Nixon, a smart politician, proved himself to be a quick learner, especially when it came to his televised appearances. He could go into a studio and talk extemporaneously without a script or a teleprompter, and he paid attention to detail. Almost overnight, Ailes had defined the modern-day political media consultant. He went on to advise both presidents Reagan and George H. W. Bush. (Today, Ailes is chairman and CEO of Fox News Channel, owned by Rupert Murdoch, and he is known to have advised President George W. Bush as well.)

Nixon's election ad spots also reflected the expertise of those who already had a long history of mastering the art of selling a product. He went on to defeat Democrat Hubert Humphrey, who declared, "the biggest mistake in my political life was not to learn how to use television."[8]

After his election, the new president created the White House Television Office. One of its first employees was TV producer Mark Goode. Among his responsibilities were choosing appropriate backdrops for presidential appearances, determining TV camera positioning for best angles, arranging lighting to complement Nixon, maximizing audio, choosing a time of day for maximum network coverage, and offering the president advice on makeup and wardrobe. This attention to detail, and the importance of the newly named White House Office of Communications, would become the hallmarks for all future presidents concerned about image control and spin.[9]

In a May 1970 memo, made available on *The Smoking Gun* Web site (http://www.thesmokinggun.com/archive/years/2007/0711073ailes1.html), to Nixon aide H. R. (Bob) Haldeman, Ailes critiqued a series of Nixon TV appearances and detailed his efforts to stage-manage the president's on-air look.

Figure 3.1

In his May 4, 1970, memo "White House Television," addressed to White House Chief of Staff H. R. Haldeman (himself a former ad executive), media consultant Roger Ailes applied his keen grasp of the power of television images to a critique of Pres. Richard M. Nixon's performance at televised events. Ailes went on to become president of the FOX News Channel and chairman of the FOX Television Stations Group. (Courtesy of the Nixon Presidential Library and Museum)

 PRODUCTIONS INC. 888 Eighth Avenue. Suite 7F New York, New York 10019

New York 212-765-3022 Washington 202-544-6449

MEMORANDUM

TO: H. R. Haldeman   cc: Dwight Chapin

FROM: Roger E. Ailes

DATE: May 4, 1970

SUBJECT: WHITE HOUSE TELEVISION

<u>HOUSTON</u>

(1) Arrival of cars in Houston was good, exciting, but a little long. Nixon's entrance through crowd looked good.

(2) There was an audio lag after the announcer introduced President and Mrs. Nixon. The networks don't seem to mike for crowd reaction so it might be good to ask the director to do a cut-away shot in these instances.

Thats why we should be inside

(3) At any outdoor event the President must assume that he is on camera at all times. There was one bad shot of him sneaking a look at his notes after he got to the platform in Houston.

indoor

— you tell him

(4) I think it is important for the President to show a little more concern for Mrs. Nixon as he moves through the crowd. At one point he walked off in a different direction. Mrs. Nixon wasn't looking and had to run to catch up. From time to time he should talk to her and smile at her. Women voters are **particularly** sensitive to how a man treats his wife in public. The more attention she gets, the happier they are.

Figure 3.1, Continued

Page Two

(5) The President looked good outdoors with his hair blowing in the wind, but I think he should wear make-up or at least beardstick even for these appearances. A double layer of beardstick should be applied to the area above the upper lip. He is especially dark there.

I disagree if he's going thru the crowd

(6) Advance men should be instructed to pay particular attention to the crowd area behind the President when he speaks outdoors. In every case people were sitting on others shoulders and raising cameras into the shot which made it distracting. Once the crowd is assembled, they should be informed that this cannot be done in the area of the camera lens. Also, whenever possible, there should be no access route back and forth behind the President. Otherwise you end up with the President in the foreground making touching remarks and people walking across in the background paying absolutely no attention. Unfortunately, this is even done through a prayer or the National Anthem.

Absolutely

HAWAII

(1) I watched the CBS playback and they lost the Dan Rather audio so Cronkite had to fill over the beginning from New York. However, this did not look too bad.

✓

(2) Again, the crowd behind the President was distracting and managed to foul up our Hawaii shot part of the time.

Right!

(3) Ron Walker did an excellent job of staging in general and the ceremony itself was good. Also, Tim Elbourn handled himself very well.

good

VIET NAM ADDRESS

(1) The Viet Nam address from the Western White House looked good. The President did the best job of reading that he has ever done. I had five or ten minutes with him prior to this broadcast and a few extra minutes to check out his lighting. During this time he seemed to loosen up considerably.

✓

Figure 3.1, Continued

Page Three

(2)   Someone said that they thought perhaps
he had a yellow cast to his make-up. On the playback I watched this was definitely not the case. In
fact, his make-up was every bit as good as Ray Voege's.

✓

(3)   At one point on the tape I could hear
crosstalk in the background at a very low level.
When I moved up to the set to try to tune it in, I
was unable to hear it. Ev Aspinwall, the pool
producer, denies any crosstalk and some people said
it was very loud and annoying. They are probably both
right.   Because of all the various inputs and outputs
involved in audio transmission of this type the
crosstalk probably did exist but was not apparent in
some cases and very apparent in others. This should
have been discovered during the audio check-out,
however, apparently did not exist at that time. I
can keep this from happening in the future, however,
as you know, I am walking a very fine line on how
much I can actually say to the networks without creating
a situation where they scream "management of news."
How firm a position would you like me to take and do
you want me to run the risk of getting these guys
angry every time. Frankly, there have been times that   *Check*
I have pushed it just short of a major blow-up. In   *this*
fact, apparently one of the networks has informed
Ziegler that I am no longer allowed in their truck
because I made them change the backlighting just prior
to broadcast. (I'm not sure which network this is and
don't really care.) I'm sure you want me to continue   *Right*
to go in the truck whenever I think it is necessary.

(4)   I finally convinced the President to
use a handkerchief (after a little bit of a go around) to
wipe off perspiration. I think he got so bugged at me   *✓*
for pushing him on this that he didn't perspire on the
air. Anyway, it worked--I noticed that he did use the
handkerchief on the Cambodia speech.

CAMBODIA ADDRESS

(1)   I hope that we can set up a more
effective way of informing me of upcoming major speeches.   *Chapin*
I learned about the Cambodia address after the press,
and only learned of it because I overheard a secretary
talking. This did not allow me adequate time to clear
my decks and be in the White House much before the speech.

Figure 3.1, Continued

Page Four

Since there is no security problem with me, could you
notify me as soon as there is a <u>possibility</u> of a
speech and I can be ready.

    (2) By the time I arrived CBS had already
lost their main camera and were setting up an alternate.
Six minutes to air and after the President had been
briefed on camera blocking they lost the second camera.
I reported this to the President and advised him on the
handling of the situation. He did it well, but the
director being more nervous than the President, blew
the shooting in my opinion. I can handle this in the
future.

    (3) Although I was advised that there would
be a map used, I was not informed that he would be
getting up and down from his desk until I arrived at
the White House. I think in the future if he uses a
map or chart, he should work from a lecturn or the
visual material should be close enough to him so that
he can turn and point it out from his seat. Getting
up and down slows down the pace, increases the possibility of a microphone cord foul-up, increases the
possibility of the President losing his place, and the
chairs squeak and rattle.

    (4) The briefing the President had just prior
to broadcast was scheduled too tight and there was not
adequate time to make him up, brief him, check out his
lighting on camera and still give him a few moments
alone to collect his thoughts and go over his speech.
Fortunately, his make-up was okay but I think we could
have done more with his lighting. I elected not to
because I didn't want to rattle him just prior to
broadcast. He should have absolutely nothing else to
do the last thirty minutes before air time.

    (5) When he lost his place, he was brilliant.
I have never seen a man on camera, including every
professional I've worked with, handle a potentially
disastrous situation so well. He did exactly the
right thing. The admiration for him by the television
industry went up 150%.

    (6) If we had had a television assistant for
me all of the above problems could have been eliminated.

Figure 3.1, Continued

```
        (7)  At some point apparently the President
decided to use a lavalier microphone.  WACA did not
have two matching lavaliers and thus a very make-
shift tape connection was made to provide him with
a back-up system.  This would have required him
carrying a cord connector and wad of tape in his
pocket the size of three golf balls.  When I saw this
I ordered the connection dismantled and elected to go
on the air with no lavalier back-up.  He didn't know
this, of course, and everything went fine.  I did put
together quickly a boom microphone back-up system
which might have been noticeable but adequate if
anything had happened.  I have asked WACA to obtain
immediately matching lavaliers with long cords and
no connectors.

        (8)  I am more convinced than ever that I
need an assistant full time on the staff.  If this
is impossible, tell me so I can at least train Tim
Elbourn to handle some of these emergencies.  I do
feel, however, that we need a television producer/
director.
```

****

MICHAEL DEAVER: POLITICAL IMAGE MAKER

Michael Deaver was one of President Ronald Reagan's top aides. Deaver had worked for Reagan since 1967, when Reagan was governor of California. Reagan biographer Edmund Morris recalled Deaver's strength: "his particular talent . . . was for the Hollywood-style production of power: statesmanship rendered as drama."[10] Former first lady Nancy Reagan agreed, saying Deaver's greatest strength "was in arranging what were known as good visuals—televised events or scenes that would leave a powerful symbolic image in people's minds."[11]

Deaver had a gift for understanding the visual rhetoric of television. It was Deaver who orchestrated and choreographed every public appearance by Ronald Reagan. He knew Reagan's strengths (as both actor and orator) and crafted press events to take advantage of both: "Everything I did was preplanned, premeditated. The background was perfect."[12]

One political event was planned to ensure that just the right message would reach the home viewing television audience. In 1984, Reagan, running for reelection, gave a speech at a B-1 bomber assembly plant in California that was facing the loss of 40,000 jobs. In creating the image for the media, Deaver had a huge banner prepared and draped along the ceiling, in just the right position, so that it could not be missed by news photographers. The sign said "Prepared for Peace," and in every news story about the speech, there was Reagan in the foreground with the word *Peace* visible just behind him. According to Deaver, people do absorb impressions rather than substance.[13]

Deaver engineered "a story for the day" for journalists, designing events around a quotable phrase and appropriate photo opportunity. Deaver said: "I noticed how people who run TV news reduced things to 'soundbites.' "[14] So he provided broadcasters and journalists with material designed to fit their medium.

One journalist went so far as to conclude: "Do you know who was the real executive producer of the television network news? Michael Deaver was the executive producer of the evening news broadcasts—yes, he was . . . (he) decided what would be on the evening news each night. He laid it out there. I mean, he knew exactly who we were, what we went for. He suckered us."[15]

In a February 2001 Cable News Network TV special about the Reagan presidency, Deaver revealed, to CNN reporter Frank Sesno some of the choreography surrounding the first meeting between the president and Soviet President Mikhail Gorbachev at the White House:

DEAVER: You look back at those films. And there is Reagan in freezing weather, standing on the steps ready to greet the general-secretary, the first Russian leader he has ever met. And Gorbachev's old Russian ZiL car comes in. And he gets out, all bundled up with hat and so forth, and there is Reagan. The symbolism was incredible.

SESNO: Did you choreograph it that way?

DEAVER: I didn't choreograph it. I wasn't there. But that's what happened.

SESNO: It was choreographed that way?

DEAVER: It was choreographed that way, absolutely.

SESNO: To convey what?

DEAVER: To convey American strength.[16]

REAGAN AT NORMANDY—SCRIPTING FOR THE MORNING NEWS

On June 6, 1984, Ronald Reagan marked the 40th anniversary of the invasion of Normandy to honor those Americans who lost their lives during World War II. The president of France, François Mitterand, wanted to speak before Reagan, but if the French president spoke first, it would mean that Reagan's speech would miss being seen by millions of people who watch the network morning news shows in America. Deaver interceded, and Reagan spoke before Mitterand.

The result was one of President Reagan's enduring moments, a speech carefully orchestrated by his media advisers and set against the cliffs of Normandy in which he honored the sacrifices of the World War II generation. "I have always believed," said Michael Deaver, "that impressions are more important than specific acts or issues . . . I believe TV is a great boon to us in judging our leaders. It lets us see all the dimensions that, in the past, people could only see in person: the body language, the dilation of the eye, the way they perspire. We see them

On June 6, 1984, against the stark and dramatic backdrop of the war memorial at Point du Hoc, Normandy, Pres. Ronald Reagan delivered an address commemorating the 40th anniversary of D-Day landing of Allied forces that launched the drive to liberate France from German occupation. (AP Photo)

when they are tired, worried, under great crises. If television focuses on somebody every day, it shows all the dimensions."[17]

In 1988 Lee Atwater, a media-savvy strategist working (along with Roger Ailes) for George H. W. Bush, spearheaded a negative advertising campaign against rival Michael Dukakis. The two-pronged ad approach arrived at two visceral images:

1. A photo of the Massachusetts governor sitting in a tank, looking goofy (Dufus in tank = soft on military)

2. Image of Governor Dukakis letting murderers go home on weekend furloughs from prison (Dukakis let black men go home early = fear for your lives)[18]

The ads worked, even though the furlough ad was factually misleading. Governor Dukakis tried to respond, but it was too late.

In May 2003, the *New York Times* published a news story highlighting the manner in which the George W. Bush administration had used the staged visual image as propaganda. In addition to the "Mission Accomplished" speech, writer Elizabeth Bumiller described these photo-ops: "It is all by design: the White House has stocked its communications operation and people from national television who have expertise in lighting, camera angles and the importance of backdrops." The reporter cites many instances of this expertise: Bush speaking against the background of Mount Rushmore with the camera angled so as to capture the monumental presidential sculptures with President Bush in the foreground; a Bush speech with the large visible "Helping Small Business" backdrop; and another

press event on trade with the sign "Strengthening America's Economy" strategically placed behind the president so that all of the photographers' photos would
include it.

HOW THE NEWS MEDIA COVER POLITICAL CAMPAIGNS

In general, the news media set the agenda by deciding who and what to report
and how to report it. In the case of covering the presidential candidates, they send
a message when they cover major candidates and ignore "second tier candidates."
In 2007, for example, the mainstream media carried regular news reports of Hillary Clinton, Barack Obama, and John Edwards regularly, but virtually ignored
the six other Democrats in the race. The same could be said of the Republicans:
the media carried many stories about Rudy Giuliani, Mitt Romney, and John
McCain, but almost nothing about the others.

To understand all of this we must really understand the role of the media as gatekeepers: that is, they control what goes through the gate, the news. They decide
what gets reported and what does not. (One of the other important critical thinking
questions is: What am I not being told/shown and why?)

One practice that has become commonplace in election coverage is what's known
as "horse-race journalism." This analogy says the election is covered by the media as
if it was really an actual race: the reporters cover it as a sport or game, reporting
mostly on who is in first place, who won last night's debate, who's first in the polls,
who's raised the most money, who attacked whom, and so on. Some journalists
defend this practice because, they say, policy issues are static, while the candidates
are in constant motion, and journalism tends to follow the candidate, not the issue.[19]

The Center for Media and Public Affairs has been tracking media coverage of
three major networks: ABC, CBS, and NBC. The information below[20] shows
how much coverage has been of the "horse-race" variety:

Focus of coverage:	1988	1992	1996	2000	2004
Horse Race	58%	58%	48%	71%	48%
Policy Issues	39%	32%	37%	40%	49%

Horse-race stories are those which report on a campaign's game plan or other
strategic choices made by the candidates. These stories deemphasize the public
policy components of the campaign. Media critic Peter Hart says reporters
assigned to campaigns seem to be more interested in handicapping a race among
frontrunners. That kind of reporting, he says, tends to obsess over poll numbers
or fundraising efforts.[21] When the news media ignore issues, they fail in their
job to provide the electorate with vital information.

Another reason the race or game analogy works for the media is that it gets audience attention. This kind of reporting borders on entertainment, which attracts lots
of viewers—and larger audiences can be delivered to advertisers, who in turn
make huge profits.

Another media critic says horse-race journalism hurts those who need the information most: "since the media coverage of a presidential campaign often bears so little resemblance to what the public might want to know about candidates' positions, one can reasonably conclude that the point of campaign journalism is not to engage the public in the political process; indeed, it's the exact opposite."[23]

Republican media consultant Roger Ailes doesn't even mention issues when he lists the five things the media *are* interested in: "They're interested in polls, they're interested in pictures, they're interested in mistakes, and they're interested in attacks ... but they're also interested in advertising."[24]

The horse-race mentality has been criticized for years.

Political reporter D. D. Guttenplan is critical of reporters who are on the "campaign bus," constantly following their candidate on the road, reporting everything that happens, whether it is substantial or trivial. Having covered candidates himself, Guttenplan says peer pressure also gets in the way:

Polls, fundraising, media strategies—that's what the insiders on the road want to know about. Ask a candidate a detailed question about health care and you're instantly marked as a yahoo. Ask about day care or job creation or the racial makeup of his staff, and you're tagged as a fanatic—some kind of "ideologue." Why this should be so is difficult to explain, except that "on the bus," naivete is the worst possible offense. Even novice reporters quickly learn the philistinism of the road—that the best way to seem sophisticated is to ask the shallowest questions, preferably with a sneer in your voice.[25]

Covering the Debates as Horse Races

Following the 1992 campaign (Bill Clinton versus George Bush), the Freedom Forum Media Studies Center Research Group issued a detailed analysis of media coverage of the campaign entitled *The Media & Campaign '92*. When researchers examined post-debate coverage, for example, they concluded: "The news media's coverage of the debates provided very little information that was different from what audiences learned through watching the events themselves. In addition, in focusing on the horse-race aspect of the contest, the media neglected their interpretative and analytical function."[26]

How the Media Feels about Horse-Race Journalism

Much of the criticism about political campaign coverage seems to point in the same direction: reporters don't cover candidates' positions on the issues nearly enough. Media critics are vocal about the problem.

A lot of political coverage seems to be aimed at a small circle of political junkies. ... The key is to make the coverage relevant. To report on differences in proposed policy, find real people and examine the impact on them. ... Ad watches and ... Web site watches help the audience sort fact from hype. Tape a conversation among six or seven people, then edit it to highlight their views. The audience identifies with people like themselves, not the pundits.

—Barbara Cochran, president of the
Radio-TV News Directors Association[27]

"Basically, journalists need to be less concerned about their peers and more concerned about the public. There's a premium," says S. Robert Lichter, president of the Center for Media and Public Affairs, "on being witty and getting inside dope" at the expense of substance. He also finds writing that "demonstrates journalists' intellectual superiority." What journalists should do, he says, is "get up every day and . . . make everyone understand how this election relates to their lives, how it affects their lives." Campaign coverage on the network evening news shows has "dropped sharply," Lichter says. "Network news executives said, 'They can go to cable and to the Internet.' . . . So clearly we are in transition. . . . It used to be that the networks were the whole ball game."[28]

The Alternative to Horse-Race Coverage

For many years, journalists have been urged to move away from the horse-race narrative so common in campaign coverage. And what would they report on, if not the horse race? Media critic Brad Delong suggests "the better . . . narrative [would be] 'which of these policy proposals would be best for the country?' and 'what did we learn today about whether so-and-so would make a good or bad president.' " New York University journalism professor Jay Rosen, who edits the blog *Press-Think,* suggests reporters need to move to what he calls "the idea race." He cites the example of the *New York Times*'s coverage of candidate John Edwards, who made the issue of poverty a central theme in his campaign for the Democratic presidential nomination. Rosen maintains that "the idea race" is not just about the candidates, either. He cites singer/activist Bono's campaign to raise awareness of global poverty, enlisting the assistance of, among others, former U.S. senators Bill Frist and Tom Daschle.[29]

Media watchdog and critic Amy Goodman goes one step further, criticizing not only the issues unreported, but also the source of the money trail:

The race for the 2008 election is on, and all we hear about is the race for the money. Presidential hopefuls are vying with each other to raise tens of millions of dollars for what is projected to be the most expensive election in history. But hardly anyone is talking about where this money comes from or where it ends up. Fewer still have asked persistent questions about corporate America's grip over not just the elections, but most policy decisions out of Washington, DC.[30]

The Problems with Polls

Almost every poll, reported by the media, leading up to the New Hampshire primary on Tuesday January 8, 2008, indicated that Barack Obama had a huge (10 percentage points or better) lead over rival Hillary Clinton. The media were starting to report the death of the Clinton campaign, especially since Clinton trailed Obama in the Iowa caucus vote. The actual New Hampshire results took everyone, including the media, by surprise. Clinton bested Obama 39 percent to 36 percent.

When interviewed by the media, Senator Clinton noted that she pays little attention to the "snapshot polls." *Snapshot polls* is a phrase which takes its meaning from photography. To take a snapshot is to literally "take a picture"—simply capturing a single moment in time. Senator Clinton makes her point by implying that polls offer a myopic, limited view of the preferences of those being polled.

Every election cycle includes reporting by the media of poll results. Unless you've hidden your head under a rock, you've seen or read about any one of a number of polls asking voters who their favorite candidate is or soliciting opinions about an issue or controversy. Large polling organizations such as Gallup, Hart, Harris, Zogby, and Rasmussen Reports are hired by political parties, campaigns, lobbyists, and news organizations. It seems as if there is a new poll released every week, especially around election time.

The news media have also collaborated to conduct and report on their own poll results. Among those partnering to produce and report poll results:

ABC News and the *Washington Post*

NBC News and the *Wall Street Journal*

CBS News and the *New York Times*

Reuters (the international news agency) and Zogby International (a polling organization)

The problems with polls are numerous. Unsuspecting news consumers may hear the results and take them to be gospel. Very few people ever read the small print at the bottom of the poll, which might say, for example, "this poll has a margin of error of plus or minus 5 percentage points." Few of us really understand polling limitations.

Former National Public Radio ombudsman Jeffrey A. Dvorkin has some excellent advice in regard to polls.

1. Sample size: He says many polls ask too few people to be significant.

2. Scope: Many polls are not local, but rather emanate from large metropolitan areas.

3. Procedures: Did the pollster attempt to call back someone if they could not be reached the first time—in other words, is the poll representative?

4. Funding: Who paid for the poll? Do you know? Might they have an agenda?

5. Timeliness: When was the poll taken? Might it be out-of-date and thus misleading?

6. Questions: How were questions phrased? Could they have been misleading?[31]

When Media Make Mistakes

When the media cover elections, it becomes one of the biggest challenges for both print and broadcast. Election day is the culmination of thousands of hours of work by politicians and their volunteers.

The broadcast industry (radio and television) relish the opportunity to be the one place everyone tunes to for the results. And, of course, each news network wants to be the first with the news. But they can't give you the results right away. On the East Coast, most polls close by 7 PM. On the West Coast, some polls close as late as 11 PM or midnight Eastern Time. As more and more states begin to report their results, broadcasters start to make predictions based on exit polling.

Based on a sample of voters' opinions, as they leave their polling places, broadcast journalists predict who will win. And sometimes those predictions/trends are simply wrong.

Newspapers are also handicapped by having to publish before all of the results are known. One paper in particular made history because of who it thought had won the presidency.

Truman versus Dewey: One Newspaper's Wrong Prediction

The election for president of the United States in 1948 was a memorable one. The incumbent, President Harry Truman, a Democrat, was being challenged by heavy favorite and New York governor Thomas Dewey. On election day, results came in right up to the deadline in which many newspapers print their final editions. One of those newspapers was the *Chicago Daily Tribune.* With Dewey predicted to win, the *Tribune* went to press.

When Truman went to bed November 2, he was losing the election. Upon arising the next morning he, of course, learned he had won. He traveled to Washington, D.C. that day by train. On a short stop in St. Louis, Truman was presented with one of the "DEWEY DEFEATS TRUMAN" papers while on the back platform of the train. It was at this moment that the now famous photo of Truman

Pres. Harry S. Truman mischievously celebrates his narrow victory in the Nov. 4, 1948, presidential election by holding up a *Chicago Daily Tribune* headline prematurely calling the election for his opponent, Thomas E. Dewey. (AP Photo/Byron Rollins)

holding up the paper was taken. When asked to comment, Truman said, "This is for the books."[32] Another one for the books occurred 52 years later.[33]

Election Night 2000 Fiasco: The Night the News Media Goofed, Badly

The race for president in 2000 was one of the closest in recent history. Polls indicated a neck-in-neck race between Republican George W. Bush and his Democratic challenger, Vice President Al Gore. As results started to come in on election night November 7, it was clear that the polls might be right. Millions of people tuned into the major news networks to watch the election returns. Little did they know how long a night it would be.

At 7 PM, most of the polls had closed on the East Coast.

Election Night Timetable. If you were watching CBS, you would have heard anchorman Dan Rather say:

7:07 PM ET: "Let's get one thing straight, right from the get-go. We would rather be last in reporting returns than be wrong. If we say someone has carried a state, you can pretty much take it to the bank."

All of the major networks (ABC, CBS, and NBC), along with cable networks (CNN and FOX) and national news organization The Associated Press, fund the Voter News Service (VNS), a national exit-polling group. The VNS workers interview voters as they leave polling locations to determine who they voted for and why. All of this information goes into a national database, which is studied by analysts who report to the networks.

7:49 PM ET: Depending on VNS data of Florida results, all of the TV networks, within minutes of each other, declared Al Gore the new president.

8:00 PM ET CBS Bulletin: Dan Rather: "Florida just got pulled back into the undecided column. Computer and data problems. Turn the lights down, the party just got wilder."

2:16 AM ET (Wednesday, November 8): Fox News Channel projects Bush as the winner in Florida. ABC's Peter Jennings announces: "Unless there is a terrible calamity, George W. Bush, by our projections, is going to be the next president."

2:18 AM ET: CBS called Florida—and the election—for Bush.

2:57AM ET: CBS pulled back Florida for a second time. Over on NBC, anchorman Tom Brokaw was heard saying: "What the networks giveth, the networks taketh away."

Near 4 AM ET: Networks start retracting the Bush "call," declaring the presidential race in limbo.

In limbo it would stay. Needless to say, the networks were left with eggs on their faces. Millions of television viewers who depended on TV news to report the winner went to bed that night either not knowing who had been elected president, or thinking they knew who won, only to find on awakening that they were mistaken. (And they would not know for several weeks, as the issue went all the way to the U.S. Supreme Court before George Bush was finally declared the winner.)

Later, news executives were called to Washington to testify before the House Committee on Energy and Commerce, which oversees television issues. Many of the networks' news division spokespersons were angered that Congress might try to intrude on what they saw as a purely journalistic problem.

Fox News executive Roger Ailes acknowledged that the VNS "gave out bad numbers that night." ABC News president David Westin said that competitive pressures led to election night faux pas.

Apparently, voters agreed. In a poll, most voters felt the bad calls were motivated by the (TV) networks' desire to be the first to declare a winner rather than serving an audience need.[34]

Despite that, all of the networks agreed that next time, they would not call any state in a presidential election until all the polls in that state had closed. They also agreed that relying on the VNS system alone was a mistake, and they promised to rely on more than one source for their exit polling data.[35] Political media consultants are the people you rarely see, but their work is seen and heard. And their work becomes the stuff of history. In the past, the tools they used were the traditional media (radio, TV, newspapers, direct mail). Today, they rely on newer tools: new media and technology. New media such as cell phones and social networks (MySpace, Facebook, Twitter, etc.) are increasingly used by consultants to reach the media and tech-savvy consumer. The job of the consultant has not changed; but the manner to which voters are reached certainly has.

Notes

1. Philip Lentz, "The Power behind the Candidate," October 23, 2000, http://www.gothamgazette.com/iotw/polptofs/doc1.shtml.

2. Personal e-mail correspondence, 4/17/2007, with researcher Larry J. Sabato, via assistant Michael Baudinet.

3. Susan Milligan, "Candidates Spending Millions for Advice," *Boston Globe,* September 2, 2007, http://www.boston.com/news/nation/articles/2007/09/02/candidates_spending_millions_for_advice/?page=2.

4. Phil Leggiere, "BT Ready for Prime Time Politics," *Behavioral Insider,* MediaPost Publications, August 29, 2007, http://publications.mediapost.com/index.cfm?fuseaction=Articles.showArticleHomePage&art_aid=66581.

5. "Campaign Ads Target Voters' Favorite Shows," Associated Press, June 16, 2004.

6. John Anthony Maltese, *Spin Control: The White House Office of Communications and the Management of Presidential News,* 2nd ed. (Chapel Hill, NC: University of North Carolina Press, 1994). "We're going to build this whole campaign around television" Nixon said, "you fellows just tell me what you want me to do and I'll do it." (*The Spot,* page 163).

7. Edwin Diamond and Stephen Bates, *The Spot: The Rise of Political Advertising on Television,* 3rd ed. (Cambridge, MA: MIT Press, 1992), 156.

8. Joe McGinniss, *The Selling of the President, 1968* (New York: Trident Press, 1969).

9. John Anthony Maltese, *Spin Control: The White House Office of Communications and the Management of Presidential News,* 2nd ed. (Chapel Hill, NC: University of North Carolina Press, 1994), 59–60.

10. Edmund Morris, *Dutch: A Memoir of Ronald Reagan* (New York: Random House, 1999), 421.

11. Nancy Reagan with William Novak, *My Turn: The Memoirs of Nancy Reagan* (New York: Random House, 1989), 239.

12. Michael K. Deaver, quoted in the documentary *American Photography: A Century of Images* (PBS, October 13, 1999). Reviewed by John Kiesewetter in the *Cincinnati Enquirer,* October 13, 1999, http://www.enquirer.com/editions/1999/10/13/loc_century _of_images.html.

13. From the PBS transcript: http://www.pbs.org/ktca/americanphotography/ filmandmore/transcript3.html.

14. Victoria Sherrow, *Image and Substance: The Media in U.S. Elections* (Brookfield, CT: Millbrook Press, 1992), 49.

15. CBS producer Richard Cohen, quoted in Martin Schram, *The Great American Video Game: Presidential Politics in the Television Age* (New York : Morrow, c1987), 33.

16. CNN Perspectives: The Reagan Years: Inside the White House: http:// transcripts.cnn.com/TRANSCRIPTS/0102/18/cgs.00.html.

17. Kenneth T. Walsh, "The Public Face," in *U.S. News & World Report,* December 13, 2004, http://www.usnews.com/usnews/news/articles/041213/13walsh.htm.

18. Joe Trippi, *The Revolution Will Not Be Televised* (2004; repr., New York: Harper-Collins, 2005), 41. The ad's complicated gestation is described at http://www.inside politics.org/ps111/independentads.html.

19. Thomas E. Patterson, *Out of Order* (New York: Knopf, 1993), 62.

20. Media Monitor, 18.6, November–December 2004, http://www.cmpa.com/files/ media_monitor/04novdec.pdf.

21. Peter Hart, "Why People Hate Politics—Blame Journalism That Isn't?," *Fairness & Accuracy in Reporting, Extra! Update,* August 2007.

23. Peter Hart, "Why People Hate Politics—Blame Journalism That Isn't?," *Fairness & Accuracy in Reporting, Extra! Update,* August 2007.

24. Roger Ailes, "The Selling of the President: An Interview with Roger Ailes," *Gannett Center Journal* (Fall 1988): 70.

25. D. D. Guttenplan, "Out of It: While Perot Gets through to the Voters, the Press Gets Lost on the Campaign Trail," *Columbia Journalism Review* 31, no. 2 (July–August 1992): 10(3).

26. Martha FitzSimon, ed., *The Finish Line: Covering the Campaign's Final Days* (New York: Freedom Forum Media Studies Center, 1993), 13.

27. Lacy Papai and Lori Robertson, eds., "Campaign Reform," *American Journalism Review* (September 2000), http://www.ajr.org/article.asp?id=686.

28. Ibid.

29. Jay Rosen, "Who's Ahead" No, Seriously," Pressthink blog, June 15, 2007, http:// journalism.nyu.edu/pubzone/weblogs/pressthink/2007/06/15/idea_race08.html.

30. Amy Goodman, quoted in "Enough Already," by Danny Schechter, Huffington Post blog, July 10, 2007, http://www.huffingtonpost.com/danny-schechter/enough-already_b_55653.html.

31. Jeffrey A. Dvorkin, "The Way Polls Can Mislead Media Matters," www.npr.org/ yourturn/ombudsman/000504.html.

32. Lewis Kramer, "The Story behind 'Dewey Beats Truman,'" History Buff, http:// www.historybuff.com/library/reftruman.html.

33. James Poniewozik, "TV Makes a Too-Close Call," *Time Magazine,* November 20, 2000, http://www.time.com/time/magazine/article/0,9171,998547-2,00.html; Neil

Hickey, "The Big Mistake," *Columbia Journalism Review* (January/February 2001), 38, http://backissues.cjrarchives.org/year/01/1/hickey.asp; Katherine Q. Seelye, "Network Chiefs Get Flogging at Capitol for Election Fiasco," *New York Times,* February 15, 2001.

34. Andrew Kohut, director of the Pew Research Center for the People and the Press, http://backissues.cjrarchives.org/year/01/1/kohut.asp.

35. *USA Today,* February 15, 2001; *New York Times,* February 15, 2001.

4

Analyzing Photographs

[Presidents] must try to master the art of manipulating the media not only to win in politics but in order to further the programs and causes they believe in; at the same time they must avoid at all costs the charge of trying to manipulate the media.
—Richard Nixon, *The Memoirs of Richard Nixon* (1978)

A democratic civilization will save itself only if it makes the language of the image into a stimulus for critical reflection, not an invitation to hypnosis.
—Umberto Eco, Italian philosopher and novelist (1979)

The camera eye has affected the democratic political process more than any other invention since the ballot box.
—Leonard Shlain, *The Alphabet versus the Goddess: The Conflict between Word and Image* (1998)

All media messages are representations. Photographs, especially, essentially preserve single moments in time. The photographer captures a very small part that represents the entire event, even though we don't see the entire event. When viewing media representations, such as photographs, it is important to ask a number of questions. What might this person or event really represent? Who or what is omitted, and why?

REPRESENTATIONS

Representation is an important concept in media literacy. In general it means "the process by which a constructed media text stands for, symbolizes, describes, or represents people, places, events, or ideas that are real and have an existence outside the text."[1] Politicians who are in office, and those who run for office, are

> **Media Literacy Core Concepts:**
> *Media messages are constructed using a creative language with its own set of rules.*
> *Different people experience the same media message differently.*
>
> **Media Literacy Key Questions:**
> *What techniques are used by the creator to attract attention?*
> *What lifestyles, values, points of view are represented in, or omitted from, this message?*

always concerned about their image. Their campaign aides and consultants try to control how the media convey their image in the press. "Photo ops" (photo opportunities) abound: specific events and times when news photographers can capture the candidate doing anything from kissing babies to eating lunch.

All candidates are interested in how they are represented. Candidates may, for example, wear a coat and tie in order to communicate a serious, business, or formal message—or they may dress down, as John Edwards did, in blue jeans and no tie, for much of his poverty tour. Or they might wear the color red, as Hillary Clinton frequently has done, to perhaps communicate patriotism. Or they may be photographed in military gear, seated in a tank, as was Democratic presidential nominee Michael Dukakis in 1988, trying to communicate his strength on America's defense. President George W. Bush sought to send the message that he was a strong leader when he appeared on an aircraft carrier to declare "Mission Accomplished" in Iraq (even though the mission wore on for years following that declaration).

PHOTOGRAPHY AND THE BIRTH OF THE CAMPAIGN PHOTOGRAPH

Direct representations of actual persons and events (as opposed to artists' renderings) became possible only in the mid-19th century. In the beginning, there was only photography: no radio, no TV. And pictures were only in black and white. Men running for office hoped that their images, along with the appropriate words, would appeal to voters. Early campaign posters incorporated photographs. The 1860 election of Abraham Lincoln was partly credited to the fact that people could now *see* the man they'd heard so much about. Today, photographers are more sophisticated: they use digital equipment and tools. Acquiring an image and delivering it to a news editor now takes minutes rather than hours. But can you believe everything you see?

MAKING LINCOLN LOOK PRESIDENTIAL

The first president to exploit photography was Abe Lincoln. An early photograph of Lincoln, taken by Mathew Brady, was credited with helping elect the 16th president. Brady's image of Lincoln made him appear more handsome and

Mathew B. Brady's February 1860 portrait of Abraham Lincoln, taken shortly before Lincoln's address at the Cooper Union Institute in New York City. Some scholars hold that this address opposing the expansion of slavery into the western territories was responsible for his victory in the 1860 presidential election. (Courtesy of the Library of Congress, Prints & Photographs Division, LC-USZ62-5803)

less gangly. Brady accomplished the task by pulling up Lincoln's collar to cover his long neck. He retouched his face to help eliminate the gauntness. The photo was reprinted and used in magazines such as the widely read *Harper's Weekly*. From that moment until today, the use of photography has been understood by presidents as a powerful way to communicate with people.[2]

Another American president to take advantage of his photographic image was Teddy Roosevelt. Even though he complained about news photographers' intrusiveness, Roosevelt also took advantage of the medium. A photograph of him as a "Rough Rider" during the Spanish-American War of 1898 was so popular that a letter with nothing but a hand-drawn copy of this picture was delivered to his

Campaign poster or banner image used by the Republican Party in the 1860 presidential campaign. Lincoln's portrait is flanked by figures representing Justice and Liberty. Baker and Godwin had supplied the same banner for Millard Fillmore in the 1856 presidential campaign, simply replacing the portrait for the 1860 version. (Courtesy of the Library of Congress, Prints & Photographs Division, LC-DIG-ppmsca-19254)

Then-Colonel Theodore Roosevelt at Camp Wikoff on Montauk Point, Long Island, in 1898, after his triumphant return from Cuba with his "Rough Riders" volunteer cavalry. After the famous charge up San Juan Hill established the "Rough Riders" image, journalists flocked to Roosevelt, now a war hero. The photograph is by Frances Benjamin Johnston. (Courtesy of the Library of Congress, Prints & Photographs Division, Frances Benjamin Johnston Collection, LC-USZC4-11819)

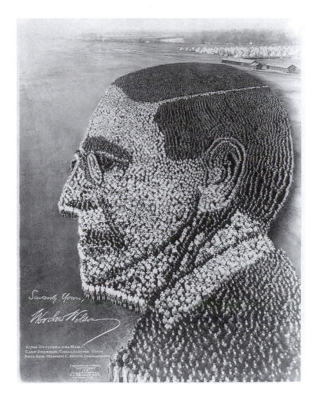

For this 1918 "living photograph" portraying President Woodrow Wilson, photographer Arthur Mole and his associate, John Thomas, assembled and posed some 21,000 servicemen at Camp Sherman in Chillicothe, Ohio. The photo was taken from a 75-foot tower erected for this purpose. (Courtesy of the Library of Congress, Prints & Photographs Division, LC-USZ62-77278)

home. Roosevelt employed photographers who captured his trips on safari, his trips out West, and his perch on a steam shovel at the Panama Canal.

Woodrow Wilson's public persona was more one-sidedly intellectual, but he too benefited from the tradition of providing leadership portraits meant to be treasured by patriotic citizens. Toward the end of World War I, in 1918, photographer Arthur Mole and his partner John Thomas arranged with the Army at Camp Sherman in Chillicothe, Ohio, to photograph some 21,000 soldiers—some in dark dress, some in light—painstakingly arranged to form a pattern that "read" at the photographer's prescribed distance as a profile of Wilson. Mole and Thomas's "living photo" captured the symbolic image of Wilson, commander in both war and peace, who, seen from the right vantage point, was revealed to be entirely composed of his loyal followers.[3]

ANALYZING POLITICAL PHOTOGRAPHS

How we interpret photographs depends on a number of factors. For example, have you had any photography training that would help you understand framing, composition, depth-of-field, focus, backlighting, and so on? Have you been exposed to any "visual literacy" education designed to help you "read" photographic images? Assuming the answer is no, then you would not necessarily have the skills needed to read the "language" of photographic images. Visual literacy has been defined as the "ability to understand, interpret, and evaluate visual messages."[4]

Questioning Photographs

Professional photographers and photojournalists who *have* had training understand how to use the tools of their trade—and how to use those tools to communicate a message to the audience. Today, those tools include the ability to digitally alter an image and the ability to capture an event and transmit it millions of miles in a few minutes. But that wasn't always the case.

Is Seeing Believing?

Take a look at the photograph that shows Senator Robert Kennedy (at the time, one of the Democrats trying to win his party's presidential nomination) walking alongside his wife, Ethel, on a beach. The location is Astoria, Oregon, and the photo was taken on May 28, 1968. The Oregon primary was just a few days later.

May 24, 1968: Senator Robert F. Kennedy and his wife, Ethel Kennedy, walk along the beach in Astoria, Oregon. (Courtesy of the John F. Kennedy Presidential Library; Burton Berinsky/Landov)

Thinking about this image and what it might represent, we might say that it could be representative of a romantic moment: two people sharing some quiet time, relaxing and alone. The fog in the distance also lends to the mood. We might speculate as to the weather, because the Senator has his hands in his pockets; his wife is wearing a coat. She has taken her shoes off in order to walk in the sand. There appear to be tire tracks in the sand, indicative of a car or some other vehicle having driven there. How did the photographer know they would be on the beach at that time? Did the Kennedy campaign issue a press release notifying the media that the candidate would be available for a photo op? What was the campaign hoping this image would communicate to voters?

The important thing to remember here is that the Kennedys were not alone. The photographer who took this picture was situated behind them. His framing of this shot, or "cropping" of it, is such that we are not allowed to see what might be to the left or right of the Kennedys. We should ask: what is outside the photographer's viewfinder? What are we not allowed to see, and why?

Now look at the subsequent image, taken by the same photographer from a different angle a short time later. Notice the number of people who can be seen in the wider shot.

How do you feel about the first photograph, now that you've seen the second one? Does this change your impression or your understanding of this staged event? We might ask, who are those people surrounding the candidate and his wife?

Some time later, another photo was taken: It reveals that the senator not only has taken off his shoes but has rolled up his pants—and he has been joined by many other people on the beach.

"A picture is worth a thousand words." That old adage might be true. But photographs, like all media, have a language all their own. Our understanding of these images depends on how much we know about how the images are created. In photography, the person shooting the picture can manipulate the image by:

- Moving higher, lower, closer to, or further from the subject
- Adjusting the lens to zoom in closer, or pull out to seem further away
- Changing the focus
- Changing the depth-of-field

When they are preparing their photographs for publication, photographers have a number of digital tools to use to improve or enhance the image. (Tools such as PhotoShop have made news of their own recently with the digital manipulation of images of models on magazine covers.)

Photographs, like writing, communicate information as much by the way a subject is photographed, as by the content that is chosen to be photographed.[5] By asking a series of questions, we can begin to better understand why the photographer took the image, what might be communicated by it, and how to better understand it. Questions to consider are:

- What is happening in the picture?
- How might the subject(s) be feeling?
- How might a person's facial expression and body posture reveal his or her feelings?
- What do you see in the background?
- What do the background details tell us about the person or action?
- Why did the photographer include these details?
- What details might be omitted, outside the frame?
- What do you know about the photograph; what don't you know; what would you like to know?

Applying Critical Thinking Questions to Political Images

Can you believe what you see? Part of being media literate about images in the news is to apply this and other critical thinking questions to the images. Questions you might consider include:

- Who took the photograph?
- How might the photographer want me to feel?
- For what purpose was the picture taken?
- For which publication/organization/Web site is it intended? (newspaper, magazine, TV, Web)
- Who is likely to be exposed to this photo? (Who is the target audience?)
- What do you know about the content of the image? (for example, from the caption or the accompanying story)
- Where can you go to locate additional reliable, relevant information?

THE PRESS AND THE PRESIDENT'S POLIO

Did you know that President Franklin D. Roosevelt had what was thought to be polio and was confined to a wheelchair for much of his adult life? If you didn't know, you are not alone. There were more than 35,000 photos taken of Franklin D. Roosevelt during his presidency, but only two showed him wheelchair-bound.[6] Most photos show him seated, not standing. In deference to the chief executive, news photographers at the time agreed to photograph him only in settings that would not include his wheelchair or his crutches. Roosevelt would arrive hours ahead of a scheduled speech or appearance in order to be in a position that would not reveal his disability.[7] Would publishing photos showing the president's actual physical condition send a message, to readers and to America's foes, that the chief executive was weak?

Acutely aware of the image he projected on camera, Franklin D. Roosevelt was photographed only twice using the wheelchair to which he was confined after a bout with polio in 1921. In this 1941 photo, he shows his Scottish terrier, Fala, to Ruthie Bie, the granddaughter of the caretaker of a cottage at his Hyde Park, New York, estate. Most photographs of Roosevelt show him standing with an unobtrusive means of support, such as a lectern, or sitting in an apparently ordinary pose, such as behind a desk, in an open car, or with a seated group of leaders. (AP Photo/M. L. Suckley/ FDR Library)

IT SOUNDED LIKE A GOOD IDEA AT THE TIME

Some carefully staged media events backfire. At the beginning of the chapter, the "strong on defense" photograph of 1988 Democratic presidential candidate Michael Dukakis was mentioned. But Governor Dukakis looked silly and out of place, not "presidential," riding around in a tank with an ill-fitting helmet on his head. Some political photos are funny—one or two of them intentionally.

Most political photos are totally forgettable. Some are memorable, and a few key images are totally unforgettable, capturing moments of high drama in ways that provide a shared sense of history for all. Who can forget the image of President Richard Nixon waving goodbye as he prepared to board a helicopter on his last day in office after being forced to resign in the wake of the Watergate scandal? When a photo captures such a moment, political life somehow escapes

The "Mission Accomplished" banner proclaiming victory served as the visual counterpart to President George W. Bush's carefully orchestrated May 1, 2003, speech announcing the end of major combat operations in Iraq. The banner's message proved to be embarrassingly premature. (AP Photo/J. Scott Applewhite)

control of the spin doctors and image masters, and manages to recover a sense of immediacy, vitality, and significance.[8]

THE "MISSION ACCOMPLISHED" SPIN

On May 1, 2003, a few months after the United States's war with Iraq had begun, the White House spin machine went into action. The president, it was decided, would give a major speech aboard the USS *Abraham Lincoln,* an aircraft carrier, as it was making its way into the port of San Diego, California. The president would tell the American people that "major combat operations in Iraq have ended." Many people will remember the image of President George W. Bush landing in one of the U.S. Navy's planes, exiting dressed in a flight suit and talking to many of the sailors on the flight deck. *New York Times* reporter Frank Rich later noted that the Bush speech was delivered at sunset, so as to give photographers the best light in which to photograph the president, and that a White House communications expert had seen to it that a huge banner declaring "Mission Accomplished" could not be missed, hovering just over the president's head.[9] Many in the media compared the depiction of the president to the popular film "Top Gun." Critics called it an expensive and embarrassing publicity stunt. Bush fans and the compliant media just swooned, thus demonstrating the point, according to media critic Norman Solomon, that the determining factor was not the choreography, but rather the perspective of those who watched the event.[10]

THE WHITE HOUSE AND CONTROLLING THE MEDIA IMAGE

The national press corps (which represents newspapers; news magazines; network, cable, and local television news operations; and others) is composed of hundreds of people who follow the president everywhere he goes and document his every step and every word. In order to control the images, the White House Office of Communications positions the photographers—in other words, determines from what angle they must shoot—in order to capture and convey just the right image/ message to American news consumers. Like NASCAR drivers in the winner's circle, President Bush was put on a stage with a colorful background setting: all of the photographers then captured the same moments and images.

In May 2003 the *New York Times* published a revealing essay about the George W. Bush White House's use of stagecraft: constructing the stage and controlling the image when President Bush traveled on location to give a speech. *New York Times* reporter Elisabeth Bumiller pulled back the curtain on White House media control.

Pres. George W. Bush delivers a speech about homeland security in August 2002, positioned at the base of the Mount Rushmore National Memorial, near Keystone, S.D., so as to capture in the photograph frame the majestic monument beyond. (AP Photo/Ken Lambert)

Bumiller reported on the hiring of a former ABC News producer and a former NBC cameraman, both of whom went on to work for the White House Office of Communications. She cited several instances in which the White House advance team worked to control the setting and the images, even going so far, at one appearance, as to ask men in the crowd to remove their ties so as to look like regular folk. "We pay particular attention to not only what the president says but what the American people see," admitted Dan Bartlett, then director of White House Communications.[11]

READING IMAGES

The next time you open up a newspaper, news magazine, or news Web site, consider the image(s) chosen by the news organization. Read the caption provided by the photojournalist, but be mindful of what is not shown—that which is outside the frame.

In order to read a photograph, you have to ask a number of important questions, many of which are common sense.

- Who took the photo, and why?
- Where was it published, and why is it there?
- From what position was the photo taken?
- How is the image framed? What might have been omitted, and why?
- What is in the background, and why are these elements important?
- What might facial and other nonverbal expressions reveal about what is happening?
- How does this make you feel?

NOTES

1. Media Awareness Network, http://www.media-awareness.ca/english/resources/educational/teaching_backgrounders/media_literacy/glossary_media_literacy.cfm#R.

2. "Presidential Image Making," *American Photography: A Century of Images,* http://www.pbs.org/ktca/americanphotography/features/pres_essay.html.

3. Vicki Goldberg and Robert Silberman, *American Photography: A Century of Images* (San Francisco: Chronicle Books, 1999), 77–78. See also Louis Kaplan's article "Dead Troops Salute" in the quarterly magazine *Cabinet,* no. 24 (Winter 2006/2007), http://www.cabinetmagazine.org/issues/24/kaplan.php.

4. Valerie J. Bristor and Suzanne V. Drake, "Linking the Language Arts and Content Areas through Visual Technology," *THE Journal (Technological Horizons in Education),* 22 (1994): 74(4).

5. Wendy Ewald, *Literacy through Photography, Teacher Guide* (Durham, NC: Duke University), http://cds.aas.duke.edu/ltp/.

6. Paul J. Maurier, "Media Feeding Frenzies: Press Behavior During Two Clinton Scandals." *Presidential Studies Quarterly,* 29.1 (March 1999): 65.

7. Stacy Anderson, "FDR Made a 'Tacit Agreement' with the Public about Disability," paraphrasing Richard Harris of Ball State University (speech, October 17, 2003), http://www.umich.edu/~urecord/0304/Oct27_03/19.shtml.

8. "Presidential Image Making," *American Photography: A Century of Images,* http://www.pbs.org/ktca/americanphotography/features/pres_essay.html.

9. Frank Rich, *The Greatest Story Ever Sold: The Decline and Fall of Truth from 9/11 to Katrina* (New York: Penguin, 2006), 90.

10. Norman Solomon, "Visual Images and How We See the World," http://www.alternet.org/columnists/story/16284/.

11. Elisabeth Bumiller, "Keepers of Bush Image Lift Stagecraft to New Heights," *New York Times,* May 16, 2003.

5

And Then There Was Radio

With electricity we were wired into a new world, for electricity brought the radio, a "crystal set" and with enough ingenuity, one could tickle the crystal with a cat's whisker and pick up anything.

—novelist and journalist Theodore H. White

The speed of communications is wondrous to behold. It is also true that speed can multiply the distribution of information that we know to be untrue.

—Edward R. Murrow (1964)

With the invention of radio, and its embrace by those running for office, politics would be forever changed. This new medium did not quickly displace the personal appearances by the candidates, but it did allow them to reach more people in a shorter amount of time.

In 1916 inventor Lee DeForest was running his own amateur "radio telephone" show of phonograph music and chats from his laboratory in Highbridge, N.Y. In November he arranged for a special line to be run to his home from the newspaper offices of the *New York American* to supply him with election returns, which he then broadcast over the air to his amateur friends, up to 200 miles away. As 11:00 PM approached on election day, DeForest decided it was time for bed. In a foreshadowing of the famous Dewey "victory" over Truman headline in 1948, DeForest, looking over the returns, duly confirmed that Charles Evans Hughes had defeated Woodrow Wilson![1]

With radio in its infancy, Woodrow Wilson would not know how many people would hear the first broadcast speech by a president in 1919. Following Wilson, Warren Harding was able to broadcast from a special transmitter built into his

Media Literacy Core Concept:
Media messages are constructed using a creative language with its own set of rules.

Media Literacy Key Questions:
Who created this message?
Why was this message sent?

campaign train. Calvin Coolidge was aware of the reach of radio: his March 4, 1925 inaugural address was transmitted by 27 radio stations to what was estimated to be about 15 million listeners. "On Dec. 6, 1923, in a conversational but nasalized tone, Coolidge delivered the first broadcast State of the Union address. So clear was the transmission that when a radio station in St. Louis called the Capitol to ask 'What's that grating noise?,' experts responded 'That's the rustling of the paper as he turns the pages of his message.' "[2]

In the early 1920s, Herbert Hoover, Secretary of Commerce under Harding, spearheaded radio's development and organized conferences that dealt with the new medium's technical issues. In 1922 there were only about 60,000 U.S. homes with radios. By 1924 there were more than one million radios in homes. Yet that represented only about 5 percent of the entire U.S. population. Radios were being mass produced by many companies and advertised in magazines such as *National Geographic* and *Ladies' Home Journal*. Radio stations were popping up everywhere. Yet radio didn't catch on quickly: many thought it a novelty, while others considered owning a radio a luxury.

In 1924 both candidates for president, Republican Calvin Coolidge and Democrat John W. Davis, bought radio time for speeches, but not ads. Republicans spent three times as much as the Democrats. Coolidge won that year.[3]

That year's broadcast of the two parties' political conventions proved very popular, according to one historian: "Convention broadcasting became a national drama as some stations not carrying the convention shut down to avoid interfering with nearby stations broadcasting it. Around the country schools closed so that students could listen, radio demonstration rooms in department stores were packed with people, and sales of radio sets hit record levels. For the first time, the American people were able to look in on a national political convention." And look in they did. Radio became the centerpiece for everyone who wanted to keep up with news, speeches, and political events. "When the 1924 campaign began, no one knew what radio would be worth as a weapon in the campaign war chest. For millions to hear the voices of the candidates was unique—it couldn't be duplicated in silent movies or newspapers. Many in both parties questioned how they could know if there was an audience listening and if their message was reaching them. By the end of the campaign, these questions and more were answered. It was clear that radio had improved politics, and, furthermore, politics had improved radio."[4]

Future president Herbert C. Hoover listens to an early radio receiver, circa 1925. Regulation of the airwaves began while Hoover was Commerce Secretary under Pres. Calvin Coolidge. (Courtesy of the Library of Congress, Prints & Photographs Division, National Photo Company Collection, LC-USZ62-111716)

THE BIRTH OF THE SOUNDBITE

By 1928 radio was in eight million American homes. When President Calvin Coolidge decided not to seek reelection, Herbert Hoover became the Republicans' nominee. That year, the *New York Times* reported, "brief pithy statements . . . will reach the emotions through the minds of millions of radio listeners."[5] And so, the soundbite was born. The soundbite would become extremely popular. Scriptwriters included soundbites in talks, knowing full well that the press and the public would remember them. The race for the presidency that year was between Hoover and New York governor (and Democrat) Alfred E. Smith, both of whom purchased ad time on radio to reach voters. Radio was a natural choice for both candidates to use, and an estimated $2 million was spent on advertising that year. The Republicans had pioneered the one-minute spot announcement. While running for office, Hoover's slogan was the popular promise, "a chicken in every pot, a car in every garage."

In the early days of radio, live presidential convention coverage was considered sufficiently exciting to provide the theme for ads from companies such as Zenith, RCA, and Westinghouse. This Zenith Radio Corporation ad dates from 1928. (Photo courtesy of Frank W. Baker)

Listen to Hoover's radio broadcast accepting the GOP nomination for president: http://www.presidency.ucsb.edu/mediaplay.php?id=23198&admin=31.

RADIO: THE INTIMATE MEDIUM

Radio historian Susan J. Douglas says politics on the radio was riveting to the 1932 audience because it created a "you are there" atmosphere: "even listening to something as dull as a Hoover campaign speech in 1932 was much more gripping on the radio. It wasn't just that the announcer evoked the scene by telling you that 'more than 30,000 people packed and jammed every available seat' in this auditorium in Cleveland—you heard the sounds of people milling around, talking, yelling and applauding . . . you heard the ovation and the rousing band music . . . [it] brought you to the hall and allowed you to participate vicariously . . . to be part of the crowd, and to envision a thriving public sphere consisting of thousands of everyday people."[6]

Hoover, meanwhile was trying to reassure a panicky population: the country was in the midst of the Great Depression, which eventually led to his downfall. By 1932, voters wanted change, and when he ran against Franklin Delano Roosevelt, he lost. It's estimated that almost $5 million was spent that year on radio advertising by both parties.[7]

Roosevelt was a natural on radio, using it extensively in what became known as the "fireside chats," beaming regular radio broadcasts from 1933–1944 into homes, where families gathered to listen. He used the radio address to mobilize support for key provisions of his New Deal.[8] His chats inspired just the surge of confidence the nation needed in the dark days of the Depression. It marked the first time American people had been spoken to simply and directly by their president.[9]

Listen to FDR fireside chats: http://www.presidency.ucsb.edu/medialist.php?presid=32and http://www.fdrlibrary.marist.edu/audio.html.

Read transcripts of FDR fireside chats: http://www.mhric.org/fdr/fdr.html, http://www.fdrlibrary.marist.edu/firesi90.html, and http://www.presidency.ucsb.edu/fireside.php.

The use of radio by politicians was not without controversy. Everyone wanted a piece of the pie. There were questions of fairness and objectivity, all of which eventually led to new legislation in the areas of equal time and freedom of speech.

In the 1950s television began to be used more and more by politicians, although radio was still quite popular.

Even though television was available, Richard Nixon used radio during his White House run in 1968. He purchased half-hour blocks of time and found them

In March 1933, Pres. Franklin D. Roosevelt delivered the first of his legendary "fireside chats," radio talks directed to ordinary citizens in which he explained New Deal policies and, later, the events of World War II, seeking to instill confidence and allay listeners' fears. Roosevelt continued these chats periodically until June 1944. (AP Photo)

In the 1930s radio transformed the lives of many Americans. Beautifully designed radio consoles were the focus of family living rooms. (Photograph by the Rural Electrification Administration; Courtesy of the Franklin D. Roosevelt Library and Museum)

to be a cost-effective way of delivering his themes.[10] Later he explained: "I did make great use of it because I have found that while naturally the primary emphasis these days in terms of any public relations program and any political program is on television because of the huge impact that it has, the radio audience is first a very large audience and a very significant audience; second, it is a growing audience—all of your advertising is, too; and, third, it is particularly a large audience in the teenage group."[11]

And radio is still used by candidates today. The radio industry promotes this medium to politicians because of its ability to "narrowcast," that is, to target listeners both by where they live (geographically), by who they represent (demographically), and by what genre of music they listen to (talk, hip-hop, rock, country, and so on). Local AM and FM radio stations have the ability to reach audiences in places television can't—in cars, for example.

In 1996 Tobe Berkovitz of Boston University's College of Communications summarized the strengths of various formats and explained their particular appeal for political advertisers in his *Political Media Buying: A Brief Guide:*[12]

Radio stations employ formats, or types of programming, which are designed to attract a narrower audience than is possible with television. Radio formatting tends to reduce waste in the audience desired in a media buy.

Radio stations sell time by appealing to the advertisers need for concentrated, narrow demographics. By judging the format used by a station, and analyzing the rating demographic data, radio buys can be made extremely cost-efficient. Radio is effective to reach defined geographic targets. It is a localized medium and concentrates in a tight geographic region. Although advertising time is sold on a limited number of network radio programs, the vast majority of radio time purchased for political campaigns is bought on a spot basis by selecting specific radio media markets. The following is a brief overview of different formats to help focus on the advantages of using radio for campaign advertising.

Middle of the Road:
   AM station with a powerful signal. Strong on-air personalities. Popular music, news, service features, traffic reports, weather updates, sports coverage or talk shows at night. Audience 35+.

News and Information:
   Usually an AM station. Efficient attracting likely voters. Night programs talk shows or sports coverage.

Talk Radio:
   Usually an AM station with a highly involved and loyal audience. This type of programming can mix with other formats such as News and Information. Live sports coverage can be featured at night.

Contemporary Hit Radio:
   Very popular skew under 35. Adult contemporary is a format similar to CHR, but attracts slightly older demographics.

Varied Rock Formats:
   Usually skew young.

Country and Western:
   Demographics relatively broad for radio, but strong ratings in most parts of the country.

Black Formats:
   Several variations to the format. Demographics vary tremendously frequently skewing young.

The radio broadcast day is also divided into sections that are called dayparts. Advertising time is placed in dayparts. The following is an overview of radio station dayparts:

AM Drive:
   Highest ratings of the day. Reaches people getting ready to go to work and commuters. Most popular personalities are in AM.

Midday:
   High ratings, reaches people at work and at home.

PM Drive:

Good ratings, reaches commuters and people at home. Evening: Includes sports and talk programs. Lower reach. Older listeners late at night.

Source: Excerpt from Tobe Berkovitz, *Political Media Buying: A Brief Guide.* http://www.hks.harvard.edu/case/3pt/berkovitz.html. Copyright © 1996, Tobe Berkovitz, Ph.D.

WHAT RADIO ADVERTISING COSTS

When candidates purchase ad time on radio, they don't buy time for one ad; they purchase multiple times for their ad, in hopes of reaching people through repetition. A number of factors depend on the cost of the ad package, including how many listeners are likely to be tuned in at a certain time. Refer to Table 5.1.

Tobe Berkovitz continues:

Radio is a medium which requires substantial frequency to achieve the goals of an advertiser. Most advertisers feel that 18 spots a week on a station is an absolute minimum necessary to have any impact on the listener. Most buys will run 24 to over 50 ads a week per station. 24 spots a week is a solid average radio buy. At least three stations should be bought to insure satisfactory reach of the target audience. Many markets have a radio

Table 5.1
Spot Radio Advertising Time

Market	Avg. weekly buy	
New York	Light	$45,000
	Med./heavy	$90,000
Los Angeles	Light	$55,000
	Med./heavy	$110,000
Chicago	Light	$33,000
	Med./heavy	$65,000
Washington, DC	Light	$33,000
	Med./heavy	$66,000
Dallas	Light	$27,000
	Med./heavy	$54,000
Seattle	Light	$22,000
	Med./heavy	$43,000
Miami	Light	$17,000
	Med./heavy	$33,000
Denver	Light	$13,000
	Med./heavy	$25,000
Phoenix	Light	$11,000
	Med./heavy	$22,000
Kansas City	Light	$6,000
	Med./heavy	$13,000

Light buy = 72 spots market total
Med./heavy buy = 144 spots market total
Source: Tobe Berkovitz, *Political Media Buying: A Brief Guide*[13]

station that dominates the ratings for the desired target demographics. This station is usually bought heavily.[14]

TAILORING THE MESSAGE TO THE AUDIENCE

In the 2008 presidential campaign, Democrat Barack Obama was one of a number of candidates to use radio to reach targeted groups of potential voters. When the Obama campaign purchased advertising time on radio stations in Nevada, for example, the ad narration was in Spanish; an estimated 24 percent of that state's population is Hispanic. Similarly, African-Americans in South Carolina were targeted using radio stations that they frequently listen to; it is estimated that 30 percent of that state's population is black.[15]

RADIO ADS FOR BARACK OBAMA AND MITT ROMNEY THAT RAN IN SOUTH CAROLINA DURING THE 2007–2008 PRESIDENTIAL CAMPAIGN

Title: Man of Hope (August 2007)
Listen to the ad: http://sc.barackobama.com/page/content/schome.

60 sec.

Transcript:[16]

Announcer:
  "Barack Obama and the politics of hope."

Barack Obama:
  "I was a young community organizer working with a group of churches that were trying to do something about the devastation of steel plants that had closed. The fact that I was working with a lot of churches led me to conclude that I probably need to start going to church. So one day I walk in to Trinity United Church of Christ. And my pastor's premise is very simple. He says, 'Listen, the easiest thing in the world is to be cynical. You look at the world as it is, with its poverty and its violence and its division, and the easiest thing is to say, there's not much we can do to change it.' "

Announcer:
  "Barack Obama found that through faith and hope and hard work we can make a change for America."

Barack Obama:
  "Although the world as it is may have its problems, that does not determine the world as it might be."

Announcer:
  "Barack Obama for the future of America. Barack Obama for President."

Barack Obama:
"I'm Barack Obama and I approved this message."

Announcer:
"Paid for by Obama for America."

Title: Exceptional (August–September 2007)
Watch the ad: http://www.youtube.com/watch?v=JoTyYgB01Bc.

60 sec.

Transcript:[17]

Announcer:
"Immigration laws don't work if they're ignored. That's the problem with cities like Newark, San Francisco and New York City that adopt sanctuary policies. Sanctuary cities become magnets that encourage illegal immigration and undermine secure borders. As Governor, Mitt Romney didn't wait on Washington. He acted to make our immigration laws work. Mitt Romney is the exceptional governor who took a stand so State Police could enforce federal immigration laws. Mitt Romney said 'No' to drivers' licenses for those here illegally. Mitt Romney insisted on teaching our kids in English. And as president, Mitt Romney will cut back federal funds to cities that provide sanctuary to illegal immigrants."

Mitt Romney:
"Legal immigration is great. But illegal immigration; that we've got to end. And amnesty is not the way to do it."

Announcer:
"Mitt Romney—an exceptional leader for exceptional new challenges."

Mitt Romney:
"I'm Mitt Romney, and I approve this message."

Announcer:
"Paid for by Romney for President, MittRomney.com."

With the famous Nixon-Kennedy debates of 1960, radio was superceded by television.

NOTES

1. Don Moore, "Radio Election of 1924," retrieved from Internet archive: http://web.archive.org/web/20040224221424/http://www.swl.net/patepluma/genbroad/elec1924.html. A slightly edited version of this article was originally published in the July 1992 issue of *Monitoring Times* magazine.

2. Kathleen Hall Jamieson, *Packaging the Presidency: A History and Criticism of Presidential Campaign Advertising,* 2nd ed. (New York: Oxford University Press, 1992), 24–25.

3. Edwin Diamond and Stephen Bates, *The Spot: The Rise of Political Advertising on Television,* 3rd ed. (Cambridge, MA: MIT Press, 1994), 36.

4. Don Moore, "Radio Election of 1924," retrieved from Internet archive: http://web.archive.org/web/20040224221424/http://www.swl.net/patepluma/genbroad/elec1924.html. A slightly edited version of this article was originally published in the July 1992 issue of *Monitoring Times* magazine.

5. *Empire of the Air: The Men Who Made Radio* (New York: Harper Collins, Perennial, 1993), 182.

6. Susan J. Douglas, *Listening In: Radio and American Imagination* (1999; repr., Minneapolis: University of Minnesota Press, 2004), 166.

7. Christopher H. Sterling and John M. Kittross, *Stay Tuned: A Concise History of American Broadcasting,* 2nd ed. (Belmont, CA: Wadsworth, 1990), 124–25, 533.

8. Shanto Iyengar and Jennifer McGrady, *Media Politics, a Citizen's Guide* (New York: Norton, 2007), 178.

9. Irving Settel, *A Pictorial History of Radio* (New York: Grosset & Dunlap, 1967), 73.

10. Theodore H. White, *The Making of the President, 1972* (New York: Atheneum, 1973), 355.

11. http://www.presidency.ucsb.edu/ws/index.php?pid=2719.

12. Tobe Berkovitz, *Political Media Buying: A Brief Guide,* http://www.ksg.harvard.edu/case/3pt/berkovitz.html#anchor572483.

13. Ibid.

14. Ibid.

15. Chris Cillizza, "Candidates Turn to 'Boutique' Firms to Reach Niche Audiences," *Washington Post,* August 19, 2007, A02; accessed via the web http://www.washingtonpost.com/wp-dyn/content/article/2007/08/18/AR2007081800905.html.

16. South Carolina for Obama: http://sc.barackobama.com/page/content/schome.

17. Provided to the author by the Romney Campaign.

6

Why Television?

The time has come for political campaigning—its techniques and strategies—to move out of the dark ages and into the brave new world of the omnipresent eye.
—H. R. "Bob" Haldeman (1968)

Television is not a gimmick, and nobody will ever be elected to major office without presenting themselves well on it.
—Roger Ailes (1968)

The most common image on television is a close up of the human face. Television is not only a mass distribution channel, but it's also a distribution of intimacy. That's changed the way people have to campaign. They have to be a lot warmer. They have to be someone you can imagine having as a neighbor.
—Dr. Roderick Hart, College of Communication,
University of Texas at Austin (2004)

In every poll I have seen in the past three years, nearly 70 percent of the American people say they get their news from television. The number alone is scary and ought to cause those of us still literate to sit down and think about the day when we will simply plug the TV cord right into our eye sockets. As a so-called image maker, I am torn between thinking about how I can best take advantage of this trend, and where it is likely to lead us.
—Michael K. Deaver (1987)

TELEVISION'S POWER

Most people would agree that television is a powerful force in society. Many of us depend on television for news, weather, and other vital information. Having a

Media Literacy Core Concepts:

Media messages are constructed using a creative language with its own set of rules.

Most media messages are organized to gain profit and/or power or both.

Media Literacy Key Questions:

What techniques are used by the creator to attract attention?

What lifestyles, values, points of view are represented in, or omitted from, this message?

television in our homes is commonplace; televisions have become part of the cultural landscape. Like the radio before it, the television has become the central focus of many a living room. Many of us gather around it to experience events we cannot see firsthand. (For example, the 2007 Super Bowl football game was seen by an estimated 97 million people, only 72 thousand of whom witnessed it at Miami's Dolphin Stadium.) On any given night, the total combined audience for the three major television network newscasts (ABC, CBS, and NBC) is about 26 million viewers. (Compare that figure to the audience of 2.2 million daily readers for the national newspaper *USA Today*.)

The introduction of television, in the late 1940s, changed the way many people understood their world. In 1951, during his first *See It Now* television broadcast on CBS, broadcast journalist Edward R. Murrow showed viewers something they'd never seen before. With one camera pointed at New York's Brooklyn Bridge and another aimed at San Francisco's Golden Gate bridge, Murrow showed viewers both scenes simultaneously. It was the first live coast-to-coast transmission. Television technology, and the addition of communication satellites, forever changed how news events are covered: now local TV stations and network and cable news operations all go "live" at a moment's notice.

The "tube" has become our primary source of news and information. America experienced the deaths of President John F. Kennedy; Martin Luther King, Jr.; and Robert Kennedy, all via television. Television showed us civil rights violence and men walking on the moon. The *CBS Evening News* anchorman Walter Cronkite brought the Vietnam War into the living room, causing President Lyndon B. Johnson to blame television as the reason the public turned against the war. Millions of Americans were riveted by the Watergate hearings, which eventually led to the resignation of President Richard Nixon. In 1991 Cable News Network (CNN) would broadcast the beginning of the Persian Gulf War, live.

The introduction of cable and satellite has meant an increase in how, when, and where we get news and information. With new media and technology, we can now access television's programs and events away from home. We can now "watch" television on the computer, cell phone, or similar wireless-capable device.

The medium of television, new in the early 1950s, also took a giant leap into politics, bringing the thrill of campaigns into the living room. Political events began to be designed for the home audience. The powerful influence of advertising was about to reach even further. Candidates discovered that one 30-second commercial could reach hundreds of thousands of people watching local TV and millions more watching nationally.

Using television to speak to millions of people was a novel idea in the early 1950s, when a future president decided he would use this new medium in a new way.

THE POWER TO PERSUADE: NIXON USES TELEVISION TO SURVIVE

In the history of that medium, his 1952 speech was probably a greater milestone than the presidential debate that came eight years later.
—Garry Wills, "The Checkers Speech," *Esquire Magazine* (June 1983)

Long before the famous debates with John F. Kennedy, Richard Nixon turned to television to reach the people, defend his reputation, and save his job. In 1952 Senator Richard M. Nixon was a young, up-and-coming politician. He had already made a name for himself and captured media attention for his service on the House Un-American Activities Committee, which investigated communism charges against Alger Hiss, among others. But after his quick rise, it looked as though Nixon was about to come crashing down. A New York newspaper charged him with accepting bribes, a charge that didn't sit well with Republican presidential nominee Dwight D. Eisenhower, who had just named Nixon as his running mate. The paper said Nixon had accepted an $18,000 "slush fund" from wealthy Californians in order to pay off campaign debts.

In an effort to assert his innocence, Nixon decided to take his case directly to the people via television. He hired experts on advertising and makeup to advise him on how to look and sound. Paid for by the Republican National Committee, his speech on September 23, 1952, was broadcast nationwide from the El Capitan Theatre in Hollywood. With millions of people watching on television and listening on the radio, Nixon offered an elaborate explanation, denying that any funds had been used for personal gain. He mentioned that a dog, whom his daughter Tricia had named Checkers, had been given to his children. Declared a confident Nixon: "I want to say right now that regardless of what they say, we're going to keep it." The so-called Checkers Speech ended with an attack on his opponents.

One commentator later called Nixon's television performance "polished."[1] By all accounts, Nixon was persuasive, and the speech was a great success. Eisenhower enthusiastically welcomed Nixon to the ticket, and they swept the election that year.[2] Other politicians took notice. You might say that the birth of television as a key ingredient in campaigns was born. But television exposure, as Nixon himself would later learn, could cut both ways. The Watergate scandal and resulting nationally broadcast Congressional hearings on it did much to force him from office in August 1974.

Watch Nixon's resignation speech: http://www.youtube.com/watch?v=BN8OfPc_aQ8.

In the so-called Checkers Speech on Sept. 23, 1952, Richard M. Nixon exploited television—then a new medium with as-yet untapped political potential—to counter corruption charges and secure his vice-presidential slot on the 1952 Republican ticket headed by Dwight D. Eisenhower. (AP Photo)

A few days after the televised speech, Nixon was photographed at his Washington, D.C., home, holding Checkers, the family's cocker spaniel—a gift from a political supporter—and surrounded by his wife, Pat, and young daughters, Julie and Tricia. The average American family image was intended to dispel any lingering hint of corruption. (AP Photo)

Favorable public reaction to the Checkers Speech appeased Eisenhower, shown campaigning with Nixon in Wheeling, W.Va. (AP Photo/stf)

DEBATES—SCRIPTED THEATER?

> It's show business . . . it's not really debating, or getting into details on issues, or what your experience has been. It's too much prompting and too much artificiality and not really debates. They're rehearsed appearances.
>
> —former president George H. W. Bush (1995)

Putting two (or more) candidates together on a stage and televising their "debate" seems like a good idea. The candidates can be seen and heard by millions of people, listening on radio and watching on television or online. Their "messages" are unfiltered, unlike slick, highly produced 30-second campaign commercials. Viewers use the debates as another opportunity to decide which of the candidates looks or sounds "presidential." The media have plenty to write about, from debate preparations to candidate faux pas to debate conclusion scorecards.

But in this context the word *debate* is a misnomer. The presidential candidates do not debate one another. The format of many of the modern-day events does not allow such direct and revealing encounters. With eight or more candidates on a stage, and a 90-minute length, the format doesn't permit a thorough, comprehensive exploration of issues. Instead, it results in a highly structured and scripted event. Candidates will have been through untold hours of preparation with staff. Every possible issue and question will have been rehearsed. Every speech and campaign appearance by an opponent will have been reviewed, looking for trends. Debate briefing books are studied as though the candidates were preparing for a final exam.

How a candidate looks on television will have been studied from every possible angle. Today, candidates are just as much concerned with how they look as they are with what they will say and how they will say it. (Richard Nixon learned the importance of appearance from his first debate with John Kennedy.)

The power of the image is, again, emphasized during debates. Media researcher Kathleen Hall Jamieson believes the viewing audience is more receptive to the visual image than to the speakers' words: "Since viewers are more disposed to respond to the impression created by a televised image than its substance, the pictures it conveys rather than the words, those who are naturally telegenic have an advantage not related to their competence or command of the issues. Unfortunately, voters sometimes leap from personal appearance of a candidate to a judgment about that person's ability to lead."[3]

Therefore, the debate of today has changed radically. Political reporter Roger Simon compares modern-day debates to stage plays, for which the "actors" have rehearsed, using scripts and briefing books, and with staff members acting as debate moderators.[4] Simon calls it a game in which everyone will be watching to see how the candidates do: will they follow the script?; will they make a mistake?

Some people are attracted to televised debates in the same way some people are attracted to NASCAR races: they watch to see who might crash and burn. According to critic Alan Schroeder, "In every debate . . . the objective has been to install an invisible safety net that keeps the tightrope artists from crashing to the ground. Campaigns engage in what can best be described as a mix of talent management and preventive damage control, doing whatever it takes to stabilize an inherently combustible production situation for the leading players."[5]

Kennedy-Nixon Debates

In 1960 Democratic senator John F. Kennedy of Massachusetts, a virtual unknown, won his party's nomination for president. His Republican opponent was the much better known vice president, Richard M. Nixon. Television was the medium that their consultants knew would reach the largest number of voters, and the candidates agreed to participate in a series of four "live" televised debates. An estimated 85 million people would see at least one of the four debates.[6]

The first debate was held on September 26, 1960. Most media commentators at that time observed the same thing: Kennedy, just back from vacation, looked tanned, rested, and relaxed. Nixon did not; shortly before arriving at the TV studio, he had reinjured a knee, and he was in considerable discomfort. Others observed that Nixon had a heavy beard; he had refused offers to put on makeup. Further, TV watchers noted that Nixon's gray suit blended too much into the debate background.[7] Kennedy, on the other hand, was described as robust and healthy, and as having a "rugged vitality."[8] Kennedy, by all accounts "won" the first debate: that was the consensus of those who watched on TV. Surprisingly, those who heard the debate on radio judged Nixon to be the winner. Three more televised debates followed: Nixon coordinated his wardrobe better with the debate sets, but Kennedy held his own with the vice president.[9] Experts say television and the images of the candidates left an indelible impression on voters: "What counted was the image projected by the tube."[10]

In 1960 the first televised "presidential debates" between the nominees of the major parties catapulted little-known Massachusetts senator John F. Kennedy to national renown. Richard M. Nixon and Kennedy are shown here during the fourth debate, held in New York City on October 21. (AP Photo/File)

Watch a two-minute clip from the second Kennedy-Nixon debate: http://www.veoh.com/videos/e87521tQJWkN7S.

Despite the favorable reaction to the four Kennedy-Nixon debates, the next presidential debate did not occur until 1976. The reason: incumbent presidents refused to debate. There was another factor as well: federal communications laws required local stations to provide equal time for all candidates, even minor ones. This provision had been suspended by order of Congress for the Kennedy-Nixon debates only.[11]

The Equal-Time Provision

Equal time dates back to early broadcasting in the United States: the Radio Act of 1927. Lawmakers said that without equal time, some in radio might try to influence elections. As one congressman put it, "American politics will be largely at the mercy of those who operate these (radio) stations." When the Radio Act was superseded by the Communications Act of 1934, the equal-time provision became enacted (paraphrased from http://www.museum.tv/archives/etv/E/htmlE/equaltimeru/equaltimeru.htm). The equal-time provision dates back to the late 1920s. Basically radio and TV stations, which produce their own programs, were required to provide equal time to qualified candidates, and charge them the same rates for ad time. Over time, stations were exempt from providing the equal time if candidates appeared in legitimate news programs, and debates were later ruled to be news events.

In 1975 the Federal Communications Commission created a "loophole" regarding the equal-time provision, ruling that debates were "bona fide news events." That meant that if debates were sponsored by some organization other than the networks, the debates qualified as "news events" and were exempt from the equal-time requirements.[12] (In 1960 the three television networks (ABC, CBS, and NBC) had cosponsored the Kennedy-Nixon debates.[13]) With the rule change, the League of Women Voters stepped in and sponsored the debates in 1976, 1980, and 1984. The nonpartisan Commission on Presidential Debates sponsored the subsequent debates.[14]

The equal-time rule should not be confused with the "fairness doctrine," which required broadcasts to provide time for contrasting viewpoints on controversial public issues. The Fairness Doctrine was abolished in 1987.

On September 6, 2007, Republican Fred Thompson, former U.S. senator from Tennessee and a well-known actor, made it official, throwing his hat into the ring for the Republican nomination for president. Thompson was quite late in joining an already crowded field of candidates, many of whom had gotten a huge jump in fundraising, debating, and name recognition.

But name recognition might have been the least of Thompson's worries. He was, in fact, already known to many for his role as District Attorney Arthur Branch in the NBC drama series *Law and Order,* which plays in repeats on cable's TNT network. That Thompson would still be seen in these repeats while at the same time running for president might have raised an interesting issue regarding the federal equal-time provision.

While candidate appearances on legitimate news programs are exempt from the equal-time provision, entertainment programs, such as *Law and Order,* are not. Voluntarily, NBC stopped airing any episodes of the series in which Thompson appeared (he asked to be released from his contract in May 2007 in order to pursue his presidential ambitions). But TNT signaled its intention to continue airing the series. The network didn't state its reasons, but clearly *Law and Order,* a popular series, draws a large audience—satisfying TNT's advertisers and thus its bottom line. Dropping the series would have meant a loss in advertising revenue.

The TNT network shows several hours of *Law and Order* reruns every day and often holds all-day marathons. Had that continued while Thompson was running for office, one of his rivals might have sought to apply the equal-time rule to cable TV. The FCC's equal-time rules were written when cable was in its infancy, and it has never been clear whether or not they apply only to broadcast stations. The rules have never been applied to cable programming. If a rival candidate had challenged Thompson's *Law and Order* appearances and demanded equal time, it would have provided a chance for the law to be clarified. Thompson, however, withdrew from the race in January 2008.

The equal-time provision has been applied previously to other actors and notable celebrities. Stations dropped *Bedtime for Bonzo* and other Ronald Reagan movies during his campaigns for governor of California and president. During the 2003 California gubernatorial race, television stations dropped all Arnold Schwarzenegger movies, fearing that showing them would require the stations to give countless hours of free airtime to all 134 other candidates for governor.

Table 6.1
Presidential Debate Audience Size[15] (as measured by average and share of audience)

Year	Candidates	Average audience[*] (millions)	Percent of households watching (share)
1960	Kennedy-Nixon	75	60%
1976	Ford-Carter	65.4	51%
1980	Reagan/Carter/Anderson	80.6	59%
1984	Reagan-Mondale	66.2	46%
1988	Bush-Dukakis	66.2	36%
1992	Bush/Clinton/Perot	66.4	42%
1996	Clinton-Dole	41.2	29%
2000	Bush-Gore	40.6	26%
2004	Kerry-Bush	53	48%
2008	McCain-Obama	51.7	NA

[*] = average audience, since more than one TV debate occurred during the campaign.

Where Did They All Go? Presidential TV Debate Audience Levels

Although debates are a good way to see the candidates answering tough questions posed by journalists, the viewing public, for the most part, has tuned out. As Table 6.1 shows, the audience size dropped roughly by half from the 1960 high to the 2000 low, with an uptick in 2004.

Great Lines from Debates: Not Always Spontaneous, Often Rehearsed

In 1980 Ronald Reagan met President Jimmy Carter in their one-and-only face-to-face debate. Reagan claimed his comeback to Carter during the debate, "There you go again"—used during a discussion of Medicare and much commented on afterward—was not rehearsed. But when Reagan used the line again (in 1984's first debate), Democratic challenger Walter Mondale was ready to respond with a challenge of his own, pointing out that Reagan had in fact cut Medicare during his term in office, although four years earlier he had promised not to.

In October 1984 President Ronald Reagan was being rehearsed for the second of his two nationally televised debates with former Vice President Walter Mondale. Most critics agreed that Reagan had performed poorly during the first debate. So his media and communications teams were convinced their man would have to do better the second time around. Helping with the coaching was media consultant Roger Ailes, who had successfully elevated Richard Nixon's image during Nixon's 1968 campaign for the presidency. In 1984 Reagan was 73 years old, and age was certainly a campaign issue—one his advisers expected Mondale or one of the questioning journalists to bring up during the debate. Ailes asked the president if he was prepared for the question should it come up, and Reagan assured him he was. Sure enough, Henry Trewhitt, a reporter for *The Baltimore Sun* newspaper, brought up the age issue. The chief executive answered that he felt up to the job, and then went after Mondale: "And I want you to know that I will not make age an issue of this campaign. I am not going to exploit for political purposes my opponent's youth and inexperience." The response brought applause and laughter and was one of the debate highlights most repeated by the media. According to Ailes, it wasn't just Reagan's words, it was "his timing, facial expression, and body language which made the moment powerful."[16]

Reagan also received high marks for his debate's closing lines, when he looked directly into the camera and asked Americans: "Are you better off than you were four years ago?" Since many Americans were not better off, Reagan said, their choice for president was clear.

In 1988, vice presidential candidates Dan Quayle (Republican running mate of President George H. W. Bush) and Senator Lloyd Bentsen (running mate of Democrat Michael Dukakis) met for a nationally televised debate. During the debate Quayle compared himself to President John F. Kennedy. Bentsen retorted: "Senator, I knew Jack Kennedy, you're no Jack Kennedy." The line brought rousing applause from the debate audience. While many thought that the line was extemporaneous, it was not. It was well rehearsed. The Bentsen team, which included political strategist Robert Shrum, knew about Quayle's frequent references to John Kennedy. So they prepared Bentsen for the likelihood that Quayle would do it again at the debate. In rehearsal, as Shrum relates, "the moment was worded, practiced, and polished." The rest is history: the Bentsen line was played over and over again by the media.[17]

Debate Limitations: Who Gets Heard and Who Doesn't

In reality, the amount of time a candidate has to fully answer a debate question is limited. Following the 1984 vice presidential debate, Democrat Geraldine Ferraro complained that she had gotten to say very little. She lamented the vigorous rehearsal process and expressed doubt about whether the public really learned anything new that they didn't know before the debates.[18] Ronald Reagan's preparation also hurt him during his first debate with Walter Mondale. He complained, after the fact, about overpreparation.

Frustrated by his lackluster showing in polls during the 2007–2008 presidential campaign, Democratic candidate Chris Dodd created the Talk Clock graphic. The graphic was designed to show potential voters, bloggers, and the media how little time he actually got to talk during each of the broadcast debates. In one instance (the June 3rd debate), Dodd spoke for 8:28 minutes, while Democratic frontrunners Barack Obama and Hillary Clinton spoke for 16:00 minutes and 14:26 minutes, respectively. *Campaigns & Elections* magazine reported that the clock had become a popular feature on the Web, "landing the site an estimated 20,000 hits and even spawning its own MySpace page."[19]

The Debate Reaction Shot

During televised debates, it is a common practice for the television technical director to "cut away" from the primary camera shot showing the candidate who is speaking in order to show the audience the reaction of his or her opponent. In TV terms, this is called the "reaction shot."

Recent debate rules have attempted to restrict the use of the televised reaction shot, which can be awkward if not embarrassing to a candidate. But broadcasters have not always complied. The reaction shot has actually become rather controversial because of some recent debate occurrences.

As some critics have noted, it is the visual image, more than what is said, that is remembered by many long after the debate has ended.

In 1960 Richard Nixon perspired visibly under the hot television lights during his first televised debate with John Kennedy, and was seen using his handkerchief to wipe his forehead. As noted earlier, Nixon was in fact unwell and looked pale, but he had refused to have makeup applied. Nixon's appearance became one of the major topics for post-debate discussion.

A study of reaction shots during the 1976 debate between Gerald Ford and Jimmy Carter found that the candidate appearing in the reaction shot had not actually reacted in any visible way.[20] Sometimes a director uses a reaction shot just to change the pace. In Carter's case, the shot demonstrates that Carter, while listening, is well aware that he is on camera, and he is responding to the medium.

An alternative to the reaction shot is the "split screen" in which both debaters are seen on the screen simultaneously, thus allowing viewers to see the reactions of both candidates at the same time.

In 1992 President George H. W. Bush repeatedly looked at his watch during a debate with opponents Bill Clinton and Ross Perot. This image of the chief executive was seen on television and printed in newspapers and magazines, giving the impression that he had somewhere else to go or could not wait for the event to conclude.

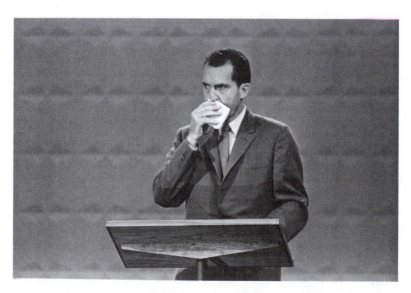

Nixon, who was unwell on the day of the first debate, in Chicago on September 26, appeared ill at ease, even furtive, handing a decisive advantage to his Democratic opponent. (AP Photo)

Various techniques have been devised to enliven the "talking heads" debate format for television audiences. One such technique is the split screen, which registers images of both the candidate speaking and the opponent listening. The "reaction shots" showing Pres. George W. Bush repeatedly frowning during the first of the 2004 debates, in Los Angeles, hurt his standing in the polls. (AP Photo/Damian Dovarganes)

During his 2000 presidential debate with Republican George W. Bush, the Democratic candidate, Vice President Al Gore, made "loud and pained sighs" that made him appear "contemptuous and condescending," according to one news account.[21]

For his part, in 2004, President George W. Bush, during a debate with Democrat opponent Senator John Kerry, "scowled, squinted, clenched his jaw and appeared disgusted as he hunched over his lectern." His various facial expressions became fodder for the Democratic National Committee, which created a video montage called "Faces of Frustration." A body language consultant said Bush's performance "made him appear smaller and less commanding" compared with Kerry.[22]

In July 2007 CNN and YouTube co-hosted a prime-time TV debate among Democratic presidential contenders in South Carolina, with CNN's Anderson Cooper moderating the debate. But instead of lining up a panel of qualified journalists to ask the candidates questions, the news organization collaborated with the video-sharing Web site to solicit videotaped questions from people all across the country. Viewers were encouraged to record their questions for the candidates and upload them to YouTube's Web site. The candidates could, of course, review the submitted video questions beforehand, but they did not know which questions would be used during the debate. Deciding which questions would be selected was the task of a team from CNN, including the head of CNN's Washington news bureau. In all of the videos except one, the questioners appeared personally on camera; the exception featured a snowman who wanted to know the candidates' positions on global warming. The effort was seen as another in a long list of ways the political process has attempted to engage young people in the political process, and also as a new application of technology to political campaigns.

Techniques of Persuasion in Debates

Candidates for president understand how to appeal to voters during debates using the same persuasive techniques used in propaganda and advertising. Here are some examples of the techniques, drawn from past televised debates:[23]

Emotional Appeals (including fear, patriotism, money issues)
Bill Clinton, Robert Dole: 1996 Debate
Senator Dole: "We're spending millions of millions of dollars on negative ads frightening senior citizens. I know this to be a fact because I had one tell me last week: 'Senator, don't cut my Medicare.' I'm trying to save your Medicare, just as I rescued Social Security with a bipartisan commission. I have relatives on Medicare. I used to sign welfare checks for my grandparents."

Generalities (not offering specifics)
Bill Clinton, George H. W. Bush, Ross Perot: 1992 Debate
Clinton: "I got into this race because I did not want my child to grow up to be part of the first generation of Americans to do worse than their parents. We're better than that, we can do better than that. I want to make America as great as it can be. And I ask for your help in doing it."
Bush: "The exciting thing is the fear of nuclear war is down. And you hear all of the bad stuff that has happened on my watch and I hope people will recognize that this is something pretty good for mankind. I hope they'll think it's good—that democracy and freedom is on the move. And we're gonna stay engaged as long as I'm president, working to improve things."

Oversimplification (making complicated issues too simple)
Bill Clinton, George H. W. Bush, Ross Perot: 1992 Debate
Perot: "In the first two years, they will learn how to learn or if they don't know how to learn, if they don't, they wind up in prison."
Bush: "When you cut capital gains, you put people to work."
George H. W. Bush, Michael Dukakis: 1988 Debate
Dukakis: "If he's serious about what he's saying, then the only place he can go to balance that budget is to raid the Social Security trust fund. We tried that in 1985, and I think he's going to try it again."

Avoidance (sidestepping an issue, perhaps due to controversy)

George H. W. Bush, Michael Dukakis: 1988 Debate

Questioner Ann Compton, ABC News, addressing then Vice President George H. W. Bush: "Mr. Vice President: Yes, we read your lips: 'no new taxes'—but despite that same pledge from President Reagan, after income tax rates were cut, in each of the last five years, some federal taxes have gone up: Social Security, cigarettes, liquor, even long-distance telephone calls. Now, that's money straight out of people's wallets. Isn't the phrase 'no new taxes' misleading the voters?"

Bush: "No, because that's because I'm pledged to that. And yes, some taxes have gone up, and the main point is, taxes have been cut and yet income is up to the federal government by 25% in the last three years. And so what I want to do is keep this expansion going. I don't want to kill it off by a tax increase. More Americans at work today, than at any time in the history of this country and a greater percentage of the workforce and the way you kill expansions is to raise taxes and I don't want to do that and I won't do that. And what I have proposed is something much better."

Testimonial (using a respected third party to bolster your case)

Bill Clinton, Robert Dole: 1996 Debate

Clinton: "Don't take my word for this, the *Economist* magazine polled lots of economists, seven Nobel Prize winners have said that if this tax scheme passes, it will require huge cuts."

Dole: "Well, the president's own CIA director has said Saddam is as strong now as he was."

Personal Attacks (character and competence)

Dan Quayle, Lloyd Bentsen: Vice Presidential Debate 1988

Quayle: "The fact of the matter is, Senator Bentsen, he's raised taxes five times —he just raised taxes this last year. And that's why a lot of people refer to him as 'Tax Hike Mike.' "

How to Watch a Debate

Media coverage[24]

- If you are watching the debate on television, are reaction shots or other techniques used to create a sense of drama or conflict?
- Are you being influenced by comments made by reporters and commentators immediately before and after the debate?

Image[25]

- Are you influenced by the age, sex, clothes, posture or other physical characteristics of the candidates? How?

- What impressions do the candidates convey as the debate progresses? Who appears more relaxed? More sincere? More confident?
- Who knows how to use television better? Do the candidates look directly at you (into the camera) or elsewhere (at the panelists, live audience, etc.)? Does this affect your overall impression of the candidates?

What Really Goes On behind the Scenes of a Presidential Debate?

That is the question I sought to answer when I requested a "press pass" from the South Carolina Republican Party to cover the Republican candidates' debate. The date was May 15, 2007, and since I live in Columbia, South Carolina, I thought I would take a look at the preparations in advance of that night's "First in the South" GOP presidential candidates' debate, originating from the Koger Performing Arts Center on the campus of the University of South Carolina.

Around lunch time, I made my first visit to the debate site, where I found several roads adjacent to the Koger Center closed. Up and down the street in front of the Koger Center were satellite TV trucks representing not only local news stations, but also cable networks such as CNN and FOX News. Each satellite truck had huge audio and video cables going to adjacent tents, where photographers and reporters were set up. They used the Koger Center building as the backdrop for their standups. Visible in the window of the Koger Center, behind the reporters, were several large banners promoting the debate. On the lawn of the center were hundreds of candidate signs, all designed to get the attention of the media and of

In May 2007 candidate John Edwards visits the stage at South Carolina State University where the first Democratic primary debate would take place hours later, to check his positioning and suggest camera angle adjustments. (AP Photo/J. Scott Applewhite)

Satellite TV trucks, representing both local and national news organizations, line up outside the Myrtle Beach, S.C. Convention Center, site of the Republican Presidential Candidates Debate on January 10, 2008. (Courtesy of Frank W. Baker)

the ever-growing, curious crowds that gathered at the debate site throughout the day.

Later in the day, I went to the official media/press tent, situated directly behind the Koger Center. Accredited media representatives had to pass through metal detectors and be signed in before proceeding. The tent was air-conditioned and contained probably about a hundred tables for visiting media. Wireless Internet access was installed, as were several monitors airing the FOX News Channel, originator of the live debate broadcast. Several FOX news personalities were on location. I saw bloggers, reporters, and news photographers all working at their computers, submitting stories/photos for their customers/readers.

Inside the tent, a group of young people caught my eye: they produce a teen radio talk show that is syndicated throughout the Southeast. They had prearranged an interview with candidate Duncan Hunter. When he walked into the tent and began his live radio interview, he attracted quite a few members of the visiting press corps. The young interviewers were well prepared: they peppered Hunter with several questions, including one about U.S. immigration policy, a timely issue in Washington and elsewhere.

A colleague of mine from the South Carolina Educational Television Network (SC ETV [PBS]) was working with the technical and engineering crew that was directing the debate. He invited me inside the "truck" to get a look at the control room. If you've never seen one of these, it is fascinating. Basically all of the video (camera) and audio (microphone) feeds from the debate event go into the truck

A large media tent provided for the use of journalists filing stories or conducting interviews quickly becomes crowded. (Courtesy of Frank W. Baker)

where the director decides which video and audio make it on the air. So if you have ten cameras, you will have at least ten monitors. Outside the truck hundreds of wires and cables run to the uplink satellite dish, which sends the signal to the satellite in Earth's orbit, from which it returns to FOX for distribution to cable and TV stations nationwide.

FOX News anchor Shepard Smith files a pre-debate report from the Koger Center. (Courtesy of Frank W. Baker)

Journalists from the *Teen Forum Show,* a Columbia, South Carolina-based nationally syndicated radio talk show run entirely by young people, interview candidate Duncan Hunter in the media tent. (Courtesy of Frank W. Baker)

The director here is really the main person in charge of the production. He or she will have spent hundreds of hours preparing for the event, including meetings with debate sponsors. The director decides the best location for the cameras, ensuring that the home audience will get the best view.

Before the debate begins, technicians monitor equipment in the control room to ensure that cameras are positioned for maximum effect. (Courtesy of Frank W. Baker)

The Republican candidates for president take the stage at the Myrtle Beach Convention Center, site of the January 10, 2008 debate. (Courtesy of Frank W. Baker)

A photojournalist captures an image of the candidates on his laptop as the January 10, 2008 debate gets under way. (Courtesy of Frank W. Baker)

TV AND THE POLITICAL CONVENTIONS

A convention is an infomercial, but they're not selling stain remover or hair treatments. They're selling a presidential candidate.
—Bill Schneider, Senior Political Analyst, CNN

[By curtailing coverage of conventions] the networks are operating as economic institutions and very minimally as public institutions.

—Tom Rosenstiel, Director, Project for Excellence
in Journalism (2004)

A Timeline of Convention Media Coverage

1844	News of the presidential convention in Baltimore is sent by telegraph for the first time.
June 10, 1924	First radio program broadcast from a convention: Republican Party Convention, Cleveland, Ohio.
1926	NBC Radio Network is launched (co-owned by RCA, Westinghouse, and General Electric).
1932	60% of U.S. homes have radios and access to that year's conventions.
June 1940	NBC's experimental TV station becomes the first to broadcast from a convention, airing filmed reports from the Republican convention in Philadelphia.
June 21, 1948	TV networks (NBC, CBS, ABC/Dumont) broadcast first live reports from the Republican convention, again in Philadelphia.
1956	32 million families see the two political conventions on television.
1968	Networks devote an average of 36 hours of live TV coverage to the two conventions (the most ever).
2004	Select group of bloggers report live from both the Republican and the Democratic conventions.

Brief History: How TV Covers Political Conventions

The gathering of all 50 states' delegates to their party's national convention is not as important an event as it was in the past. Most observers agree that the result of the current primary process is that the drama of who will be the party's presidential nominee has been decided months before the convention. Over time, the number of viewers who tune into TV coverage of presidential conventions has fallen steadily. Sadly, voter turnout declined at the same time as television convention viewership.

Yet since its inception, television has been there to witness the proceedings, and it has clearly changed the complexion of the events. Those whose job it is to plan a national political convention for a large nationwide audience must always ask themselves, "How will it look on TV?"

Today, though, the major networks have all but abandoned prime-time convention coverage, complaining that there is little news in these scripted events. Over time, audiences have migrated to cable and public television coverage. The CNN political analyst Bill Schneider justifies the enduring importance of the national convention: "We're covering the convention as a news event. Because we think our obligation is to give the voters the information they need to make a wise choice. The parties are in the business of selling their candidates. We're like *Consumer Reports*. We're in the business of trying to tell the voter, 'Well, here's something you didn't know that the party didn't say and here's a way to put what you just heard in perspective.' You gotta find sources you trust that will give you reliable information. And it's like we're providing a consumer guide in politics."[26]

News inside and outside the Convention Hall

"The whole world is watching," shouted peace protesters outside the Chicago arena that was the site of the August 1968 Democratic Party political convention. The protesters had come to send the message to the party's nominee (not yet selected) that America needed to get out of Vietnam. The massive protests were planned not only to voice disapproval of America's continued involvement in the Vietnam War but also to gain media attention, since the nation's media were in place to cover the convention. Clashes between police and protesters were widespread. And the media brought it right into America's living room, in color: "Television cameras recorded a bloody riot as police arrested over 500 people in clashes that injured more than 100 police and 100 demonstrators."[27] Television drew a lot of criticism because of the amount of time devoted to the protests. But NBC News' president Reuven Frank, writing in *TV Guide* magazine, defended his network's coverage. He said of the 35 hours NBC devoted to the convention, only 65 minutes presented demonstration images.[28]

That year, the networks broadcast more hours of the convention, generating the largest TV audience in the history of the event. But 1968 would be the last time a political convention would get such concentrated attention from the broadcast media and home viewers. While in an unusually active election year, such as 2008, the conventions might attract a larger audience, it will not reach the levels of the past.

Today, television network (ABC, CBS, and NBC) coverage of political conventions has all but disappeared. The year 1980 was the last time the major networks carried "gavel to gavel" prime-time coverage.[29] The reasons are many. By the time conventions are held in the summer prior to the elections, the parties' nominees are known, and so the dramatic suspense is gone. Former NBC anchorman Tom Brokaw says the conventions have become "infomercials," nothing more than carefully scripted and choreographed events.[30] Andrew Heyward, the president of CBS News, labeled the convention "a political pep rally."[31] The networks maintain that no real news emanates from the conventions. They also argue that the audience has decreased, and thus the ratings. (Let us not forget that the networks are still advertiser supported, and without an audience, you don't attract sponsors.)

Accordingly, over time, the three major networks have drastically reduced the amount of prime time they allocate to convention coverage. Another reason for the network's reduced coverage: cable networks such as CNN, FOX, MSNBC, and C-SPAN helped fill the void. Public Broadcasting Service (PBS) is another alternative to commercial network coverage.

A veteran political TV watcher is startled by network claims that conventions are boring: "The irony," says Rick Shenkman, "is that television executives in the 1950s at the birth of the industry thought that politics was so exciting that people would want to buy sets to watch the conventions. Buy a Stromberg-Carlson (television), proclaimed one newspaper advertisement and you "can see and hear more of the Presidential Conventions than the delegates themselves . . . . You're in the scenes and behind the scenes-with history in the making!"[32] There was a major push to get televisions in homes with advertisers like Westinghouse, RCA and Stromberg-Carlson all encouraging consumers to purchase a TV so they could watch the political process in action.

Just four years after the first live convention broadcasts of 1948, the advertising appeared to have worked: television had become a staple in most homes. By 1952, the networks estimated that 65 million people watched all or part of the conventions.[33] But by 1956 the networks' love affair with the live events had faded. Then CBS News vice president Sig Mickelson said the agenda and format of the convention would have to change. The public, he concluded, would not sit and watch "hour after hour of deliberations in which the significant developments are only a small part of the proceedings."[34] In order to placate the networks, convention organizers made sure that subsequent conventions (1960, 1964, 1968) were considerably shorter, and more choreographed.

What Can Happen on the Convention Floor . . .

Two network correspondents found themselves *in* the news while trying to report the news from the convention floor. In 1964, at the Republican Convention, NBC reporter John Chancellor was trying to report on a disturbance on the convention floor when he found himself arrested. As he was reporting live from the floor, security personnel literally lifted him up, and Chancellor was heard to say: "Here we go down the middle aisle. . . . I've been promised bail, ladies and gentlemen, by my office. This is John Chancellor, somewhere in custody . . . ."[35]

Dan Rather, CBS's floor reporter during the 1968 Democratic convention in Chicago, found himself in a similar situation. While trying to follow up a report on a dispute involving the Georgia delegation, Rather was roughed up. While he was being led away, anchorman Walter Cronkite was heard saying, "I don't know what's going on, but this—these are security people, apparently, around Dan."[36]

The selection of Miami Beach, Florida, as the location of the 1972 Republican Convention was no accident. A narrow road led to the site, and police could control those who had access. (They didn't want any repeats of the scenes enacted four years earlier.) To say this convention was a scripted event would be an understatement: each night was highly choreographed. The networks were given copies of each night's script, which provided minute-by-minute details of music, applause, and the movements of the speakers.[37] Richard Nixon sailed to renomination.

A Trend That Takes Hold: Shorter Network Convention Broadcasts

Instead of going full gavel-to-gavel for the 1968 conventions, ABC went on the air with convention coverage at 9:30 PM (Eastern time), and did a 90-minute (or longer, if that night's session ran past 11:00 on the East Coast) program, mixing tapes of earlier events and live coverage of some major moments, such as the keynote addresses and candidates' acceptance speeches. The network would again cover the conventions in this manner in 1972 and 1976. From 8:00 PM Eastern (7:30 PM Eastern in 1968) until 9:30, ABC ran regular programming. In 1972, and 1976 especially, ABC's early-evening counterprogramming won an increasing number of viewers.[38]

Conventional Network Coverage

As recently as 1976, the three major networks provided more than 50 hours of convention coverage. But by 1996, coverage had dropped to 12 hours. Only about four million Americans at any time watched the 1996 conventions. One ratings analyst offered another reason why people tuned out: viewers had more options than ever on cable.[39] In 2000 and again in 2004 , NBC broadcast only an hour of coverage—from 10 to 11 PM—on three of the four nights at the GOP and Democratic conventions.

According to Democratic National Committee statistics, the total amount of ABC, CBS, and NBC coverage at each convention fell from about 20 hours in 1992 to only 11 hours in 2000, while ratings dropped by about one-third in that period. Nielsen numbers indicate that the average viewership of the 2000 Democratic National Convention on both broadcast and cable outlets was 20.6 million each night, while the Republican event attracted 19.2 million viewers each night.[40] Refer to Table 6.2.

The Vanishing Voter

Political scientist Thomas E. Patterson has assessed what he calls the "vanishing voter" in his book of the same name. "In 1952, the typical television household watched 25 hours of convention coverage, often in the company of friends and neighbors. Even as late as 1976, the typical household viewed the conventions for 11 hours. Since then, the ratings have hit the skids. By 1996, the average had fallen to less than 4 hours. A new low was reached in 2000: 3 hours of convention viewing for the typical household. In 1976, 28 percent of television households had their sets on and tuned at any given moment to the convention coverage. Only 13 percent were watching in 2000, down from 17 percent in 1996."[41]

Table 6.2
Audience Levels and Ratings for Selected Year Conventions

Year	Party	Audience rating (millions)	Average hours viewed by household	Network hours telecast
1968	Republicans	26.4	6.5	34.0
	Democrats	28.5	8.5	39.1
1980	Republicans	21.6	3.8	22.7
	Democrats	27.0	4.4	24.1
1988	Republicans	18.3	2.2	12.6
	Democrats	19.8	2.3	12.8
1992	Republicans	22.0	NA	7.3
	Democrats	20.5	NA	8.0
2000	Republicans	19.2	2.0	7.2
	Democrats	20.6	2.0	7.2
2004	Republicans	22.6	NA	7.2
	Democrats	20.4	NA	7.2

Using Cellphones as News Gathering Devices to Cover a Convention

As of 2007, neither major U.S. political party had allowed bloggers to cover one of its presidential conventions firsthand—in real time and without prior filtering. Firsthand blogging seems, in fact, to run counter to the carefully orchestrated nature of the contemporary political convention, which appears to be intended to ratify the party's candidate of choice and reposition the nominee for the ensuing general campaign. "Independent blogs—especially those focusing on politics—are far more freewheeling, their authors frequently mixing fact with opinion and under no obligation to be either fair or accurate."[42] It is safe to assume that some blogging will occur again at conventions, but the parties that run them won't have any control over what is sent out into the blogosphere.

But a bold experiment began in 2004, when college students were recruited to be "citizen reporters" from the Republican Presidential Convention in New York City.

Using cell phones to send text and images, students from several colleges and universities documented each day's happenings and transmitted their moblogs (mobile weblogs) to Newsplex, a news-gathering hub at the University of South Carolina, where their transmissions were prepared and posted on the Cingular Wireless Election Connection Web site.

Cingular promoted the initiative as "a program encouraging young people to vote and play an important role in the political process."

One student participant reported on how the technology made access to news easier: "The phone's size enabled me to get in on the action unobtrusively. I got a dynamic shot of Katherine Harris (the Florida Secretary of State) at a Life-timeTV/Rock The Vote party because I could intrude my camera's eye into the hive of fans . . . ." She concluded that the information she gathered had its limitations and could not be mistaken for news. "What we created was mainly a picture show. It was comprehensive—we showed a lot, but in the main, the telling was left to other's Web sites."[43]

In May 2007 the cable network MTV received a $700,000 grant from the John S. and James L. Knight Foundation to create a Knight Mobile Youth Journalist (Knight "MyJos") in each of the 50 states and the District of Columbia. The goal was to recruit 51 young people to become "citizen journalists" covering the 2008 presidential election and other political news stories that would be of interest to their peers. The new "MTV Mobile" service allowed these new "citizen reporters," dubbed Street Team '08, to use laptops, cell phones, and video cameras to document stories that would be posted on MTV's Web sites and streamed on-line.[44] Later, MTV diffused the most popular stories to other media, such as cell phones and MTV stations.

LATE-NIGHT TV AND PRESIDENTIAL CANDIDATES

On any given night, *The Tonight Show with Jay Leno* (NBC) and *The Late Show with David Letterman* (CBS) can attract between 4 and 6 million viewers. That fact alone makes the networks happy: they can deliver a large and desirable audience (mostly young people) to their advertisers. Jon Stewart on cable's Comedy Central pulls in another 1.6 million people.[45]

Large viewership is the reason why candidates clamor to be guests on any one of a half dozen late-night television shows. Those running for president know that

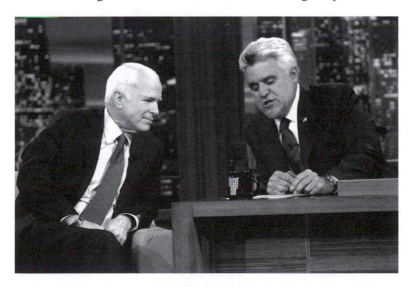

As a venue for capturing the attention of large numbers of younger voters, late-night TV programs attract politicians of every stripe. On Aug. 25, 2008, Sen. John McCain, Republican candidate for president, appeared on *The Tonight Show with Jay Leno*. (AP Photo/Mary Altaffer)

an appearance on these programs is highly desirable, because they want to reach the young, potential voter. It is also an opportunity to show off their lighter, humorous side.

"As modern political figures attempt to embrace popular culture and expand the methods by which they reach potential voters, the line between politics and entertainment can occasionally be blurred," says political science professor Larry Sabato.[46] Some candidates have even made major announcements during late-night TV. Senator John McCain used his appearance on David Letterman's show to announce his candidacy. "The influence of these (late-night talk) shows is naturally greater because the candidates themselves have added to that credibility."[47]

Today, an effective appearance on late-night TV also extends long after the television is turned off. Snippets of candidate appearances can also show up on the candidate's Web site, as well as on YouTube and a host of other video streaming Web pages. Comedy Central's *The Daily Show with Jon Stewart* created the Web page, Indecision 2008, specifically to post host Jon Stewart's musings about politics as well as clips of special guests.

Candidate appearances on late-night television are a natural fit, according to a top executive of Comedy Central, whose *Daily Show with Jon Stewart* has become one of the most popular places for presidential candidates: "Jon makes these guys feel comfortable. He provides them with an opportunity to reach an audience they don't always reach, which is young men," said Michele Ganeless, Comedy Central's executive vice president and general manager.[48]

Reaching Youth by Staying Up Late

In 1992 candidate Bill Clinton made a surprise visit to the late-night TV program *The Arsenio Hall Show.* Wearing sunglasses, the Democratic candidate played his favorite song, "Heartbreak Hotel," on the saxophone. Some critics suggested that his appearance captured the imagination of not only young people, but of a lot of older Americans as well. Clinton was not the first, and certainly was not the last, to use television in this way; refer to Table 6.3.

While late-night TV has become an attractive venue for all of those running for president, a 2003–2004 poll found the biggest audience for those programs, young people ages 18-24, are those least likely to vote.[49]

Despite that fact, politicians' enthusiasm for late-night appearances has not waned.

Do Young People Learn from Late-Night TV?

Studies continue to show young people are flocking to the broadcast (and streamed) venues for their political news and information. What do politicians hope young people will take away from their appearances on late-night television? It's pretty clear that they are not only hoping to reach large, young audiences, but also to influence them. "A 2004 survey by the Pew Research Center for the People and the Press found that 21 percent of people age 18 to 29 cited comedy shows

Table 6.3
Staying Up Late to Get Their Attention

Politician	Year	Late-night TV program
President Gerald Ford	1976	In videotape, Ford says the opening line for the popular late-night NBC program: "Live From New York, It's Saturday Night"(*Saturday Night Live*)
Candidate Bill Clinton	1992	Clinton plays "Heartbreak Hotel" on the sax during *The Arsenio Hall Show*
Senator Bob Dole	1997	*The Tonight Show with Jay Leno* (NBC)
First Lady Hillary Clinton; Vice President Al Gore; George Bush; Ralph Nader; John McCain	2000	*The Tonight Show with Jay Leno*
George Bush; Hillary Clinton; Vice President Al Gore; Ralph Nader	2000	*The Late Show with David Letterman* (CBS)
Vice President Al Gore	2002	*The Late Show with David Letterman*
Senator John Kerry	2004	Kerry presents a Top Ten List during an appearance on *The Late Show with David Letterman*
Senator John Edwards	2004	*The Tonight Show with Jay Leno*
Former Vice President Al Gore	2006	*The Daily Show with Jon Stewart* (Comedy Central)
Former Vice President Al Gore	2006	*Saturday Night Live*
Senator John McCain; Senator Barack Obama; Rudy Guliani	2007	*The Late Show with David Letterman*
Senator John McCain; Senator Hillary Clinton; Ex-Senator Fred Thompson	2007	*The Tonight Show with Jay Leno*
Senator John McCain; Senator Chris Dodd; Governor Bill Richardson; Senator John Edwards; Senator Joe Biden; Governor Tommy Thompson; Senator Barack Obama	2007	*The Daily Show with Jon Stewart*

such as *The Daily Show* and *Saturday Night Live* as places where they regularly learned presidential campaign news. Startlingly, this percentage is nearly equal to the 23 percent who regularly learned something from the network nightly news or from daily newspapers."[50]

Democratic presidential candidate Bill Clinton plays the saxophone at the opening of *The Arsenio Hall Show* on June 3, 1992. Other politicians had appeared on television variety shows, but Clinton's appearance on a popular late-night program acknowledged the growing political power of a new voter demographic: young people. (AP Photo/Reed Saxon)

Another major study, which the authors dubbed "*The Daily Show* Effect," found that viewers of the program reported increased confidence in their own ability to understand the complicated world of politics.[51] A more recent study indicates that whether or not they did learn from his show, Stewart's viewers are well-informed. An April 15 (2007) Pew survey gauging Americans' knowledge of national and international affairs found that 54 percent of regular viewers of *The Daily Show* and its Comedy Central spinoff, Stephen Colbert's *The Colbert Report,* scored in the high-knowledge category, tying with regular readers of newspaper Web sites and edging out regular watchers of *The NewsHour with Jim Lehrer* (PBS). Overall, 35 percent of people surveyed scored in the high-knowledge category.[52]

"Whether (an appearance by a candidate on these shows) translates into votes, we don't know," said Bob Lichter, a professor of communications at George Mason University and president of the Center for Media and Public Affairs. "What we do know is these shows have political impact, and they transform the voters. It's counterprogramming: journalists define candidates in their own terms, but when a candidate goes on with a comedian, that's his chance to make a definition for himself."[53]

When Stewart was asked if his youthful audience gets more journalism from his show rather than from the Sunday news talk shows, Stewart told interviewer Bill Moyers:

I can assure them they're not getting any journalism from us. We are, if anything—I do believe we function as a sort of editorial cartoon. That we are a digestive process, like so many other digestive processes that go on. . . . People are very sophisticated consumers of information, and they're pulling all different things.

It's the same argument people say about the blogs. The blogs are responsible. No, they're not. The blogs are like anything else. You judge each one based on its own veracity and intelligence and all of that. And if you like, you could cherry pick only the things that you agree with from various things. Or, if you want, you can try and get a broader perspective, or you can find people who are absolutely out of their minds, or find people that are doing incredibly complex and interesting and urgent journalism. And the same goes for our show. It's a prism into people's own ideologies, when they watch our program. This is just our take.[54]

REACHING OUT TO WOMEN ON MORNING AND AFTERNOON TALK SHOWS

When you get on a stage like this, you can be asked a question you might not be able to plan for, and sometimes those are the most revealing answers. I think these shows help define the character of the person who will be president, and that's probably more important in this election than any in the past.

—Terry Wood, President of Creative Affairs and Development,
CBS Television Distribution

Just as candidates reach out to young people at night, they can also reach a large female audience on morning and afternoon talk shows. Just like late-night television, these programs are nonthreatening to the candidate and allow for a friendly exchange with the host.

Appearing on *Oprah, The Ellen DeGeneres Show,* or *Live with Regis and Kelly,* among many others, is another way for presidential candidates to reach potential voters. During the 2008 election cycle, Senator Hillary Clinton appeared on Ellen's program; Senator Barack Obama appeared on model Tyra Banks's show; both candidates appeared on ABC's *The View. Live with Regis and Kelly* has hosted many candidates over the years, including George W. Bush, Bill Clinton, Al Gore, John Edwards, and John Kerry.[55]

IS TV TO BLAME FOR LOW VOTER TURNOUT?

Fast fact: 18–24-year-olds are the largest group of nonvoters in America.

—U.S. Census Bureau

With fewer and fewer people showing up to vote on election day, a lot of attention has been paid to the question of why voter turnout is so low. Public apathy, cynicism, and negative advertising have been cited as reasons, and so has television in general. But television is not solely to blame. Researchers have found that since the 1950s more people have been staying home to be entertained, a trend encouraged by demographics (the suburban migration), by new at-home options (cable, VCRs), and at least partly by fear (crime in the streets).[56] This stay-at-home trend may also have affected voter turnout.

Communications specialist Hank Sheinkopf, who worked on President Clinton's reelection media team, says the media have not done enough to encourage people to vote.[57] But journalist Jack Germond, long-time columnist for the *Baltimore Sun* and a frequent pundit on CNN and PBS, disagrees. He says it's not the job of journalism to be the cheerleader for voting, but rather simply to report what happens.[58]

According to Harvard University political media scholar Thomas E. Patterson, author of *The Vanishing Voter,* the media are to blame for trivializing politics and turning elections into beauty contests with no real issues. In Patterson's view, the rise of the Internet and round-the-clock television news has made matters worse; thoughtful analysis has been replaced by instant theater.[59]

But "the media are only reacting to a recent trend in the management and execution of political campaigns," claims Tom Rosenstiel, author of *Strange Bedfellows: How Television and the Presidential Candidates Changed American Politics.* "Today's campaigns," he says, "are run by professionals who conduct research and who are paid to insert adjectives and adverbs and other rhetorical devices into a candidate's speeches. In turn, the press have become like specialists with gigantic microscopes looking into the many intricate aspects of a campaign."[60] As a result, Americans only rarely glimpse the real person inside the packaged candidate.

One international study found that the news media may be encouraging a disengaged citizenry by representing the public as generally passive and apolitical. The researchers acknowledge that many in the news media and politics are concerned about public apathy in politics and that there is now a willingness among the media to broadcast citizens playing a more active role in political debate.[61]

There are those who believe the Internet—with its social network sites, blogs, and user-generated digital material—is already invigorating the political process, by engaging people more than the passive television ever could.

Finally, the explosion in the availability of TV choices, on both cable and satellite, means viewers have more programming to choose from. The menus of those channels reveal more of them are devoted to entertainment than to news or analysis. Voters have to search long and hard to locate real news about politics on television, if they want to find it at all.

MUSIC TV AND ENGAGING THE YOUTH VOTERS

Music TV (MTV) launched a campaign in 1992 dubbed "Choose or Lose." It was designed and targeted to reach the 18- to 30-year-old crowd by informing them of the political process and encouraging their participation. The network claims to have registered 350,000 voters that year.[62]

In 2004 the slogan was again part of the network's voter registration drive. The president of MTV, Van Toffler, said, "The political and social environment of the past three years has created an amazingly active and informed group of young voters with issues ranging from the war on terror and the U.S. involvement in Iraq to education and the economy. The goal of 'Choose or Lose 2004' and '20 Million Loud' is to give this enormous pool of potential voters the tools they need to make informed choices, get involved in the political process, and become motivated to make the ultimate choice in our democracy."[63]

In 2007–2008, MTV partnered with MySpace to create a series of "live" dialogues with the candidates and young people. With a studio audience and MTV hosts, the town-hall-style events were designed to allow the candidates to address young people's concerns and to let MTV and MySpace fans ask questions. The first event was held in September 2007 and featured former North Carolina Senator John Edwards; the second, in October 2007, featured Senator Barack Obama; and the third, in December 2007, featured Senator John McCain. The music network encouraged audience participation: users were able to submit questions for the events through MySpace, IM, mobile devices, and e-mail while they watched the live Webcast.

YOUTH VOTER TURNOUT

The high point of the past 30 years came in 1992—when 48.6 percent of the 18- to 24-year-olds and 52 percent of the 18- to 29-year-olds voted.

Turnout among 18- to 24-year-olds grew by nearly one-third between 2000 and 2004 (from 36 percent to 47 percent). And 2006 (the off-year election) saw significant gains in young voter participation as well.[64]

Will more young people vote in the 2008 presidential election? That is something many researchers will be watching and analyzing carefully. Some say the large participation by young people in the primary process may be an indicator of their future participation in civic duties, including voting.

NOTES

1. Dan Nimmo, *The Political Persuaders: The Techniques of Modern Election Campaigns* (1970; repr., New Brunswick, NJ: Transaction Publishers, 2001), 1.

2. Transcript of the Checkers Speech: http://www.historyplace.com/speeches/nixon-checkers.htm.

3. Kathleen Hall Jamieson and David S. Birdsell, *Presidential Debates: The Challenge of Creating an Informed Electorate* (New York: Oxford University Press, 1988), 183.

4. Roger Simon on CNN's Reliable Sources (transcript of show for June 3, 2007), http://transcripts.cnn.com/TRANSCRIPTS/0706/03/rs.01.html.

5. Alan Schroeder, *Presidential Debates: Forty Years of High-Risk TV* (New York: Columbia University Press, 2000), 23.

6. Joel L. Swerdlow, ed., *Presidential Debates, 1988 and Beyond* (Washington, DC: Congressional Quarterly, 1987), 36.

7. Judy Fireman, ed., *TV Book: The Ultimate Television Book* (New York: Workman, 1977), 194–95.

8. Sig Mickelson, *From Whistle Stop to Sound Bite: Four Decades of Politics and Television* (New York: Praeger, 1989), 122.

9. Judy Fireman, ed., *TV Book: The Ultimate Television Book* (New York: Workman, 1977), 194–95.

10. Irving Settel and William Laas, *A Pictorial History of Television* (New York: Grosset & Dunlap, 1969), 148.

11. "Presidential Debates," *Detroit Free Press,* September 14, 2004.

12. Presidential Debate History: How We Got Them and What They Mean, CNN: http://www.cnn.com/ALLPOLITICS/1996/debates/history/index.shtml.

13. Joel L. Swerdlow, ed., *Presidential Debates, 1988 and Beyond* (Washington, DC: Congressional Quarterly, 1987), 65.

14. Alan Schroeder, *Presidential Debates: Forty Years of High-Risk TV* (New York: Columbia University Press, 2000), 22.

15. Jeffrey McCall, *Viewer Discretion Advised: Taking Control of Mass Media Influences* (Lanham, MD: Rowman & Littlefield, 2007), 88; *Television: The Great Equalizer,* http://www.museum.tv/debateweb/html/equalizer/stats_tvratings.htm; Commission on Presidential Debates: http://www.debates.org/pages/his_1976.html.

16. Commission on Presidential Debates, 1988 Debates: Transcript: http://www.debates.org/pages/trans84c.html; Roger Ailes with Jon Kraushar, *You Are the Message: Secrets of the Master Communicators* (Homewood, IL: Dow Jones-Irwin, 1988), 19–20.

17. Commission on Presidential Debates, 1988 Debates: Transcript, http://www.debates.org/pages/trans88c.html; "The Man behind the Curtain: Political Strategy and Spin," *New York Times Book Review,* June 4, 2007, B4.

18. Alan Schroeder, Presidential Debates, *Forty Years of High-Risk TV* (New York: Columbia University Press, 2000), 61.

19. National Journal/The Gate: "Dodd: Take That, MSM!," June 8, 2007, http://thegate.nationaljournal.com/2007/06/take_that_msm.php.

20. Paul Messaris, *Visual "Literacy": Image, Mind, and Reality* (Boulder, CO: Westview Press, 1994), 159.

21. Dana Milbank, "Reaction Shots May Tell Tale of Debate," *Washington Post,* October 2, 2004, A10, http://www.washingtonpost.com/wp-dyn/articles/A1574-2004Oct1.html.

22. Ibid.

23. Commission on Presidential Debates, Techniques of Persuasion (video, 2004), http://www.unitedstreaming.com/ (retrieved July 28, 2007).

24. How to Watch a Debate, League of Women Voters: http://www.lwv.org/AM/Template.cfm?Section=Voter_Information2&TEMPLATE=/CM/ContentDisplay.cfm&CONTENTID=2177.

25. How to Watch a Debate, League of Women Voters of the Cincinnati Area: http://www.lwvcincinnati.org/voting/Watch_a_Debate.html.

26. Political Literacy: Sifting Thru the Spin, "In The Mix" special, PBS. Transcript: http://www.pbs.org/inthemix/shows/transcript_politics.html.

27. Going Back to Chicago, NewsHour with Jim Lehrer, PBS; the Online NewsHour: http://www.pbs.org/newshour/convention96/retro/chicago.html.

28. Reuven Frank, writing in *TV Guide,* August 1968. Reprinted in *TV Guide: The First 25 Years,* comp. Jay S. Harris (New York: Simon & Schuster, 1978), 153.

29. Martin Plissner, *The Control Room: How Television Calls the Shots in Presidential Elections* (New York: Free Press, 1999), 55.

30. Tom Brokaw, quoted in Bill Carter, "Faced with Poor Ratings, Networks Soul Search," *New York Times,* September 3, 2004, http://www.nytimes.com/2004/09/03/arts/television/03network.html?scp=1&sq=tom+brokaw+conventions+sept+3+2004&st=nyt.

31. Andrew Heyward, interviewed in Unconventional Coverage, NewsHour with Jim Lehrer, July 31, 2000, http://www.pbs.org/newshour/bb/media/july-dec00/convention _7-31.html.

32. Rick Shenkman, Why the Networks Should Still Be Covering the Conventions, History News Network, George Mason University, July 28, 2004, http://hnn.us/articles/6535.html.

33. Zachary Karabell, *The Rise and Fall of the Televised Political Convention,* discussion paper, the Joan Shorenstein Center, John F. Kennedy School of Government, Harvard University, 3: downloaded from www.ksg.harvard.edu/presspol/research_publications/papers/discussion_papers/D33.pdf.

34. Zachary Karabell, *The Rise and Fall of the Televised Political Convention,* discussion paper, the Joan Shorenstein Center, John F. Kennedy School of Government, Harvard University, 5: downloaded from www.ksg.harvard.edu/presspol/research_publications/papers/discussion_papers/D33.pdf.

35. Recounted in John Chancellor's obituary, July 13, 1996, at the CNN Web site: www.cnn.com/US/9607/13/chancellor/; also available as a post: http://www.poynter.org /forum/?id=ConventionTales.

36. All about Dan, On the Media, NPR: Transcript: http://www.onthemedia.org/transcripts/2006/06/23/08.

37. Zachary Karabell, *The Rise and Fall of the Televised Political Convention,* discussion paper, the Joan Shorenstein Center, John F. Kennedy School of Government, Harvard University, 7: downloaded from www.ksg.harvard.edu/presspol/research_publications/papers/discussion_papers/D33.pdf.

38. Joseph Gallant, Democracy in Our Living Rooms: Television Takes Us to the Political Conventions: http://jeff560.tripod.com/tv7.html.

39. "Dems at Least Win in TV Ratings," *Houston Chronicle,* August 31, 1996, 25A.

40. Mark Jurkowitz, "NBC Gives 3 Hours to Convention Coverage," *Boston Globe,* July 9, 2004, http://www.boston.com/news/nation/articles/2004/07/09/nbc_gives_3 _hours_to_convention_coverage/.

41. Thomas E. Patterson, *The Vanishing Voter: Public Involvement in an Age of Uncertainty* (New York: Knopf, 2002), 16.

42. Brian Faler, "Parties to Allow Bloggers to Cover Conventions for First Time," *Washington Post,* July 6, 2004, A04, http://www.washingtonpost.com/wp-dyn/articles/A29588-2004Jul5.html.

43. Personal correspondence from Randy Covington, Ifra Newsplex Director and Assistant Professor at the University of South Carolina School of Journalism & Mass Communications.

44. "Knight News Challenge First-Year Winners Announced," John S. and James L. Knight Foundation press release, May 29, 2007, http://www.pnnonline.org/article.php?

sid=7477&mode=thread&order=0; "MTV Recruits Youths to Cover Elections," Associated Press, December 20, 2007.

45. "Can Leno and Friends Pick Our Next President?," *NewsMax,* August 2007, 52.

46. Ibid., 53.

47. Ibid.

48. "Candidates Line Up to Visit Jon Stewart," Associated Press, August 5, 2007; archived on the Internet at various sites, including the NewsMax.com Wires: http:// archive.newsmax.com/archives/articles/2007/8/5/191852.shtml.

49. Adam Clymer, "Young People Watch More Late-Night Television," National Annenberg Election Survey (NAES) 04, May 3, 2004, http://www.annenberg publicpolicycenter.org/Downloads/Political_Communication/naes/2004_03_late-night-comedy_05-02_pr.pdf.

50. Rachel Smolkin, "What the Mainstream Media Can Learn from Jon Stewart," *American Journalism Review,* June/July 2007, http://www.ajr.org/Article.asp?id=4329.

51. Jody Baumgartner and Jonathan S. Morris, "*The Daily Show* Effect: Candidate Evaluations, Efficacy, and American Youth," *American Politics Research,* 34, no. 3 (May 2006): 341, http://apr.sagepub.com/cgi/content/abstract/34/3/341.

52. Rachel Smolkin, "What the Mainstream Media Can Learn from Jon Stewart," *American Journalism Review,* June/July 2007, http://www.ajr.org/Article.asp?id=4329.

53. Madison Gray, "Campaigning in Late Night," *TIME Magazine,* August 29, 2007, http://www.time.com/time/politics/article/0,8599,1657421,00.html.

54. *Bill Moyers Journal,* PBS; April 27, 2007, http://www.pbs.org/moyers/journal/ 04272007/watch.html.

55. Paige Albiniak, "Candidates Court Daytime," *Broadcasting & Cable,* August 20, 2007, http://www.broadcastingcable.com/article/CA6470005.html.

56. Stephen Bates and Edwin Diamond, "Damned Spots: A Defense of Thirty-Second Campaign Ads," *New Republic,* 207, no. 11/12 (September 7, 1992).

57. "The Future of Journalism: Should Political Advertising Have a Future?," The New School, New York City, recorded June 26, 2007, http://www.fora.tv/fora/ showthread.php?t=1236.

58. "Breaux Symposium Probes Issue of Declining Voter Participation," http:// www.lsu.edu/lsutoday/010330/pagetwo.html.

59. Steve Schifferes, "The Vanishing Voter," BBC News World Edition, November 6, 2002, http://news.bbc.co.uk/1/hi/world/americas/2371963.stm.

60. "Breaux Symposium Probes Issue of Declining Voter Participation," http:// www.lsu.edu/lsutoday/010330/pagetwo.html.

61. Anna Hinds, "Does TV Turn People Off Politics?," Press Release, May 12, 2003, for an Economic and Social Research Council report written by Justin Lewis, Karin Wahl-Jorgensen, and Sanna Inthorn, http://www.eurekalert.org/pub_releases/2003-05/ esr-dtt050903.php.

62. Henry Jenkins, "Photoshop for Democracy," *Technology Review,* June 4, 2004, http://www.techreview.com/Biotech/13648/.

63. Choose or Lose, MTV, http://www.mtv.com/chooseorlose/headlines/news.jhtml? id=1484712.

64. Aaron Blake, "Poll Shows Youth-Vote Boost Favoring Obama, Giuliani in Presidential Race," *The Hill,* posted April 19, 2007, http://thehill.com/campaign-2008/ poll-shows-youth-vote-boost-favoring-obama-giuliani-in-presidential-race-2007-04-19 .html.

7

Popular Appeals and Techniques of Persuasion in Political Advertising

Large scale efforts are being made, often with impressive success, to channel our unthinking habits, our purchasing decisions, and our thought processes by the use of insights gleaned from psychiatry and the social sciences. Typically these efforts take place beneath our level of awareness, so that appeals which move us are often, in a sense, "hidden." The result is that many of us are being influenced and manipulated, far more than we realize, in the patterns of our everyday lives.
—Vance Packard, *The Hidden Persuaders* (1957)

Candidates are pretty much sold like toothpaste today, with marketing techniques taken from the business world.
—Ken Warren, College of Public Service, St. Louis University

The bottom line is that an ad has to work emotionally. Fear is a primal emotion, and if an ad strikes a deep chord, it's effective.
—political consultant Tony Schwartz (1973)

In early May 2007, ten candidates for the Republican nomination for president appeared together at Ronald Reagan's Presidential Library in California for their first nationally televised debate. The MSNBC network carried it live. Host Chris Matthews opened the broadcast by noting that a recent poll indicated that only 22 percent of the American people believed this country was on the right track. The question, directed to candidate (and former New York City major) Rudy Giuliani, was, "How do we get back to Ronald Reagan's 'Morning in America'?"

> **Media Literacy Core Concepts:**
> *Media have embedded values and points of view.*
> *Most media messages are organized to gain profit and/or power or both.*
>
> **Media Literacy Key Questions:**
> *Who created this message?*
> *What lifestyles, values, points of view are represented in, or omitted from, this message?*

To many in the audience, the reference to Reagan's 1984 campaign advertisement was clear. But many others were not old enough to recall it, and the reference may have gone right over their heads.

"Morning in America" was Ronald Reagan's famous campaign spot. The spot used words and images that said virtually nothing about the issues or the candidate, but instead used music and feel-good images designed to appeal to the emotions of the television viewers.

"Morning in America Ad": Transcript

It's morning again in America. Today more men and women will go to work than ever before in our country's history. With interest rates at about half the record highs of 1980, nearly 2,000 families today will buy new homes, more than at any time in the past four years. This afternoon 6,500 young men and women will be married, and with inflation at less than half of what it was just four years ago, they can look forward with confidence to the future. It's morning again in America, and under the leadership of President Reagan, our country is prouder and stronger and better. Why would we ever want to return to where we were less than four short years ago?

" 'Morning in America' set the standard for enthusiasm-eliciting political advertising and remains largely unparalleled for its combination of evocative symbolism and minimal discussion of politics."[1]

View "Morning In America": http://www.youtube.com/watch?v=YYs8KKWU_Ms.

Few people realize that Reagan's media consultants were actually former advertising creators, responsible for Gallo Wine and Pepsi commercials, among others. "The makers of the [Reagan] ads quite openly modeled them on successful campaigns for companies such as Pepsi Cola and McDonald's,"[2] because commercial testing methods indicated voters would respond best to this style of advertising.

Running for president in the United States has become a "spectacle," according to media critic Mark Crispin Miller: "The presidency is a purely symbolic thing now, it's a purely visual thing, it's a spectacle."[3] Media scholar Stuart Ewen adds, "The Reagan presidency exemplified a period when image-making and merchandising techniques were coupling in nearly every arena of American life."[4]

IT'S AN AD, AD, AD WORLD

> Television spots . . . create auditory and visual stimuli that can evoke a voter's deeply held feelings . . . . The real question in political advertising is how to surround the voter with the proper auditory and visual stimuli to evoke the reaction you want from him.
>
> —political consultant Tony Schwartz

From the moment we wake up in the morning, until we go to sleep at night, we are exposed to literally hundreds of thousands of messages. Some estimates say between 1,000 and 3,000 of them pass our "radar screens" daily. Sources include radio, TV, billboards, the Internet, movies, newspapers, and magazines. Broadcasting and print journalism are advertiser-supported mediums. Without ads, they would not exist.

By the time we graduate from high school, we have been exposed to millions of ads: for alcohol, clothes, cosmetics, deodorant, food, shoes, tobacco, and more. Many people believe they are immune from the influence of advertising: most believe they have the skills to see through, and thus are protected from, ad techniques. (This is known as the "inoculation theory.") Advertisers use a variety of proven methods, all designed to get us to feel good or simply remember the product or service. So even though most people feel ads don't work on them, advertising *does* work—it helps make connections between consumers and goods. Think about the last time you went to the grocery store: why did you choose this brand of soap or that toothpaste? The answer may be that your family always uses that brand. But deep down inside, you've relied on that brand because your family or someone close to you trusted it. And they trusted it probably because they were unknowingly influenced by an ad campaign for the product.

Today, many of us are more skeptical of ads than in the past, and (in keeping with the inoculation theory) believe we are not affected by them. But in the early days of advertising, many people did not have the critical thinking or viewing skills necessary to question ad claims, so they believed them.

It might surprise you to learn that advertising has been around for quite a while. And the people who created some of the very first print ads learned one thing very quickly: if you want the customers to remember your product, you must appeal to their emotions. Consider this case history of a product that's been around more than 100 years.

HOW LISTERINE USED FEAR IN ADS TO BOOST PRODUCT SALES

One of the most successful campaigns in American advertising history was for Listerine, a brand name for mouthwash. "The history of Listerine dates back 120 years to 1879. The original amber-colored Listerine was formulated by Dr Joseph Lawrence and Jordan Wheat Lambert. But it wasn't designed as a mouthwash; it was actually a disinfectant for surgical procedures. It was first used as a multipurpose antiseptic. But soon it was discovered to be excellent for killing germs commonly found in the mouth. So, in 1895, the Lambert Company extended the sale of Listerine to the dental profession as a powerful oral antiseptic."[5]

In 1923 Listerine's ad agency decided to introduce a new tactic: fear. "The famous ad campaign featured poor Edna, who was 'often a bridesmaid but never a bride.' It tells the sad tale of how she was approaching her 'tragic' 30th birthday, still unmarried because of her affliction: halitosis, which the ad explains, 'you, yourself, rarely know when you have it. And even your closest friends won't tell you.' "[6]

Using Listerine, of course, would solve the problem, and Edna could be assured of snagging a husband. Sales of Listerine took off—primarily because the advertising made women afraid to be left alone and single. The American Medical Association disputed the claim that using Listerine would kill mouth germs. But "annual sales for Listerine went from $100,000 in 1921 to over $4 million in 1927—a 40x increase in six years."[7] The advertising message was firmly fixed in the minds of gullible consumers.

LISTERINE® is a registered trademark of Johnson & Johnson. Used with permission.

The slogan "often a bridesmaid, but never a bride" was recognized as the 48th most popular ad slogan by the producers of *Advertising Age* magazine in their survey of the *Top 100 Advertising Campaigns of the Century*.[8]

HOW ADS WORK

Some of the best questions to consider about today's ads are:

- How does the ad attract consumer/voter attention?
- What are its emotional appeals? How do they work?
- How does the ad make the product/candidate look appealing and believable?
- What other ad techniques should I be aware of?

All advertising messages, even those produced for politicians, use specific techniques designed to make the product or candidate appealing, attractive, and/or believable. The more you understand about these ad techniques, the better you will be at seeing through the sales pitch. Thousands of studies have been conducted about advertising's appeals and how viewers react to or comprehend these marketing techniques. Entire magazines (*Advertising Age, Ad Week, Promo*) and journals (*Journal of Advertising Research, Journal of Marketing Research*) devoted to this subject are published regularly. Today, intricate brain-research studies, called neuromarketing studies, are being conducted in order to give advertisers more information about how we react to visual stimuli. The results help advertisers create products that are more appealing to consumers.

Millions of dollars are spent by the people behind the product/candidate to develop, test, and produce just the right message to get the intended effect: buy me, vote for me.

Like products, candidates have become "branded." Voters can find their preferred candidate's name on everything from bumper stickers to T-shirts to campaign buttons to mugs. And the techniques used to sell candidates resemble commercials for the latest car, soap detergent, or cell phone. As we will see, the people behind the politicians' ads themselves come from advertising and marketing. They've simply transferred to the political arena what they know about what works in conventional advertising.

PROPAGANDA TECHNIQUES USED IN POLITICAL ADS AND CAMPAIGNS

Most political ads use one or more techniques designed to appeal to voters' emotions rather than intellect. The more familiar you are with the techniques, the better equipped you will be to comprehend how they work. Table 7.1 presents some of the more popular propaganda persuasion techniques along with some examples from present and past presidential campaigns.

Keep these in mind, because some of these same techniques have been used today by the candidates themselves during speeches and live debate situations. A further explanation of scare tactics and other appeals to emotions follows.

Table 7.1

Techniques of Persuasion Used in Presidential Campaigns and Advertising

Technique name	Description	Examples
Bandwagon	Claiming that everybody likes the candidate. Shouldn't you, too?	1950: Dwight Eisenhower's early ads used the slogan : "I like Ike; everybody likes Ike." 1994: Ronald Reagan's "Morning in America" implied that everyone was pleased with America under Reagan.
Glittering generalities	Using emotionally appealing words and phrases that can mean different things to different people.	1992: George Bush's phrase "a kinder, gentler nation." 1996: Bill Clinton's phrase "a bridge to the 21st century." "Family values": a phrase used by almost every politician.
Name-calling	Attaching a not-so-kind label to an opponent, hoping that the label will stick in the mind of the voters.	1972: Richard Nixon's opponents labeled him "Tricky Dick." 2000: Opponents said: "Al Gore is a tax-and-spend liberal." "George W. Bush is an elitist who's in the pocket of big oil companies." 2002: Bill Clinton was called "Slick Willie" by his challengers.
Plain (everyday) folks	Implying I'm one of you, or just like you, which means that you can feel very comfortable with me and my ideas; you can easily relate to me.	2007: Former Senator John Edwards's fondness for repeating that he was the son of a mill worker, that he came from humble origins, and that he knew what life is like for those who struggle to make a living.
Scare tactics	Using words and/or images to create an immediate or lasting sense of fear in the audience.	1964: President Johnson's "Daisy spot" used the threat of nuclear war against GOP opponent Barry Goldwater. 1988: President Bush's "Furlough ad" painted Democratic opponent Michael Dukakis as giving murderers weekend furloughs from prison while he was governor of Massachusetts.
Testimonial	Presenting an endorsement from a well-known person whom the audience will recognize and whose opinion the audience will presumably respect.	2007: Televangelist Pat Robertson endorsed GOP presidential candidate Rudy Giuliani. In California, Oprah Winfrey held a fundraiser for and endorsed the candidacy of Senator Barack Obama. Actor Chuck Norris appeared in an ad in support of GOP candidate Mike Huckabee.
Transfer	Referring to an event or using an image that has symbolic value—thus transferring the voter's emotion or allegiance to the candidate.	2007: Republican Rudy Giuliani's consistent references to his leadership and strength as New York City's mayor following the terrorist attacks of September 11, 2001.

DO ADS PERSUADE VOTERS?

So, are voters and viewers persuaded by the techniques used by political ad producers? Two long-time researchers don't think so. Writing in their 1976 classic *The Unseeing Eye: The Myth of Television Power in National Elections* (1976), Thomas E. Patterson and Robert D. McClure said:

Symbolic manipulation through televised political advertising simply does not work. Perhaps the overuse of symbols and stereotypes in product advertising has built up an immunity in the television audience. Perhaps the symbols and postures used in political advertising are such patently ridiculous attempts at manipulation that they appear more ridiculous than reliable. Whatever the precise reason, television viewers effectively protect themselves from manipulation by staged imagery."[9]

In fact, a Fall 2006 *USA Today*/Gallup Poll found that "Americans are highly skeptical of what they see in ads for political candidates."[10]

But others might disagree. Advertising, in general, does influence people. Some of us are persuaded more than others. Critical thinking/viewing and critical inquiry (questioning) are important strategies when considering how advertising influences consumers.

> 49%: The number of those surveyed who said "not much" when asked in a 2006 Gallup poll, "How much of what is said in (political) commercials, for or against candidates, do you believe?"

USING REPETITION TO REMIND THE VOTERS

One of the things advertisers know is that if you want your customer to remember your product, you must repeat its name over and over again. In 1960 Senator John F. Kennedy was not very well known outside his home state of Massachusetts. So when he ran for president, his image makers used a commercial designed to get him name recognition. Kennedy was challenging the very well known incumbent vice president, Richard Nixon.

Kennedy's spot mixed animation with actual newsreel footage. In order to get voters to remember his name, his media experts resorted to the proven advertising technique of repetition. The one-minute ad featured a catchy jingle in which the Kennedy name was repeated throughout.

Watch the Kennedy ad: http://www.easehistory.org/castream.asp?id=2.

FOUR RULES FOR MAKING EFFECTIVE POLITICAL (OR PRODUCT) ADS

Researchers have enough of a history of political advertising on TV (more than 50 years) to be able to provide guidance to candidates and their media consultants. Professor Arthur Sanders, author of *Prime Time Politics* (2002) sums up what the research says about how to make an effective ad, whether it be for dish detergent or a candidate:

1. Ads must grab our attention . . . so the best ads are dramatic, that is, they must tell a story using techniques like good visuals, catchy music, memorable slogans and compelling images (Verizon's cell phone campaign slogan "Can You Hear Me Now?" comes to mind).

2. Use of common genres that allow viewers with limited knowledge of the details of politics (or products) to understand the message. In other words: familiar themes and storylines (examples include political ads with visuals of terrorism, poverty, dirty waterways, crime).

3. Ads that emphasize a personal quality or characteristic rather than policy (common ads include those that introduce the candidate or his family).

4. Simple is better than complex appeals (30 seconds is just not enough time to explore complicated issues).[11]

TV IS A BUSINESS, AND ADVERTISING MAKES MONEY

In 1860 candidate Abe Lincoln spent $100,000 on his campaign, and that might have been the beginning of the idea that the one who spends the most wins. Lincoln's opponent Stephen Douglas spent only $50,000—and lost.

The idea certainly took hold. "In the 1998 elections, well over $1 billion was spent on political advertising on broadcast and print media. More than $500 million was spent by candidates to buy airtime on local broadcast stations, not including national networks, and cable channels, up some 40 percent from the total for 1994."[12]

Do the TV stations' bottom lines increase because of political ads? You bet they do. In 2006 the total TV revenue for all of the U.S. stations combined equaled $22.5 billion, according to media research firm BIA Financial Network. According to industry trade publication *Broadcasting & Cable,* these huge numbers were buoyed by political money.[13]

In the 2004 election, Florida was one of the "battleground states." Polls indicated that the race in Florida was a dead heat between incumbent president George W. Bush and his Democratic challenger, former Vice President Al Gore. No wonder the TV airwaves in the Sunshine State were bombarded by political messages. Local television ad purchases in Florida during the 2004 and 2000 presidential campaigns were:[14]

	Primary	**General Election**
2004 (Bush v Kerry)	$ 3.5 million	$119.8 million
2000 (Bush v Gore)	$ 4.3 million	$ 25.4 million

Clearly, during political campaign races, the media benefit. Those same media executives, with powerful Washington lobbyists, lead the effort against any campaign finance reforms, especially those that advocate for free airtime for candidates. After all, free airtime takes dollars away from the station's bottom line.

Table 7.2
The Rise in Political Ad Purchases, 1972–2004[15]

Year	Network	Spot/Local	Total
1972	$6,519,100	$18,061,000	$24,580,100
1976	$7,906,500	$42,935,700	$50,842,200
1980	$20,699,700	$69,870,300	$90,570,000
1984	$43,652,500	$110,171,500	$153,824,000
1988	$38,520,700	$189,379,500	$227,900,200
1992	$73,816,000	$225,807,400	$299,623,400
1996	$33,824,000	$366,661,900	$400,485,900
2000	$772,600	$611,172,500	$611,945,100
2004	$144,000	$637,831,900	$637,975,900

Figures above include presidential race years in which half of the Senate, all of the House of Representatives, and about one-quarter of the state governors were elected.

Is TV where it's at? You bet! Refer to Table 7.2. It shows the tremendous rise in ad purchases during the election campaigns from 1972–2004. Television continues to be a hot property for candidates.

So how much does it cost for a presidential candidate to purchase 30 seconds of advertising time on a local TV station? The answer is: that depends. Several factors have to be considered by the media buyer representing his/her candidate, the most important of which may be: how many people can I reach when I want to advertise?

First a little background—there are about 210 TV markets in the United States. Markets are ranked by size: that is, by how many homes have TV sets in the market. Obviously, the more homes with people watching, the larger the market. And the larger the market, the more that can be charged for ad time.

The Nielsen Company is the nation's most dominant ratings organization. Table 7.3 lists the top ten U.S. markets in 2007. Table 7.4 presents what one 30-second commercial might cost if one purchased time in one of the top network television programs listed.

Table 7.3
Nielsen Media's Top 10 Largest U.S. TV Markets (2007)[16]

Television market rank and name	Number of TV homes
1. New York	7,366,950
2. Los Angeles	5,611,110
3. Chicago	3,455,020
4. Philadelphia	2, 941,450
5. San Francisco-Oakland-San Jose	2,383,570
6. Dallas-Ft. Worth	2,378,660
7. Boston (Manchester)	2,372,030
8. Washington, DC (Hagerstown, MD)	2,272,120
9. Atlanta	2,205,510
10. Houston	1,982,120

Table 7.4
30-Second Ad Costs in Network TV (2007–2008 TV Season)[17]

Program title	Network	30-second ad cost
Grey's Anatomy	ABC	$419,000
Sunday Night Football	NBC	$358,000
The Simpsons	FOX	$319,000
Heroes	NBC	$296,000
Desperate Housewives	ABC	$370,000
CSI	CBS	$248,000
Two And A Half Men	CBS	$231,000
Survivor: China	CBS	$209,000
Survivor: Private Practice	ABC	$209,000

TARGETING THE AUDIENCE

One of the more popular places to place campaign commercials is around local television news. Local television news is very popular with candidates around the country. Over time, candidates have developed relationships with local TV news staffs, and stations cover candidates on the stump (free time). So it's natural that politicians would purchase airtime locally to reach their constituents. During the 2004 race for the White House, with TV continuing to reach the most people, ad time was purchased by candidates on specific TV programs designed to reach the audiences the candidates were trying to connect with. Media buyers were scooping up time (for example) during *The Oprah Winfrey Show,* watched by millions of women on local TV stations. Crime shows appealed to the Bush Republican campaign because the campaign was trying to reach men, whereas the Kerry Democratic campaign went after women heavily.

Before purchasing ad space, a candidate's media buyer must consider:

- Who is the target audience? (men, women, minorities, new, young voters)
- What TV shows do they watch? (football, soap operas, BET, Jon Stewart)
- Which TV shows attract the largest possible audiences? (reality, news, sports, talk, drama)
- How many of the target audience members are actually watching?
- Is this ad purchase the most effective use of my ad spending dollars?

In the 2008 race, Iowa, with its early January primary date, attracted a lot of candidate advertising. One ad tracking service found most of the presidential ads were purchased within these top five television programs:

1. Local News: $16.1 million
2. *Wheel of Fortune:* $1.4 million
3. *The Today Show:* $862,2007
4. *The Oprah Winfrey Show:* $577,860
5. *The Tonight Show with Jay Leno:* $480,551[18]

In the 2008 race, the Obama campaign purchased ad time in Manchester, New Hampshire during the following ABC series: *Ugly Betty, Private Practice, Grey's Anatomy, Dirty Sexy Money,* and *The Women's Murder Club.* The Clinton camp, meanwhile, purchased time on *Desperate Housewives, Boston Legal,* and daytime programs such as *The Martha Stewart Show* and *Who Wants To Be A Millionaire.* According to politico.com, all of the candidates bought time on Sunday's *Good Morning America, The Oprah Winfrey Show,* and the local news.[19]

Additionally, candidate Mike Huckabee purchased ad time on *The Ellen DeGeneres Show, Divorce Court,* and *Dr. Phil.* John McCain placed his spots in *People's Court, The Bold and the Beautiful,* and *Family Guy.* Mitt Romney bought time during *Friday Night Lights, Wheel of Fortune,* and *The Tyra Banks Show.* Rudy Giuliani's ads aired on *Poker after Dark, Law and Order,* and *Jeopardy.*[20]

The *New York Times,* using data from a political ad spending firm, reported on the total number of spots (TV commercials) aired in all TV markets in the campaign through December 23, 2007.[21]

The list for total number of spots aired follows:

Republicans	Democrats
Romney: 24,189	Obama: 13,834
Giuliani: 2,676	Clinton: 10,674
McCain: 2,547	Edwards: 7,735
Richardson: 5,714	Huckabee: 1,985
Thompson: 1,964	Dodd: 3,576

The *Times* also reported that of the Democratic candidates, Barack Obama had spent the most in Iowa ($8.3 million); and of the Republicans, Romney had spent the most ($6.5 million on more than 8,000 spots).[22]

For the first time, Nielsen (the ratings company) and the Wisconsin Advertising Project, used audience and TV program surveys to track political ads in every one of the 210 television markets in the United States.[23]

WHAT A 30-SECOND AD COULD COST A CANDIDATE

In Washington, D.C. (a top-10 market), during slower times of the year, a spot on a daytime show might cost under $100. But the cost of a spot on a Washington Redskins game aired in prime time might be as high as $10,000–$25,000. The price also depends upon the available inventory, the prices charged by the competition, the size of the overall package and its component parts, the anticipated ratings, and the skill of the sales staff.[24]

During the 2004 election, Ohio was one of the key battleground states. Polls there indicated that the race for president was very close. Millions of ad dollars went to every TV station. As an example, prices for a 30-second commercial on WHIO-TV (Dayton, market size 58) ranged from $185 for a low-rated program to $5,200 for a spot on highly rated television programs such as *Crime Scene Investigation (CSI).* Between March and September (2004), some 14,273 ads about the Bush/Kerry presidential race aired on Toledo's (market size 71) four leading TV stations.[25]

One question we might ask about spending by presidential candidates is: Who benefits from their purchases of ad time? Clearly the media themselves are the primary beneficiaries. Competitive campaigns, using TV to reach their audiences, benefit by broadcasting their ads at the most opportune times. The millions of dollars in ad revenue clearly helps the bottom line of the broadcast companies who own the stations, and that satisfies board members and investors.

PURCHASING AD SPACE ON WEB SITES

Consultants for candidates are also aware that many of us get our news and information online, rather than from printed newspapers and magazines. An ongoing practice involves purchasing advertising space on Web sites that millions of people are known to visit.

ADVERTISING BENEFITS NEWSPAPERS, TOO

Television is not alone: many candidates still use newspapers to reach voters. According to the *Wall Street Journal,* advertising by candidates has helped many newspapers' bottom lines, at a time when many papers are struggling to survive. Political consultants say that benefits of advertising in newspapers are that readers vote at above-average rates, and that newspapers allow for more sophisticated arguments than can be delivered in the typical 30-second television campaign spot.

As overall spending on campaigns doubled to $3.1 billion between 2002 and 2006, the amount spent on newspapers, including their online editions, tripled to $104 million, according to PQ Media.[26]

THE POWER OF THE IMAGE OVER THE WORD

Throughout the history of political advertising, there are images that stick out: images that people remember. And they remember them for a long time.

Some might remember the little girl seen plucking the petals off a daisy in the infamous "Daisy Spot" ad created in 1964 by President Lyndon B. Johnson's election campaign. Others might recall the image of Democratic candidate Michael Dukakis dressed in military fatigues atop a tank. And still others might remember the "Dean Scream" video and images of Democratic presidential contender Howard Dean reacting to his favorable New Hampshire primary showing—a spontaneous moment seized on by the opposition and the media for purposes of their own.

Each image designed to appeal to the senses, each designed to communicate something important to the voter, each a moment in time.

TYPES OF ADS HAVEN'T CHANGED MUCH OVER THE YEARS

Some of the first political ads aired on television more than 55 years ago. It may come as a surprise to learn that the types of political ads you see today do not differ very much from those seen in 1952. Descriptions of the fairly common techniques follow.

Common Political Ad Techniques[27]

Profile Spots ("the biography"): Commonly used at the start of a campaign to introduce voters to the candidate.

Examples: The Jimmy Carter profile spot from 1976 depicted the former Georgia governor as the ultimate nonpolitician, a nonlawyer tiller of the soil possessed of common sense found everywhere but inside the D.C. Beltway; Bill Clinton's "The Boy from Hope" (1992) is a more recent example.

Testimonial Spots: The "plain folks" or well known personalities who talk about why they support the candidate.

Example: Eleanor Roosevelt, widow of President Franklin D. Roosevelt, endorsed John F. Kennedy for president in 1960, and the effort was seen as a major boost from those who respected the former first lady.

Accomplishment Spots: The candidate lays out what he or she has already done in office, using memorable visuals.

Example: Ronald Reagan's "Morning in America" is the classic example here.

Negative Record Spots: Increasingly, candidates go after each other's record, using a variety of techniques. Watch for how candidates use quotations or newspaper headlines to prop up their argument against an opponent's voting record.

Example: There are so many examples that it is difficult to choose.

Response Spots: A candidate who has been criticized responds.

Example: Democrat Michael Dukakis responded (but too late) to many of challenger George H. W. Bush's ads (some say that led to his defeat).

Character Challenge Spots: Challenging your opponent's character can be a risky strategy, complex and delicate.

Example: Democrat Hubert Humphrey's "Weathervane" ad (1968) so angered Richard Nixon that he called on Humphrey to take it off the air. Humphrey did remove it. But Nixon didn't think twice about utilizing the same tactic four years later against rival George McGovern.

Issue Spots: Candidates do talk about issues, even if only for 30 seconds.

Examples: Take your pick: you'll find everything from crime, education, poverty, immigration, terrorism, and more. Both Hilliary Clinton and Barack Obama used health care as an issue in the 2008 Democratic primary race.

Scare Tactic Spots: Using fear as a vehicle has become a popular persuasive technique in ads.

Examples: LBJ's "Daisy Spot" (against Barry Goldwater, 1964); Ronald Reagan's "Bear in the Woods" spot (1984) about Soviet domination; the more contemporary use of 9/11 imagery in many political candidate ads.

SYMBOLIC IMAGERY IN POLITICAL ADVERTISING

Every media producer knows that images and related techniques can be used as symbols. Tobacco companies show young people happy and in bright colorful settings to imply smoking will lead to friendship and fun times. Political ad producers have also employed symbols for years.

In political ads, symbols such as the American flag are often used. The colors chosen for the onscreen titles or slogans will often be in red, white, and blue, all designed to communicate American values. (The "transfer" technique in propaganda says that viewers will transfer their patriotic feelings toward the flag to the candidate whose ads use such symbols and images.)

Ads which feature ordinary people—for example, senior citizens, crime victims, welfare recipients, immigrants, unemployed workers—can heighten the sense of authenticity, identification, and emotional impact, for those of us who are exposed to these types of ads.[28]

THE USE OF COLOR AND HOW THE BRAIN REACTS TO IT

Experts also know that utilizing the right color can achieve the desired response. So the use of color both in campaign events and in advertising is given a lot of time and attention.

According to one brand executive, Chuck Pettis of BrandSolutions, Inc., "Color is one of the key tools used to communicate to the amygdala and emotional portal between the three brains. Color can evoke subconscious and unconscious emotional responses that then send signals to the cortex brain, which then comes up with rationalizations for decisions already made unconsciously."[29] As an example,

At his presidential transition Web site, president-elect Barack Obama's team made crisp and effective graphical use of the traditional "patriotic" colors red, white, and blue. The president-elect sought to adapt his highly successful Internet campaign strategy to the demands of his new office. (AP Photo/change.org)

Obama's widely praised campaign logo "branded" the candidate on campaign ads of all sorts, from his ubiquitous Internet ads to bumper stickers and lawn signs. The logo, shown here in a TV ad, featured subtle use of red, white, and blue and an evocative emblem. (AP Photo/Clinton Campaign)

Pettis associates President George W. Bush with the "ruler archetype" (commonly known as the leader, the commander, the boss). Most "ruler" brands (Microsoft, IBM, Polo) have blue in their color palette. President Bush was often seen wearing a blue tie, for example.

Candidates might be shown walking or talking with farmers, housewives, business people, or children—another way of connecting with voters as the common person. Republican media consultant John Brabender pulls back the curtain on what he calls the "visual shorthand" used by ad makers to communicate to voters. If the candidate is pro-business, for example, you show him wearing a hard hat on a construction site: that's the universal code for jobs. If the candidate is trying to influence senior citizens, he or she will be shown at a nursing home, smiling with older folks. To show a candidate's support of K–12 education, multiracial kindergartners are preferred. And to invoke middle American values, the commercial will contain lots of flags, a universal sign of strength and patriotism, especially since 9/11.[30]

Music is specially chosen to make the viewer feel soothed and comforted, especially in times of stress or anxiety.

WHY DO CAMPAIGN ADS LACK QUALITY OF INFORMATION?

Media critic and historian Robert W. McChesney maintains that political ads are "dreadful" because they emulate the best (or worst) of conventional advertising. In his *Rich Media, Poor Democracy* (1999), McChesney notes that political ads are protected from regulation by the First Amendment, so their content cannot be legally challenged. Thus candidates can (and usually do) say anything in their political messages. An ad executive who compared the accuracy of presidential TV spots in 1976 to that of commercial messages found that ads for candidates

Jimmy Carter and Gerald Ford would not have met the standards the government places on the most trivial product commercial.[31]

APPEALING TO EMOTIONS

Most advertising today is still designed to appeal to the emotions. Advertisers and political media advisors have known for years that the best ads appeal to emotions.

Psychophysiologist Thomas Mulholland (Veterans Hospital in Bedford, Massachusetts) found that after just 30 seconds of watching television the brain begins to produce alpha waves, which indicates torpid (almost comatose) rates of activity. Alpha brain waves are associated with unfocused, overly receptive states of consciousness. A high frequency of alpha waves does not occur normally when the eyes are open. In fact, Mulholland's research implies that watching television is neurologically analogous to staring at a blank wall . . . . When Mulholland's research was published, it greatly impacted the television industry, at least in the marketing and advertising sector. Realizing viewers automatically enter a trance state while watching television, marketers began designing commercials that produce unconscious emotional states or moods within the viewer. The aim of commercials is not to appeal to the rational or conscious mind (which usually dismisses advertisements) but rather to implant moods that the consumer will associate with the product when it is encountered in real life. When we see product displays at a store, for instance, those positive emotions are triggered. Endorsements from beloved athletes and other celebrities evoke the same associations. If you've ever doubted the power of television advertising, bear this in mind: commercials work better if you're not paying attention to them![32]

In his book *Campaigning for Hearts and Minds: How Emotional Appeals in Political Ads Work* (2006), political science professor Ted Brader describes some of the common beliefs shared by those who create messages for politicians:[33]

Belief #1. Politicians routinely appeal to the emotion of voters, especially in campaign ads.

Belief #2. Emotional appeals strengthen the power of campaign ads as to sway voters.

Belief #3. Much of the emotional power of campaign ads derives from images and music.

Belief #4. Emotional appeals influence voters by getting their attention and evoking emotions that will then be associated with a candidate.

Belief #5. Campaign ads that rely on emotional appeals are manipulative, lacking in substance, and antithetical to reason or rationality.

Belief #6. Emotional appeals are most effective at influencing uninformed or uneducated voters.

> (Political) commercials make the American public captive in two respects. Since they occur in the midst of regular programming, they can't be readily shut off. And since their primary appeal is not to reason but rather to emotions, they are virtually unanswerable.
>
> —Curtis B. Gans, Director, Committee for the Study of the American Electorate (1973)

NEGATIVE ADVERTISING: HOW DOES IT AFFECT VOTERS?

Years of negative campaigns conducted almost exclusively by thirty-second television ads have gridlocked our political process and made the compromises necessary to govern all but impossible. Worse, it has soured our politics to the point that too many people no longer want anything to do with it.

—CBS newsman Bob Scheiffer

How do you feel about negative advertising? Does it turn you off? Does it confuse you over which candidate to vote for, if you vote at all? Is it possible that negative ads might actually be good for the election process?

Negative campaigning and advertising have been around for a long time, in one form or another.

One major study found that negative advertising does, in fact, drive down voter turnout. Researchers Stephen Ansolabehere and Shanto Iyengar documented this trend in their 1995 book *Going Negative.* Their study says that political campaign consultants intentionally use these ads to turn off voters. By their calculation, more than 6 million votes were lost to negative campaigns during the 1992 presidential election.[34]

Yet another study found that negative ads are actually good for the election process. Attack ads and negativity are healthy for campaigning, according to other researchers, if for no other reason than the need on the part of voters for solid information so they can make choices among partisan alternatives.[35]

THEMES IN 2008 ADS

Campaign ad watcher Evan Tracey of the Campaign Media Analysis Group, a firm that tracks political advertising, says themes in the ads for the 2008 presidential race followed predictable patterns: a vote for the GOP is the same as a vote for Bush (bad) and special interest groups are the cause of both global warming and inadequate health care for all Americans. "By and large the themes (up to this point) are very similar to those of four years ago: 'GOP equals Bush equals bad.' And: 'Evil special interests in Washington are the cause of global warming and the reason we don't have health care for all,'" says Tracey.[36]

CRIME SYMBOLISM—BUSH VERSUS DUKAKIS (1988)

Experienced media consultants and ad producers have also figured out how to indicate their candidate is strong on crime: showing him or her talking to law enforcement officials. This technique has been used in countless ads.

One negative ad on crime has gone down in political ad history. Many voters saw not only the ad, but also the ensuing massive press coverage about it.

The ad was created by Bush media specialist Roger Ailes, and it was used by President George H. W. Bush in his 1988 reelection campaign. The ad was designed to paint Bush's opponent, Democrat Michael Dukakis (who was governor of Massachusetts), as being soft on crime. With images of prisoners walking through a revolving prison gate, the ad (known as the "Furlough Ad") said "many first-degree murderers escaped" as the words "268 escaped" were superimposed on the screen. The problem was, the facts didn't add up. Massachusetts actually had one of the best prison records among the states. But that didn't matter. According to media scholar Kathleen Hall Jamieson, "it depended on innuendo and visual images to link Michael Dukakis with the supposed dangers of a prison furlough program and therefore . . . a dangerous breed of liberalism." Jamieson also charged that the media failed to challenge the inaccuracies of the furlough ad, thus failing in one of its primary responsibilities.[37]

"Furlough Ad": Transcript

As Governor of Massachusetts, Michael Dukakis vetoed mandatory jail sentences for drug dealers. He vetoed the death penalty. His revolving door prison policy gave weekend furloughs to first-degree murderers not eligible for parole. While out, many committed other crimes like kidnapping, and rape. And many are still at large. Now Michael Dukakis says he wants to do for America what he's done for Massachusetts. America can't afford that risk.

Watch the "Furlough Ad": http://www.youtube.com/watch?v=-lFk78R _qYM&mode=related&search=.

A similar ad also portrayed Dukakis as weak on crime, but this second ad was not funded by the Bush campaign, but rather by an independent political action committee.

"Willie Horton Ad": Transcript

Bush and Dukakis on crime: Bush supports the death penalty for first-degree murderers. Dukakis not only opposes the death penalty, he allowed first-degree murderers to have weekend passes from prison. One was Willie Horton, who murdered a boy in a robbery, stabbing him 19 times. Despite a life sentence, Horton received ten weekend passes from prison. Horton fled, kidnapping a young couple, stabbing the man and repeatedly raping his girlfriend. Weekend prison passes: Dukakis on crime.

Watch the "Willie Horton Ad": http://livingroomcandidate.movingimage .us/election/index.php?ad_id=944 and http://www.youtube.com/watch?v= EC9j6Wfdq3o.

The impact of both the "Furlough" and "Willie Horton" ads was devastating: Bush surged ahead of Dukakis in the polls. The shift in public opinion was widely attributed to the broadcast of these two ads and the subsequent media coverage of them.[38]

IMPRESSIONS OF NEGATIVE ADS

A Pew research poll[39] found that voters and consultants had very different concerns when asked about the impact of negative ads.

What bothers the American public:

	Very much	Somewhat	Not much/Not at all
Negative campaigning	69%	17%	21%
What politicians promise	53%	25%	21%
Amount of money spent	56%	17%	26%
Political ads on TV	32%	24%	43%
News coverage	15%	26%	57%

What consultants say causes voter cynicism:

	Very much	Somewhat	Not much/Not at all
News coverage	63%	28%	9%
Politician performance	27%	46%	26%
Fundraising practices	25%	36%	38%
Negative campaigning	24%	43%	33%

REAGAN AND SYMBOLISM OF FEAR IN POLITICAL ADVERTISING

The Reagan campaign ran a commercial during the 1984 campaign that subtly told voters that Democrats of the era didn't appreciate the dangers of the world in which they lived. It suggested that Reagan's opponents were convinced the woods were safe because they harbored no bears, but asked a simple question of those watching it: What if they're wrong, and there *are* bears in the woods?[40]

"Bear in the Woods Ad": Transcript

There is a bear in the woods. For some people the bear is easy to see. Others don't see it at all. Some people say the bear is tame. Others say it's vicious and dangerous. Since no one can really be sure who is right, isn't it smart to be as strong as the bear? If there *is* a bear . . . .

The ad ends with a visual: a photo of Reagan with the words: Ronald Reagan Prepared for Peace.

Watch the "Bear in the Woods Ad": http://www.4president.us/tv/1984/reagan1984bear.htm.

Media scholar Ted Brader explains, "The entire script is a metaphorical reference to the Cold War standoff with the Soviet Union (the bear is a traditional symbol of Russia.) Like *Daisy,* the Bear ad counts on viewers to fill in what is missing. The audiovisual packaging of the ad does nothing to help clarify the message. For nearly thirty seconds, a bear lumbers over the rocks, through bushes, and into streams, until finally meeting a man with a gun atop a grassy ridge. At first, the bear walks directly toward the man but then pauses several feet away and takes a step back. The ad never cuts away to images of Soviet tanks, missiles, or other visual evidence that might help viewers who miss the point. Just as the *Morning in America* ads use a sentimental tune to elicit an emotional reaction from viewers, the Bear ad uses disquieting string chords with the 'thump-thump' of a drum at regular intervals."[41]

The ad is impressive for what it *doesn't* show or say:

- It never references Reagan's Democratic opponent, Walter Mondale.
- It never mentions the Soviet Union (the "bear," then thought to be the threat).
- It says nothing about nuclear powers or weapons.
- It makes no reference to spending on American defenses.

The ad was created by renowned adman Hal Riney, the same man who produced Reagan's "Morning in America" spot. Many critics are fond of Riney's approach: "Riney has the ability to cloak a strong message inside of a softer approach . . . . Most political advertising hits viewers over the head, while his work makes just as strong a point but in a less confrontational and a more soothing manner."[42]

In 2004, the Bush-Cheney campaign took a page directly from Reagan's campaign playbook, creating an updated version of the bear ad. Their version showed wolves, preparing to strike, in the woods.

"Wolves Ad": Transcript

In an increasingly dangerous world . . . . Even after the first terrorist attack on America . . . John Kerry and the liberals in Congress voted to slash America's intelligence operations. By 6 billion dollars. Cuts so deep they would have weakened America's defenses. And weakness attracts those who are waiting to do America harm.

Watch the "Wolves Ad": http://livingroomcandidate.movingimage.us/election/index.php?nav_action=election&nav_subaction=overview&campaign_id=178://www.sfgate.com/cgi-bin/article.cgi?f=/c/a/2004/06/09/BUGBI72U8O1.DTL.

This time, the Republicans were not referencing Russians as our foes, but rather terrorism. The ad used ominous music and implied that Democratic challenger John Kerry would not be strong on terrorists. Kerry's response to the wolves ad: "Instead of giving voters even one good reason to vote for him, George W. Bush has chosen to scare the American people with images of wolves."[43] But as Kathleen Hall Jamieson notes, such "allegorical" ads can be powerful.[44]

SWIFT BOAT VETERANS NEGATIVE AD CAMPAIGN CHALLENGES DEMOCRAT KERRY

In May 2004, a "527" (independent interest) group called Swift Boat Veterans for Truth unveiled a campaign designed to discredit Vietnam veteran and Democratic presidential candidate Senator John Kerry. The group, partially composed of veterans who had served with Kerry, raised millions of dollars to create a Web site and to broadcast their "issue ads" claiming Kerry had lied or misled voters about his war record and events that had occurred during Kerry's Vietnam War tour of duty. In August of that year, several ads sponsored by the group aired across the country. The ads created a great deal of controversy and publicity, both in

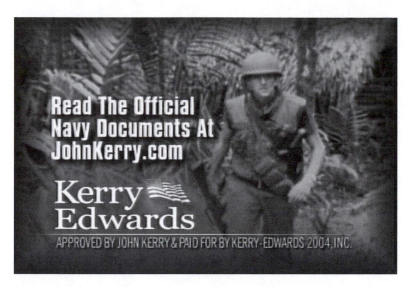

In August 2004 the John Kerry campaign countered Swift Boat Veterans for Truth attack ads impugning Kerry's military record with this ad showing Kerry in action in Vietnam in the 1960s. (AP Photo/Kerry-Edwards 2004)

newspapers, news programs, and online. Senator Kerry was slow to respond to the charges in the ads, and some claim this hurt him in his bid to unseat President Bush.

Charges made in these ads, and others, caused many in the media to return to their roles as "fact checkers." Tom Hannon, CNN political director, says, "I think the Swift Boat Veterans for Truth [ad campaign] is really what caused the rebirth or certainly the explosion of fact-checks. It sort of gave a second life to some of the tools that maybe hadn't been used as much in recent campaigns."[45]

THE AD WATCH: NEWS MEDIA ANALYSIS OF CAMPAIGN SPOTS

How are voters supposed to know what's accurate and what's not in a candidate's slick 30-second commercial? Careful and critical viewers apply a good deal of skepticism when they watch. The negativity of the 1988 presidential campaign bothered a lot of people. The result was a move to provide the electorate with a new tool for analysis: the ad watch, which was designed to help voters see through manipulative, inaccurate, and misleading information in ads.[46] In this digital media age it is important for unsuspecting viewers to understand the unique techniques of persuasion used in polished political advertising.

Since 1992, the news media has sought to help readers and viewers deconstruct these sophisticated visual production techniques and claims made by candidates (and their public relations/advertising agencies) in commercials. "Some political ads leave out important information that would help voters make a better decision about which candidate they prefer or which position on an issue to support. Others provide confusing information that misleads voters. The job of a good 'adwatcher' is to find ads that are misleading or uninformative and correct any misinformation."[47]

One of the pioneers of the advertising watchdog was Cable News Network reporter Brooks Jackson. His bosses at CNN offered him a chance to review misleading or false ads by presidential candidates. "The news media had been letting candidates and their paid consultants get away with it. We covered the often high-toned speeches the candidates were making to audiences numbering in the hundreds and thousands, while ignoring the down-and-dirty statements their ads were making to audiences numbering in the millions and tens of millions."[48]

And so the "ad watch" was born. (Some television and news operations simply call their analyses "truth checks," "truth tests," "for the record," or "just the facts.") The ad watch is an analysis, typically prepared by a reporter who deconstructs the words and images of a 30- or 60-second commercial. Typical elements in a print ad watch include a transcript of the ad script, one or more images taken from the commercial, an explanation of the techniques of persuasion used, and an explanation of the claims made. Many newspapers also publish "ad watches" on local campaigns as well as on the ads of the presidential candidates. Elements of a broadcast ad watch include snippets of the ad itself. Typically, the broadcast ad watch is part of a station's local news.

HELPING NEWS VIEWERS UNDERSTAND BROADCAST AD WATCHES

Studies have proved that TV viewers are more likely to remember the campaign ads in political news stories, even if the reporter in the story is critical of the information in the ad. Researcher Kathleen Hall Jamieson asked groups of voters during the 1988 presidential campaign what they remembered seeing from the news of the previous week, during which ABC News had debunked distortions in ads used by both the Republican nominee, George H. W. Bush, and the Democrat, Michael Dukakis. Surprisingly viewers remembered the content of the ads, but *not* what the ABC reporter said about those same ads. A subsequent study found viewers likewise recalled more about the ad than the reporter's commentary of the ad. Why did this occur? Jamieson says ABC filled the TV screen with the ad while the reporter was commenting on it. To help solve viewer comprehension, Jamieson and the Annenberg Public Policy Center have recommended that future news reports place the ad within a smaller box on the screen, so that viewers don't confuse the ad's message with the reporter's message. Another recommendation: superimpose graphics over the ad to reinforce criticism.[49]

Researchers say the success of the broadcast ad watches lies not simply in replaying the ad being analyzed and offering commentary, but rather in interrupting the ad with commentary and repositioning the ad on the screen.[50]

Broadcast news organizations have been encouraged to conduct and air ad watches by the large Radio-TV News Directors Association. Brooks Jackson of CNN, co-creator of the FactCheck.org political ad watchdog Web site, provides recommendations and guidance to those news journalists who might be ready to label an ad as either "false" or "misleading":[51]

"False." This is the most serious charge you can make about an ad, and I have used this word in only a very few cases. I use it when I can prove a statement is factually incorrect, and when there is no reasonable way it can be interpreted otherwise. In the 1996 presidential campaign Bob Dole ran an ad accusing Lamar Alexander of raising Tennessee's sales taxes 85% while he was governor. In fact, sales taxes increased only 22%. Dole's ad was false and I said so.

"Misleading." Much more often an ad uses facts selectively, or quotes out of context, in a way designed to leave an incorrect impression. Not a lie, exactly. But the sort of dishonesty that might get a journalist fired in a heartbeat if presented as a news story. Example: in 1992 Pat Buchanan ran a primary ad accusing some key George Bush advisers of being "foreign agents" whose names appeared in "Justice Department files." Wow! And it was all true! But the Bush aides were not spies or criminals, as the ad seemed to imply. They were merely lobbyists for foreign corporations, and had filed the required disclosure reports with an obscure office of Justice. A classic case of an ad that was factually true, but clearly misleading. And I said so. I probably use the word "Misleading" ten times more often than the word "False."

WAYS TO CONSIDER AND QUESTION POLITICAL ADS

- Understand the type of ad you are watching
- Identify any claims made by the candidate or issues made
- Look for evidence in the ad for the claims that are made
- Find outside evidence for the claims
- Verify that evidence presented in an ad is true
- Correct any misleading statements
- Figure out if there are any visual arguments
- Identify the sponsor

While many believe ad watches help voters better understand these spots, not everyone agrees. One study disputed the contention that ad watch columns are good for the electorate. In *Going Negative, How Political Advertisements Shrink and Polarize the Electorate,* the researchers found that ad watch journalism fails, because the candidate whose ad is being profiled gets more support rather than less from viewers who see the analysis.[52]

WAYS OF DECONSTRUCTING AND ANALYZING POLITICAL ADS

Project Vote Smart, a national election education initiative, invites us to consider these questions[53] when studying political advertising:

- What are the key messages communicated in each advertisement?
- Which type of ad was more memorable? Why?
- Which do you think would be most effective in convincing viewers to vote for (or against) a candidate?

- Did you learn from the ads? Did they help you to decide which candidate to support?
- What do all types have in common? Do they provide factual information or do they evoke an emotional response?
- During which programs do the ads play? What time of the day do you see the most ads?
- What are the limitations of a 30-second commercial?
- How important is a candidate's look in these ads? What type of image are they trying to create?
- If you were the campaign manager for a candidate for Congress in your district, what type of ad would you try to create?

So what do you need to know in order to see through the spin and techniques of persuasion in political advertising? University of Maryland political science professor and media educator John Splaine offers advice on how to better understand what you see. Dr. Splaine suggests two models[54] for better understanding political advertisements. The TAPPER Model is presented in Table 7.5.

Splaine's SNAILS model is as follows:

Symbols

What symbols are being used to convey the candidate's message (flags, monuments, etc.)? What meanings do the symbols have?

Narration

What is the narration? What qualities does the narrator's voice have? What effect does that voice have on your perception? What effect do the words have?

Table 7.5
The TAPPER Model

T	Target	Who is the target audience?
A	Affect	How do viewers respond to the ad emotionally?
P	Proof	Was any proof offered for the claims in the ad?
P	Pictures	What did pictures convey? Images? Symbols? Music? Do these elements work together to support the central message of the ad?
E	Errors	Are there any errors of fact or omissions? How can you find out?
R	Remain	How many different images did you see and how long did those images remain on the screen? Was the ad fast-paced or slow?

Angles

What camera angles are used in the ad? What effect do they have?

Implied

Sometimes the most important message is not openly stated. Instead, it is implied. Is there an implied message? If so, what? Is the implied message so clear that you can't miss it or do you have to look for it? Do the individuals or groups that appear in the ad represent an implied message?

Lighting

What kinds of lighting are used? What effect does the lighting in the ad have on your perception and emotions? Is anyone or anything spotlighted? If so, how does this affect what you feel?

Scare Tactics

When a commercial is negative, is it trying to scare you? How does it attempt to scare you (what scare tactics are used)? Were the scare tactics obvious or did you have to look for them?

HOW VIDEO CONFUSES VIEWERS

Media scholar Kathleen Hall Jamieson, who has studied how TV viewers comprehend political ads, found that television's use of visuals and editing techniques does not click with voters. According to Jamieson, "Rapid intercutting of visuals can short circuit the normal logic of viewers' thought processes. Viewers are also slow to recognize that most ads feature actors and are highly sophisticated marketing tools using professional directors and the latest high-tech editing techniques. As viewers, we react mainly to their emotional content."[55]

To be better prepared for political campaign messages, Jamieson recommends that we:

1. *Be informed.* Because it enhances the ability to evaluate campaign advertising knowing what goes in the body politic is the best protection against misleading communication of all kinds.

2. *Watch for counter advertising.* A responsibility of the candidates and their supporters, well-planned and produced responses to unfair attacks have a good chance of reaching the same low-involvement, inadvertently exposed audience that has been influenced by other ads. But—they require money and expertise that may not be equally available to both sides.

3. *Watch debates.* Although often criticized for shallow questions and self-serving answers, debates do provide a televised opportunity for viewers to hear candidates' arguments face-to-face. When candidates are willing to take the risk, they also provide a forum for making opponents responsible for unfair political advertising.

4. *Watch the news.* Political analysts do serve a watchdog role over unfair political advertising. Some drawbacks: their criticisms usually only air once while ads appear

repeatedly; most vulnerable viewers may not follow news programs; critics may give additional exposure to unfair criticisms; and commentary may not be as visually evocative and effective as the ads themselves.

Common Ad Techniques of Persuasion[56]

What are the common ad techniques and what do you need to know about them?

In general, these are some of the techniques of persuasion commonly used by advertisers:

SYMBOLS are larger than reality, usually emotional, idea-conveyances; symbols can be words, designs, places, ideas, music, etc. They can symbolize tradition, nationalism, power, religion, sex, or any emotional concept. The fundamental principle of persuasion is to rub the emotional content of one thing onto another. Thus, a beautiful woman can be used on TV to promote lust, romance, killing of police, or Snickers' nutrition.

HYPERBOLE is exaggeration or "hype." Glittering generalities is a subset of hype that utilizes impressive language. Vague and meaningless, it leaves the target impressed emotionally and, therefore, more susceptible to the next sales pitch. For example, "The greatest automobile advance of the century . . . ."

DEFENSIVE NATIONALISM uses fear (usually of an enemy) although it can be a political opponent, sickness, or any threat. For example, calling statements "McCarthyism" or "communism" brings up fear of demagogues and dictatorship.

SCAPEGOATING is a powerful subset of defensive nationalism that blames many problems upon one person, group, race, religion, etc.

HUMOR is a powerful emotion. If you can make people laugh, you can persuade them.

LIES work—on cereals boxes, ads and on television "news." Most people want to believe what they see. According to Hitler, people are more suspicious of a small lie than a large one.

"MAYBE, MIGHT, AND COULD" can make outrageous claims sound okay. Listen to infomercials.

TESTIMONIALS use famous people or respected institutions to sell a person, idea, or product. They don't need to have anything in common. A dangerous trend: we seem to be increasingly conditioned to accept illogic as fact.

REPETITION drives the message home many times. Even unpleasant ads work. Chevy trucks are "like a rock," and smoking Marlboro can make you tough and independent (fact: it used to be a cigarette for girls.)

PLAIN FOLKS RHETORIC is popular with advertisers and politicians: it's the strategy of promoting oneself or one's products as being of humble origins, common —one of the gals/guys. Unfortunately, plain folks reinforces anti-intellectualism (a common tendency of all electronic media), implying that to be "common" is good (an' hit ain't, dude, ya no?)

FUHRERPRINZIP means "leadership principle." (The term was first used in this manner by Josef Goebbels.) The idea is basically, "Be firm, bold, strong; have dramatic confidence." Many cultural icons emphasize the strong, yet plain, super-hero (for example Clint Eastwood, Bruce Willis, Arnold Schwarznegger). Some think this role modeling leads to a great deal of male aloneness, and, perhaps, less ability to cooperate. The strategy is frequently combined with plain folks.

AD HOMINEM is name calling. It can be direct or delicately indirect. Audiences love it. Our violent, aggressive, sexual media teaches us from an early age to love to hear dirt (just tune in to afternoon talk TV). Name calling is frequently combined with hype, truth, lies, etc. Remember, all is fair in love, war, political dirty tricks, and advertising, and suing for libel is next to impossible!

FLATTERY is telling or implying that the members of your target audience are something that makes them feel good or, often, something that they want to be. And, I am sure that someone as brilliant as yourself will easily understand this technique.

BRIBERY seems to give something desirable. We humans tend to be greedy. Buy a taco; get free fries.

DIVERSION occurs when one seems to tackle a problem or issue, but, then, throws in an emotional non sequitur or distraction. The straw man technique is a subset that builds up an illogical (or deliberately damaged) idea which one presents as something that one's opposition supports or represents. Then one proceeds to attack this idea, reducing one's opponent.

DENIAL is the practice of avoiding attachment to unpopular things; it can be direct or indirect. An example of indirect denial was when Dukakis said, "Now I could use George Bush's Willie Horton tactics and talk about a furloughed federal (the President's jurisdiction) prisoner who brutally raped a mother of five children, but I would not do that."

CARD STACKING is using statements or facts in a context that gives a false and/or misleading impression—telling only part of the story. Read the quotations from the critics in any movie ad.

BANDWAGON is the persuasive strategy that says "everyone is doing it." It plays upon the universal loneliness of humankind. In America with our incredible addiction to sports, it is often accompanied by the concept of winning. "Wear Marlboro gear."

SIMPLE SOLUTIONS avoid complexities (unless selling to intellectuals). This strategy attaches many problems to one solution.

"SCIENTIFIC" EVIDENCE uses the paraphernalia of science (charts, etc.) for "proof," which often is bogus. A classic example is Chevy's truck commercial chart of vehicles on the road after ten years.

GROUP DYNAMICS replaces that "I" weakness with "we" strength—concerts, audiences, rallies, pep rallies.

RHETORICAL QUESTIONS get the target "agreeing," saying "yes," building trust; then try to sell them.

NOSTALGIA is the idealization of and longing for the past. A nostalgic setting can make a product seem more attractive—Forrest Gump!

TIMING can be as simple as planning your sell for when your target is tired. In sophisticated propaganda, it is the organization of multiple techniques in a pattern or strategy that increases the emotional impact of the sell.

NOTES

1. Ted Brader, *Campaigning for Hearts and Minds: How Emotional Appeals in Political Ads Work* (Chicago: University of Chicago Press, 2006), 6.

2. Frank I. Luntz, *Candidates, Consultants and Campaigns: The Style and Substance of American Electioneering* (New York: Blackwell, 1988), 207.

3. Consuming Images, The Public Mind with Bill Moyers, PBS (November 1989).

4. Stuart Ewen, *All Consuming Images,* rev. ed. (New York: Basic Books, 1990), xvi.

5. "Listerine," http://www.superbrands-brands.com/volII/brand_listerine.htm.

6. http://www.rigneygraphics.com/lunchmeat/archive/04-11/04-11.php.

7. Ibid.

8. "The Advertising Century," http://adage.com/century/campaigns.html.

9. Thomas E. Patterson and Robert D. McClure, *The Unseeing Eye: The Myth of Television Power in National Elections* (New York: Putnam, 1976).

10. James Joyner, "American Skeptical about Political Ads (but They Work)," Outside the Beltway, http://www.outsidethebeltway.com/archives/2006/10/americans_skeptical_about_political_ads_but_they_work/.

11. David A Schultz, ed., *Lights, Camera, Campaign!: Media Politics and Political Advertising* (New York: P. Lang, 2004), 3–5.

12. Robert W. McChesney, *Rich Media, Poor Democracy: Communication Politics in Dubious Times* (Urbana, IL: University of Illinois Press, 1999), 263.

13. Malone, Michael, "Report: TV Revs Up 8.2%," *Broadcasting & Cable,* May 24, 2007, http://www.broadcastingcable.com/article/CA6446456.html?display=Breaking+News&referral=SUPP&nid=2228.

14. Evan Tracey of TNS Media Intelligence/CMAG, in sidebar accompanying Mike Vogel, "Election Results," *Florida Trend Magazine,* July 2007, http://www.floridatrend.com/industry_article.asp?cName=Government/Politics%20&%20Law&cID=7&aID=17896271.223385.610701.4955364.1463063.229&aID2=46968.

15. Television Bureau of Advertising, TVB Online: http://www.tvb.org/nav/build_frameset.asp.

16. Source: http://www.nielsenmedia.com/nc/portal/site/Public/menuitem.3437240b94cacebc3a81e810d8a062a0/?vgnextoid=130547f8b5264010VgnVCM100000880a260aRCRD#.

17. Source: http://adage.com/mediaworks/article?article_id=120838 (available by subscription).

18. Jim Kuhnhenn, "Campaigns Prepare for Big Spending," Associated Press, September 25, 2007, http://www.policyontv.com/Publications/PR_20070925.pdf.

19. "A Look at Ad Spending in NH"; Politico: "Campaigns Target Their Ad Messages to Shows Watched by Their Favorite Voting Bloc," http://www.cbsnews.com/stories/2008/01/07/politics/politco/main3680802.shtml.

20. "Who's Buying Where?" *Campaign & Elections* magazine, February 2008, 15.

21. Amanda Cox, Farhana Hossain, Vu Nguyen, "In Their Ads: The Words They Use," TNS Media Intelligence/CMAG data, *New York Times,* December 27, 2007, http://www.nytimes.com/interactive/2007/12/27/us/20071228_ADS_GRAPHIC.html#.

22. Patrick Healy, "Iowa Saturated by Political Ads," *New York Times,* December 28, 2007, http://www.nytimes.com/2007/12/28/us/politics/28ads.html?_r=1&ref=us&oref=slogin.

23. Jim Rutenberg, "The 2004 Campaign: Advertising; Campaigns Use TV Preferences to Find Voters, *New York Times,* July 18, 2004, http://www.nytimes.com/2004/07/18/politics/campaign/18ADS.final.html?hp.

24. Howard J. Blumenthal and Oliver R. Goodenough, *This Business of Television,* 2nd ed. (New York: BillBoard Books, 1998), 24.

25. Nielsen Monitor-Plus and the University of Wisconsin Ad Project.

26. http://www.mediainfo.com/eandp/news/article_display.jsp?vnu_content_id=1003 617310 (accessed August 2, 2007); http://online.wsj.com/article/SB118541344062578440 .html?%20mod=todays_us_marketplace.

27. Based on *The Classics of Political Television Advertising* [videorecording], written and produced by David Beiler (Campaign & Elections, Inc. Teacher Guide; Garden City, NY: Focus Media, 1986).

28. Ted Brader, *Campaigning for Hearts and Minds: How Emotional Appeals in Political Ads Work* (Chicago: University of Chicago Press, 2006), 37.

29. Personal e-mail correspondence with Chuck Pettis, BrandSolutions, Inc.

30. Joshua Green, "Dumb and Dumber: Why Are Campaign Commercials So Bad?" *The Atlantic Monthly,* July/August 2004, 84.

31. Robert W. McChesney, *Rich Media, Poor Democracy: Communication Politics in Dubious Times* (Urbana, IL: University of Illinois Press, 1999), 262.

32. Wes Moore, "Television: Opiate of the Masses," Disinformation, posted May 5, 2001, http://www.disinfo.com/archive/pages/article/id1149/pg2/.

33. Ted Brader, *Campaigning for Hearts and Minds: How Emotional Appeals in Political Ads Work* (Chicago: University of Chicago Press, 2006), 23–38.

34. Stephen Ansolabehere and Shanto Iyengar, *Going Negative: How Political Advertisements Shrink and Polarize the Electorate* (New York: Free Press, 1995).

35. David A. Schultz, ed., *Lights, Camera, Campaign!: Media Politics and Political Advertising* (New York: P. Lang, 2004), 55–56.

36. Elizabeth Wilner, *Candidates' Refrains Sound the Same,* August 16, 2007, http://www.politico.com/news/stories/0807/5398.html.

37. Media & Values, Spring 1992, Center for Media & Values, Los Angeles, CA; Kathleen Hall Jamieson and Paul Waldman, *The Press Effect, Politicians, Journalists and the Stories That Shape the Political World* (New York: Oxford University Press, 2003), 2.

38. Stephen Ansolabehere and Shanto Iyengar, *Going Negative: How Political Advertisements Shrink and Polarize the Electorate* (New York: Free Press, 1995).

39. Don't Blame Us: The Views of Political Consultants, survey by The Pew Research Center for the People and the Press, June 17, 1998, http://people-press.org/reports/display.php3?ReportID=86.

40. David Keene, *The Forgotten Past, The Hill,* June 5, 2007, http://thehill.com/david-keene/the-forgotten-past-2007-06-05.html.

41. Ted Brader, *Campaigning for Hearts and Minds: How Emotional Appeals in Political Ads Work* (Chicago: University of Chicago Press, 2006), 9–10.

42. Republican strategist Dan Schnur, quoted in "Creating Reagan's Image," *San Francisco Chronicle,* June 9, 2004.

43. "President George W. Bush Gives Thanks in Re-Election Acceptance Speech," http://blog.4president.org/2004/george_w_bush/index.html.

44. Julian Borger, "Bush Sets Wolves on Kerry Campaign, *The Guardian,* October 23, 2004, http://www.guardian.co.uk/uselections2004/story/0,13918,1334228,00.html.

45. CNN political director Tom Hannon, quoted in "Campaign Trail Veterans for Truth," *American Journalism Review,* December 2004/January 2005, 40.

46. "Adwatch: Covering Campaign Ads," in *Politics and the Press, The News Media and Their Influences,* ed. Pippa Norris (Boulder, CO: L. Rienner Publishers, 1997), 166.

47. How to Do an Adwatch, Candidates in Their Own Words, Unit 3, Annenberg Public Policy Center, 2005, 12: http://student-voices.org/teachers/curriculum/campaign/Unit3 Handouts.pdf.

48. Appendix C, A Newsroom Guide to Political Advertising, Radio TV News Directors Foundation, 1999; a publication of the Political Coverage Project, funded by the Carnegie Foundation and Ford Foundation: http://www.rtndf.org/resources/politics/cfs.PDF.

49. Brooks Jackson and Kathleen Hall Jamieson, *UnSpun: Finding Facts in a World of Disinformation* (New York: Random House, 2007), 52–53.

50. Joseph N. Cappella and Kathleen Hall Jamieson, "Broadcast Adwatch Effects," *Communication Research,* 21, no. 3 (1994): 342–365.

51. "Show Me the Money," http://web.archive.org/web/20070705201807/http:// www.rtnda.org/resources/politics/smtmoney.shtml.

52. Kathleen Hall Jamieson, *Everything You Think You Know about Politics, and Why You Are Wrong* (New York: Basic Books, 2000), 122.

53. http://www.vote-smart.org/resource_classroom_01.php#Ads.

54. www.ciconline.org/viewsmart.

55. Kathleen Hall Jamieson, "The Paradox of Political Ads: Reform Depends on Voter Savvy," *Media and Values,* Spring 1992, 58.

56. Excerpt from *Media Investigations Specific Tools for Analysis* © 1999 New Mexico State University Board of Regents - Legal Information NMSU College of Extended Learning: New Mexico Regional Technology Assistance Program. This module created by Jill Brown, Clint Fisher, Kd D'Port, and Fred Lackey, RETA instructors.http:// reta.nmsu.edu/traincd/media/tools.html.

8

Analyzing Campaign Events

TV, of course, has transformed the primaries from regional popularity contests into national image-making shows.

—Marshall McLuhan (1968)

It looks dazzling.

—CBS News analyst Jeff Greenfield (2008)

Stagecraft has always had an essential role in presidential conventions—and this is no exception.

—Steven Heller, *Staging Obama* (2008)

In every political campaign, candidates appear at events that are highly choreographed. These staged events are designed like clockwork, with specific things happening that are intended to appeal to and attract potential voters and viewers.

The events can be neighborhood gatherings, "town hall" meetings, press conferences, or even debates. In media circles, these events are sometimes labeled "photo-ops," short for photo opportunities.

Controlling every aspect of an event is very important to the candidate and his or her media consultant. By controlling the event, you almost guarantee that the media will document what you want them to see and hear. For example, every day, candidates—and their aides—decide to concentrate on one issue, and so all campaign appearances on that day are designed around the "topic of the day." The campaign might even distribute a press release to local or national media that not only emphasizes the topic but also draws attention to the candidate's previous record or quotes dealing with the issue.

Media Literacy Core Concept:

All media messages are constructed using a creative language with its own set of rules.

Media Literacy Key Questions:

What techniques are used by the creator to attract attention?

What lifestyles, values, points of view are represented in, or omitted from, this message?

Table 8.1

Using the STAGE Approach to Deconstruct Campaign Events

S	Symbols	What are the symbols; what effect might they have?
T	Techniques	What effects do lighting, camerawork, and music have on the event?
A	Actions	What activity or action is occurring?
G	Groups	What group or target audience is the event designed to appeal to?
E	Engaged	How might the televised event be designed to engage the audience?

Seeing through the staged media events is an important part of media literacy. Once you begin to understand these events, you can better comprehend the way campaigns shape the message and how the media report these events as "news."

One way to understand campaign events on television is to apply the View Smart to Vote Smart "STAGE" approach[1] to better "read" political constructions (as presented in Table 8.1).

DECONSTRUCTING A NEWS PHOTOGRAPHER'S IMAGE

Take a look at the widely distributed news photograph of Democratic candidate Hillary Clinton. The photographer, Charlie Neibergall, is situated rather low, making the foreground (Senator Clinton) the center of attention and consequently more important. This position has allowed him to include not only the large audience at ground level, but also those standing along the railings on the second-level tier. He has deliberately captured the stage onto which Senator Clinton is standing; notice that her name is positioned facing the camera in the center. Her Web site address is also clear. The scene is full of color: red, white, and blue, not only on the stage, but also scattered around the room in the way American flags are also positioned, to the left and right of the larger American flag in the background. Senator Clinton appears to be looking up, but we don't know where. She is clapping, and several of the members of the audience appear to be doing so, too.

STAGING A CANDIDATE'S ENTRANCE INTO THE NATIONAL POLITICAL CONVENTION

> A convention is an infomercial, but they're not selling stain remover or hair treatments. They're selling a presidential candidate.
>
> —Bill Schneider, political analyst

Democratic candidate Hillary Clinton, campaigning at a "town hall meeting" in Mason City, Iowa, in May 2007, appears in a carefully composed yet seemingly spontaneous photograph. (AP Photo/ Charlie Neibergall)

During the 1988 Democratic National Convention, carried live by C-SPAN and other networks, Democratic presidential candidate Michael Dukakis is seen entering Atlanta's Omni Arena to the music of Neil Diamond's song "Coming to America," an obvious reference to the candidate's Greek heritage. As he enters the arena, a spotlight follows him. He's seen smiling, making his way through the crowd, shaking hands. Knowing that millions of people are watching on television, one of his handlers is seen (on camera) telling the candidate to "wave them off," a reference to the live television cameras, which are clearly focused on his rousing arrival. Dukakis suddenly pays attention and looks up to where the cameras are situated and waves in that direction. He proceeds to climb a long set of stairs to get up to the convention platform, where he shakes hands with dignitaries there. Table 8.2 applies the STAGE approach to these convention moments.

Live coverage by C-SPAN of the 1995 Republican Iowa Straw Poll in Ames, Iowa showed the candidates entering one at a time to music that resembled something you'd hear when NBA basketball players are introduced. One by one, each Republican candidate was called on stage by an enthusiastic announcer as flashbulbs flashed and music played loudly. The American flag was big and visible to those inside and those watching on television.

ANALYZING CAMPAIGN EVENTS ON TV NEWS

When television news covers campaign events, it has to be selective. Obviously, during a 30-minute newscast, the news organization cannot afford to broadcast a

Table 8.2
Applying the Word STAGE to the 1988 Democratic National Convention Clip

S	Symbols	What are the symbols; what effect might they have?	Climbing stairs is like climbing up a mountain
T	Techniques	What effects do lighting, camerawork, and music have on the event?	Music of Neil Diamond; the American dream of immigrants (in this case, the son of immigrants) making it in America
A	Actions	What activity or action is occurring?	The nominee is being cheered and celebrated
G	Groups	What group or target audience is the event designed to appeal to?	People watching TV at home and the delegates
E	Engaged	How might the televised event be designed to engage the audience?	The event is broadcast at a time when most people are likely to be watching

long story. Most TV news stories are less than two minutes in length. So a reporter has to decide what is important, following a "script" and editing the video images to give the viewers the essence of the event and what the candidate had to say.

Even while watching television news, we can and should utilize "critical viewing" and media literacy questions to better understand what is happening. Here,

At the Democratic National Convention in Atlanta in July 1988, former Massachusetts governor Michael Dukakis ascends a short flight of steps to the podium to accept his party's nomination for president. (AP Photo/Charlie Kelly)

In August 1995 a crowded field of candidates is introduced to the audience at the Iowa Republican Party Straw Poll in Ames, Iowa. (AP Photo/John Gaps, Jr.)

again, a series of critical viewing questions[2] can be used as a guide to these highly constructed campaign events and edited news stories.

- What words or phrases are being used to get your attention?

- What soundbites and quotes are used?

- How long are the soundbites, and why are they so short?

- What soundbite or slogan might be used in tomorrow's news reports?

- What kinds of images and graphics are shown?

- What might be omitted, and why?

- How can you tell if what is said or shown is accurate?

- How are opinions presented by the candidates; the reporters?

THE DISAPPEARING 30-SECOND SOUNDBITE

When politicians can get away with talking like bumper stickers, we get used to listening for slogans—and not much else. Sadly, our attention span tends to parallel our thinking span.

—Norman Solomon, media critic

As we noted earlier, television has been the number one choice of politicians who want to deliver their messages to millions of voters simultaneously.

Politicians use television in many different ways. Of course they can purchase ad time, which is costly. Or they can usually depend on a certain amount of "free air time." Over the years, politicians have become dependent on broadcasters showing up whenever they have something to say.

Historian Daniel Boorstin, writing in his classic text, *The Image* (1961), labeled these " 'pseudo-events'—events that are not genuine . . . they are, rather, spectacles created for the sole purpose of creating an image."

Boorstin describes the four basic characteristics of pseudo-events:

1. They are not spontaneous. [The event] results from careful planning or having been planted.

2. They are primarily intended for immediate reporting or reproduction: arranged for the convenience of the reporters . . . . Success is measured by how many take the hook and run with it.

3. Their relationship to the underlying reality of the situation is ambiguous.

4. Usually they are intended to be a self-fulfilling prophecy.[3]

After the "live" event has concluded, many reporters' jobs involve "retelling" the story for later newscasts, intended for audiences who did not see or hear the original event. Reporters frequently create short (usually less than two minutes) news "packages" with stand-ups and interviews or excerpts from the candidates' prepared remarks. These packages air on the nightly news and are oftentimes streamed on broadcast stations' Web pages. This happens every day and night in local TV news in America. The reporter decides what to include and what to exclude. The reporter and usually a news producer are the gatekeepers: deciding what details the news consumer will get to see and hear.

So politicians will call press conferences knowing that the reporters and photographers will show up. The "event," sometimes manufactured, will get a mention in the newspaper, on radio, and certainly on the evening news. Bloggers will also reference it or post a link to some other media coverage. In fact, politicians now know that if they schedule their "event" for noon or 6:00 PM, it might even warrant a local TV or cable news broadcast going "live," showing the audience the event as it happens.

THE INCREDIBLE SHRINKING SOUNDBITE

But a funny thing happened on the way to the editing room: politicians' soundbites (unedited segments of recorded interviews or speeches) have become shorter. So short, in fact, that it's amazing anybody can understand what they're trying to convey.

In the early 1990s, two researchers reported on this trend. With the assistance of the Vanderbilt University TV News archive, cultural historian Kiku Adatto secured copies of all three of the major networks' nightly newscasts from 1968–1988 (ABC, CBS, and NBC). She watched newscasts from Labor Day (early September) until election day (early November). Using a stopwatch, she methodically timed each politician's unedited "talking head."

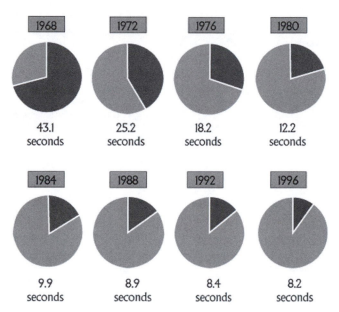

Figure 8.1
The Incredible Shrinking Soundbite, 1968 to 1996. *Source: Government in America: People, Politics, and Policy,* 8th Edition, by George C. Edwards, Martin P. Wattenberg, and Robert L. Lineberry. Copyright © 1999–2000 by Addison Wesley Longman, a division of Pearson Education. Reprinted by permission of Pearson Education, Inc.

Adatto was shocked by what she discovered: the average length of the soundbite had fallen from 42.3 seconds in 1968 to only 9.8 seconds in 1988. Subsequent studies showed that in later years, soundbites grew even shorter: 8.2 seconds in 1996.[4]

To demonstrate how brief 8 seconds is, re-read aloud the first sentence in this section.

Communications professor Daniel Hallin conducted a similar study. He offered the following reasons why soundbites in news coverage have been reduced: "This change is interpreted as part of a general shift in the style of television news toward a more mediated, journalist-centered form of journalism." Three factors help explain this change:

1. the evolution of television 'know-how'

2. the weakening of political consensus and authority during the last 20 years

3. changes in the economics of the industry

A more recent study in 2004 indicated the soundbite length had actually increased, but not much.[5]

Results from three studies are shown in Table 8.3.

So what is a news consumer to do, if television newscasts continue to deliver shorter soundbites from politicians? Is the audience being hurt by an 8-second soundbite? Where might news viewers go to get more information?

One alternative to the ever-present edited nature of local or cable news is C-SPAN, the cable-created network, which captures events unedited and airs them

Table 8.3

Average Length (Seconds) of "Soundbites" as Measured during TV News Coverage of Presidential Elections, 1968–2004[6]

Year	Candidates	Length (Hallin Study)	Length (Adatto Study)	Length (USC/Univ of Wisconsin Study)
1968	Richard Nixon/Hubert Humphrey	43.1	42.3	
1972	Richard Nixon/George McGovern	25.2		
1976	Gerald Ford/Jimmy Carter	18.2		
1980	Ronald Reagan/Jimmy Carter	12.2		
1984	Ronald Reagan/Walter Mondale	9.9		
1988	George H. W. Bush/Michael Dukakis	8.9	9.8	
1992	George H. W. Bush/Bill Clinton	8.4		
1996	Bob Dole/Bill Clinton	8.2		
2000	Al Gore/George W. Bush	7.8		
2004	George W. Bush/John Kerry			10.3

without commentary. The C-SPAN cameras frequently cover Congressional hearings, press conferences, and other noteworthy events, including presidential candidate appearances. During the campaign season, C-SPAN airs continuous coverage of the candidates on *American Politics: Road to the White House.*

Today C-SPAN provides many cable (and satellite) systems with three separate networks. Its Web site, http://www.cspan.org, also contains a wealth of information and resources for news consumers and citizens. And C-SPAN Radio is now streamed on the Web and is available to satellite network XM Radio subscribers. (In fall 2007 XM premiered Politics of the United States '08—a new channel devoted to the presidential campaign.)

Another alternative is the nightly PBS *NewsHour with Jim Lehrer,* an hour-long newscast and news interview program that is carried by most PBS stations. Typically, three to four stories are covered, thus giving interviewees much more time (and unedited time) to respond to questions.

Other alternatives to the soundbite society include the long-running ABC News *Nightline* program (aired after the late local news in most markets) and the traditional Sunday morning-afternoon talk shows:

- ABC News' *This Week with George Stephanopoulos*
- CBS News' *Face the Nation with Bob Scheiffer*

- Cable News Network's *Late Edition with Wolf Blitzer*
- FOX News' *Live with Chris Wallace*
- NBC News' *Meet the Press*

FREE AIR TIME

We simply have to take American democracy off the auction block, and this is a way of getting it done.

—Walter Cronkite

For years, many have advocated for free broadcast air time so that candidates could have more air time to explain their views than permitted by the current 30- or 60-second ads. The argument has been made that if broadcasters gave candidates free time, they wouldn't have to raise enormous sums of money to purchase broadcasting ad time.

In 1996 free air time was made available to the major candidates for the first time, thanks to a ruling by the Federal Communications Commission. The free air time amounted to just one or two-and-a-half minutes. Both presidential candidates at the time, Bill Clinton and Bob Dole, took advantage of the FCC ruling. Each of the two campaigns produced a short speech with the candidate talking directly into the camera.[7]

Efforts to expand free air time beyond the current short speeches have been opposed by both Congress and the nation's broadcasters. The head of the Radio-TV News Directors Association, Barbara Cochran, appeared to defend the practice of less politics inside newscasts: "It's not because news directors are evil or lazy or don't understand what their audience wants. It's because they do understand what their audience wants, and I'm sorry to tell you that news about politics is rather far down on the list of things that the public is interested in."[8]

Read a typical news script from a CNN[9] broadcast about John Edwards' July 2007 appearance in New Orleans:

From *360 with Anderson Cooper*

(BEGIN VIDEOTAPE)

COOPER (voice-over): John Edwards is walking through the Lower Ninth Ward. Not many voters here, but for him the pictures speak loudly. New Orleans is what he says his campaign is all about, a glaring symbol of presidential failure and governmental neglect.

JOHN EDWARDS (D), PRESIDENTIAL CANDIDATE: It's infuriating.

COOPER: Infuriating?

J. EDWARDS: Just the idea that—that people are still living like this and nothing's being done, when billions of dollars have been appropriated. Where is the money? Stuck in some bureaucrat's desk somewhere? I mean, where is it?

ELIZABETH EDWARDS, WIFE OF JOHN EDWARDS: So, I had this idea when we were in there. And that is, you put a FEMA trailer on the grounds of the White House, and we told the president he can live there until Winnie (ph), who isn't here, gets to move back into her house.

COOPER: We joined John and Elizabeth Edwards for the opening leg of their three-day, eight-state tour, spotlighting his signature issue, poverty in America.

UNIDENTIFIED FEMALE: One, two, and three.

COOPER: It's a political photo-op and at the same time, a political risk. In these times of war and uncertainty, it's unclear the plight of the poor will resonate with voters.

Emphasizing poverty, however, sets Edwards apart from his higher-profile, better-funded opponents.

(on camera): Do you think the other Democratic candidates are doing enough to focus attention on New Orleans, on the Gulf Coast?

J. EDWARDS: I think that—that the truth of the matter is, America is not paying enough attention.

COOPER (voice-over): Edwards insists this is not a campaign swing.

J. EDWARDS: Hey, how are you?

COOPER: There are no rallies, no cheering crowds. A small gaggle of reporters follows him from stop to stop as he struggles for traction.

(on camera): How much time are you on the phone trying to actually raise money?

J. EDWARDS: Except for the fact that you're in the car now, I would be on the phone right now.

COOPER: That's— that's incredible.

COOPER (voice-over): Edwards is used to the fund-raising and the constant campaigning. He's been doing it in some form for nearly six years.

(on camera): Your campaign, raised $9 million this quarter, down from the first quarter. You're running third in the polls. Why aren't you doing better?

J. EDWARDS: Well, I would—I would gently argue with you about some of that. And, at least for now, I appear to be ahead in Iowa, very competitive in the early states. But that's all politics.

I think, at the end of the day, what will matter to voters in those early states, who are paying very close attention, is, are you seasoned and experienced enough to be a good candidate for president? And, secondly, for the Democrats, they want to win. So, they want to have a candidate that they know can win the general election.

COOPER (voice-over): With him much of the time, his wife, Elizabeth, a celebrity in her own right, fighting a personal and public battle with cancer. She's a top adviser and her husband's chief defender.

(on camera): How angry do you get when you read about his $400 haircut or criticism of the house you guys are building?

E. EDWARDS: Well, you know, you don't want to sound defensive about it, because the—John thinks that he—if he had known that he was getting a $400 haircut, he—he probably wouldn't have done that. So, you know, you don't want to sound—you don't want to blame somebody else for a mistake that you made.

And, if somebody cares about the haircut and focuses on that, then they're not focusing on the real issues, where he can change, change this country. And, so, that angers me. It angers me that it's used as a political poking stick by our opposition.

COOPER (voice-over): On the road again, another van, another plane, off to Mississippi now, then Arkansas and Tennessee. All along the way, they're talking with small groups of working poor, far away from the states that matter, at least in the campaign game.

J. EDWARDS: I hope that America sees that what they saw in New Orleans is not just in New Orleans. It's in rural areas in the South. It's in big cities in the North. And it is still a pervasive—poverty is still a pervasive issue in America.

COOPER: A candidate hoping to be lifted by a cause.

Former senator and vice presidential candidate John Edwards pursued the 2008 Democratic presidential nomination by reinforcing his identification with poverty issues, making highly publicized walking tours with his wife, Elizabeth Edwards, and residents of New Orleans still struggling to recover from the effects of Hurricane Katrina. (AP Photo/Bill Haber)

IMPROVING TV COVERAGE OF CAMPAIGN EVENTS

There appears to be no shortage of people or organizations who have complaints concerning the manner in which television news covers political campaigns. Most of the complaints have to do with the common practice of reporting about the "horse race" (who's in first, who's ahead in the polls; who's raised the most money) instead of giving more time and weight to substantive coverage. Many TV stations (and some viewers) feel that political coverage is a turn-off, and worse—it turns off viewers, and thus hurts advertising.

One group that hopes to convince broadcast journalists to alter their ways is the Norman Lear Center, based at the Annenberg School of Communication at the University of Southern California. The center recognizes local TV stations and reporters who have gone beyond the usual to make political coverage interesting, enlightening, and informative. In its recommendations for local TV stations,[10] the center describes in detail how to improve television political coverage:

- Reporters should try to minimize the horse race type coverage and focus more on campaign issues
- Focus news coverage on the substance of a candidate's policy or plan, not on the staged media event
- Plan before the event by determining what policy or plan might be unveiled and look for ways to add depth to the coverage before the candidate can spin it
- Don't allow the candidate to set the coverage agenda

As you watched the political coverage from the most recently concluded presidential campaign, did you notice any changes? Is the old media still following what the candidates give them, or has the new media age, and the rise of citizen journalism, meant a change in how candidates are covered and how you view them?

NOTES

1. View Smart to Vote Smart cable TV curriculum: http://www.ciconline.org/cable-resources.

2. From the video *View Smart to Vote Smart:* http://www.ciconline.org/viewsmart.

3. Richard W. Waterman, Robert Wright, and Gilbert St. Clair, *The Image-Is-Everything Presidency: Dilemmas in American Leadership* (Boulder, CO: Westview Press, 1999), 15.

4. Kiki Adatto, "The Incredible Shrinking Soundbite," *The New Republic,* May 28, 1990, http://www.arts.mcgill.ca/programs/history/faculty/TROYWEB/Courseweb/TheIncredibleShrinkingSoundBite.pdf.

5. Micah L. Sifry and Andrew Rasiej, "Welcome to the Age of the Sound Blast," March 26, 2008, www.politico.com/news/stories/0308/9222.html.

6. Daniel C. Hallin, "Sound Bite News: Television Coverage of Elections, 1968–1988," *Journal of Communications* 42, no. 2 (Spring 1992): 5, http://occawlonline.pearsoned.com/bookbind/pubbooks/edwards8e/chapter98/medialib/edvisch07.html); David A. Schultz, ed., *Lights, Camera, Campaign!: Media, Politics, and Political Advertising* (New York: P. Lang, 2004), 226.

7. Kathleen Hall Jamieson and Karlyn Kohrs Campbell, *News, Advertising, Politics, and the Mass Media: The Interplay of Influence,* 5th ed. (Belmont, CA: Wadsworth, 2000), 298.

8. Barbara Cochran, *NewsHour with Jim Lehrer* segment, June 30, 2000, http://www.pbs.org/newshour/bb/media/jan-june00/free_air_3-30.html

9. Transcript: http://transcripts.cnn.com/TRANSCRIPTS/0707/16/acd.01.html.

10. Norman Lear Center, Annenberg School of Communication at the University of Southern California: http://reliableresources.org/RRTipsheet.pdf.

9

The Role of New Media and New Technology Tools

You and I are entering the information age—and the Washington politicians are stuck in the Stone Age.

—Steve Forbes, presidential candidate (1999)

The Internet is a powerful new tool in the arsenal of democracy, but it is so vast and the information comes from so many unknown places it requires extra vigilance on the part of citizens in determining what's credible and what's not.

—Tom Brokaw, NBC News (2007)

Ads produced by ordinary folks (are) the future of the Internet. The handheld camera and producing it at no cost mean that people not tied to political structures can create content. The moment they get exposure . . . they have formed a political communication venue that can be very effective.

—Kathleen Hall Jamieson, media scholar

Candidates are beginning to see that they don't control their message anymore.

—Carol Darr, Director, Institute for Politics,
Democracy and the Internet, George Washington University

This is a new way of communicating, and honestly, it is the most democratic of communication.

—Elizabeth Edwards, wife of presidential candidate John Edwards (2007)

You could tell something was different about the 2007–2008 election cycle: presidential candidates used new media more, and in more innovative ways, to connect

> **Media Literacy Core Concepts:**
> *Media messages are constructed using a creative language with its own set of rules.*
> *Media have embedded values and points of view.*
>
> **Media Literacy Key Questions:**
> *Who created this message?*
> *Why was this message sent?*

with potential voters. Consumers also got into the act, using new technologies themselves to showcase the power of media production and distribution.

Consider the following:

- Mitt Romney invited supporters to create and submit their own television commercials.
- Fred Thompson announced his candidacy in a video released on the Internet.
- Hillary Clinton solicited advice on which theme song her campaign should use; then her campaign created a parody of the popular TV drama *The Sopranos* for a YouTube video promoting the song.
- Barack Obama sent text messages regularly to subscribing cell phone users.
- CNN and YouTube broadcast consumer-created video questions in their two nationally televised presidential debates.
- A Barack Obama fan's music video tribute had the nation buzzing.
- John Edwards used his blog to post his personal thoughts.

It doesn't take a rocket scientist to figure out that if you're trying to reach young people with your message, you need to pay attention to their culture, including the media and technology they use. Young people rely on their cell phones, for example, for many purposes. They not only talk on them, they text, watch videos, and share photos. It's no accident, then, that advisors to many of the current presidential candidates are young and media savvy. They also know that their peers read and respond to new media. So new media played a major role in the 2008 race for the White House.

What's hot right now? Web.2.0—user-generated content such as blogs and videos (posted on YouTube and other video Web sites); photographs (posted on sites such as Flickr); virtual cyberworlds (such as Second Life); and social networking Web sites (such as MySpace, Facebook, and others). One study found that more than 70 percent of Americans aged 15–34 are active users of social networks.[1]

"The role of the Internet in politics has grown with such speed and scope that it is well on its way to becoming the dominant media force in political campaigning." So begins the Digital Future Project's latest report on the influence of the Web in the political process. The report implies that television won't continue to be the dominant political medium: politicians can and will reach more voters with online media than with traditional media.[2] But for now, TV does still dominate. An analysis of political ad purchases by the TNSMI/Campaign Media Analysis

Group found that those candidates highest in the polls were the ones still purchasing ads on television.[3]

Advertisers have already figured out that social networking Web sites attract millions. (News Corporation president Rupert Murdoch purchased MySpace in 2005 for $580 million, because he wanted to convert the social networking site into a huge marketing machine, driving eyeballs, and dollars, to many of his own brands.[4]) So candidates in the 2008 presidential race, anxious to raise money, made their presence known on MySpace and Facebook. These candidates knew that money could be made by appealing to potential young voters, many of whom would be willing to donate on a secure Web site. And donate they did: during the first quarter of 2007 (January–March), Democratic presidential candidate Barack Obama raised $25 million in campaign contributions, of which an estimated $7 million came from online donors.[5] Hillary Clinton, meanwhile, had raised $8 million from online donations, based on her third-quarter report to the Federal Election Commission.[6] Republican candidate Ron Paul surprised analysts when he raised more than $5 million online during the third quarter.[7] (For a full report on campaign fundraising, go to http://www.fec.gov/ or http://www.opensecrets.org.)

By 2007, candidates' Web sites had become dynamic, with links to current ads, news stories, blogs, Flickr photo collections, and more.

One-time presidential candidate Howard Dean (later chairman of the Democratic National Committee), who is generally credited with being among the first to harness the Internet for politics, connecting with people and raising millions of dollars, now observes: "The Internet is not just a tool, it is a community of human beings who are tired of what I call the 'one-way campaign,' which began essentially during the Kennedy-Nixon debates, where everything is on television. Well, it's not about communicating our message to you anymore; it's about listening to you first before we formulate the message."[8]

THE NEW MEDIA ELECTION

Three incidents during the race for the presidency in 2007–2008 defined what has become known as the new media election and revealed the role "ordinary people" using media technology are now playing in American politics:

1. At an August 2006 campaign appearance, U.S. Senator George Allen (R-Va.) saw a young volunteer for his opponent's campaign videotaping the event (which has become a common *campaign* practice). Allen pointed out the volunteer (who was of Indian descent) to his audience, using the word *macaca* (a racial slur in some cultures) to *ridicule* him. The volunteer caught it all on video and uploaded it to the Web, where the incident received prominent attention in the mainstream media. Allen later apologized. This "YouTube moment" made national news and foretold the importance of citizen journalism: anybody with a video camera can capture news events, become a "news reporter," and distribute "news" worldwide via the Web. Allen eventually lost in his reelection bid.

2. "Obama Girl," ostensibly a fan of Democratic candidate Barack Obama expressed her love for the candidate in a music video posted on the popular video site YouTube.com. *I Got a Crush on Obama* quickly became a nationwide sensation

when millions watched her video tribute online. Shortly afterwards, imitators got on the bandwagon, creating videos for other candidates. "Obama Girl" Amber Lee Ettinger, a model, did not work alone: her video was the brainchild of some marketing geniuses, and Ettinger lip-synched the vocals.[9]

Commenting on this trend, GOP political consultant Mark McKinnon observed: "The impact that [user-produced video] has on us [political media consultants/producers] is that we've lost control. It used to be that we could control our message and control the political messages out there. Now it's just the Wild West out there."[10] Never was this more apparent than when a rash of malicious e-mails made several false claims about Barack Obama in the winter of 2008. The Obama campaign spent a lot of time just defending their candidate, setting the record straight and putting out fires ignited by the false claims.

To announce the winner of the competition to determine the best popular song to be used in her campaign, the Hillary Clinton campaign created a video parody of the final episode of the popular Home Box Office series *The Sopranos.* The campaign selected Celine Dion's "You and I." The timing of the contest and the announcement coincided with the final episode of *The Sopranos,* which had a large cable TV audience.

3. In July 2007 CNN, YouTube, and Google collaborated to sponsor the Democratic candidates' nationally televised debate. But instead of having journalists query the candidates, the sponsors had viewers submit their own questions on video. The videos were uploaded by viewers to the YouTube site. Even though the candidates could

Innovative formats for major-party primary debates were introduced in the 2008 campaign cycle. At the July 2007 Democratic primary debate sponsored by CNN, YouTube, and Google, held at The Citadel military academy in Charleston, S.C., candidates fielded videotaped questions submitted by viewers via the Internet. Here, Rev. Reggie Longcrier of Hickory, N.C., poses his question. (AP Photo/Charles Dharapak)

watch the submitted questions beforehand, they did not know which ones would be used during the debate. An estimated 3,000 video questions were submitted; only a fraction were actually chosen by CNN. Question topics ranged from gay marriage to global warming to the war in Iraq. Afterwards CNN said that the debate had drawn the biggest audience of viewers between the ages of 18 and 34—the demographic most coveted by advertisers—for a cable news debate since measurements began in 1992.[11] Many critics agreed that the event added a different dimension to the traditional debate format. Questions submitted were often personal in nature, with some having been recorded in family settings. A similar debate was held in November 2007 for the GOP contenders.

OTHER DEVELOPMENTS

YouTube added an interactive feature on its You Choose '08 site: allowing presidential candidates to post video questions that encouraged user-generated responses. The first candidate to post a question was Republican Mitt Romney, who posed the question, "What do you believe is America's single greatest challenge, and what would you do to address it?"[12] The site was unique in its ability to allow users to choose a candidate and an issue and view a video featuring that candidate explaining his or her position.[13]

Watch YouTube's You Choose '08 web page and political "vlog" Citizentube: http://www.youtube.com/watch?v=oBYdDZX5aoU.

MySpace Joins the Political Conversation

The CEO of MySpace, Chris DeWolfe, announced proudly in March 2007, "MySpace will play a powerful role in the upcoming election." With that, MySpace unveiled the Impact Channel, a Web site featuring candidate profiles, a voter registration tool, and public service job announcements. DeWolfe told *Newsweek* magazine online that digital candidate banners will be the yard signs of the 21st century and that political "viral videos" and vlogs are the campaign ads of the future.[14] On MySpace Impact pages, candidates such as Democratic contender Senator Joseph Biden filled their sites with links to music, photos and videos, cut-and-paste banners, and links to other sites such as Facebook and YouTube.

User-Generated Content

Do you own a digital still or video camera? Then you're a reporter. So announced the international news organization Reuters and the Internet giant Yahoo. Shortly after purchasing the photo-sharing site Flickr, Yahoo, along with its Reuters partner, launched a user-generated news video/photo-sharing Web site, dubbed You Witness. Yahoo encouraged contributions by what it labeled "citizen photojournalists." Using digital cameras, users uploaded their pictures and/or videos to the site, adding captions and photo credits.

Comedy Central's Political Page with Streaming Video Clips

Not to be outdone by YouTube and other video streaming sites, Comedy Central, home to both Jon Stewart and Stephen Colbert, established Indecision2008.

com, a Web page from which viewers can download clips from previous pro-grams, read their blogs, and more. The Web page says it is "dedicated to making fun of the American Democratic process, in all of its ceremony and pomposity."

WHAT HAPPENS WHEN NEW MEDIA ARE DETRIMENTAL TO CANDIDATES?

The media labeled it a "YouTube moment" when a video camera caught Vir-ginia Senator George Allen's "macaca" faux pas. "YouTube moment" refers to a politician's statement or action, caught on video and then uploaded to YouTube for everyone to see. With any luck, as one blogger wrote, the mainstream media will pick up the embarrassing video and run it on the evening news, where it will be seen by millions of viewers. "Every appearance by a top Republican official or candidate should be recorded. Every one of them. All it takes is one 'macaca' incident to transform a race or create one where one didn't exist. ... And this is no longer about finding one big blunder to put on a campaign commercial. It's about using video and (free) technologies like YouTube to build narratives about opponents, using their own words, at their own events."[15] Today, more than ever, young people are seeking political news and information about candidates and their positions online.

GETTING CAMPAIGN NEWS ONLINE

Have you gone online to read news? If so, you're not alone. This new media age in which we live has resulted in a dramatic shift in the numbers of people who live (and work) in cyberspace. With access to information via computers, cell phones, personal digital assistants (PDAs), and other devices, more of us have access to news. Advertisers have been watching this trend too, because they want to go where the eyeballs are. And the audiences have drifted away from traditional print to online sources. Newspapers, magazines, and even the big three networks' nightly news broadcasts have all seen changes in their audience sizes. One of the reasons for such changes involves technology: more people have access to news and information at their fingertips.

- In the 1996 presidential campaign, Internet users said they were looking for things not available from traditional media sources and liked the convenience of getting political material online.[16]

- In 1998, an off-year election, three in ten people who went to a political Web site were seeking information about a candidate's record, making that the top motivation for election news seekers.[17]

- A study of the online news habits during the Campaign 2000 found that nearly one in five Americans (18 percent) said they went online for election news during the cam-paign, up from 4 percent who did so in the 1996 campaign. Nearly seven in ten of those who went online for election news sought out information on the candidates' positions.[18]

- In 2002 the annual Pew study found that the Internet was a principal source of cam-paign news for only about one in ten online users. The same survey found that while the Internet has not made significant gains in recent years as a primary outlet of election news, it does serve as an important source for young people who go online.[19]

- The Internet became an essential part of American politics in 2004. Fully 75 million Americans—37 percent of the adult population and 61 percent of online Americans —used the Internet to get political news and information, discuss candidates and debate issues in e-mails, or participate directly in the political process by volunteering or giving contributions to candidates.[20]

"A post-election, nationwide survey by the Pew Internet & American Life Project and the Pew Research Center for The People & The Press shows that the online political news consumer population grew dramatically from 18% of the U.S. population in 2000 to 29% in 2004. There was also a striking increase in the number who cited the internet as one of their primary sources of news about the presidential campaign: 11% of registered voters said the Internet was a primary source of political news in 2000, and 18% said that in 2004."[21]

A study conducted by the Pew Internet & American Life Project (2007) found that some 15 percent of all American adults said the Internet was the place where they got most of their campaign news during the 2006 campaign elections. That figure was double from just four years earlier.[22] But when young people were asked about the source of their campaign news in 2004, television remained the top choice.

WHAT HAPPENED BEFORE THE INTERNET?

In the days prior to blogs, cell phones, Blackberries, and the Internet, candidates sought out exposure in "traditional media": magazines and TV programs, both popular venues attractive to the youngest voters.

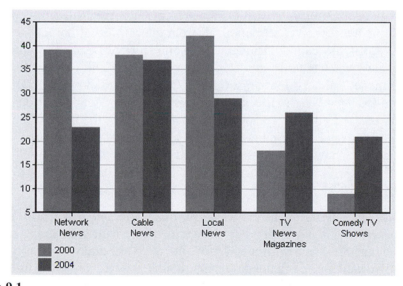

Figure 9.1
Young People and Campaign News Sources. *Source:* "Cable and Internet Loom Large in Fragmented Political News Universe, Survey, January 11, 2004," Pew Research Center for People and the Press.

Richard Nixon surprised a lot of political pundits in 1968 when he made a cameo appearance on the prime-time NBC comedy *Rowan & Martin's Laugh-In.* One of the most popular phrases of the late 1960s, "Sock It to Me," originated on *Laugh-In,* and the producers even persuaded Nixon to say it. Critics at the time say it showed Nixon had a softer side, and his appearance, brief as it was, received a lot of positive press.

One popular magazine long read by young people, *Rolling Stone,* has profiled many presidential candidates, in good times and bad. Not all appearances in the magazine have been positive: the May 2006 issue, for example, blasted the presidency of George Bush ("The Worst President in History?") showing him seated in the corner of a room, brandishing a dunce cap, as if he had been punished.

EARLY INTERNET USE

When the Internet was new, in the mid-1990s, the presidential candidates started creating their own Web pages and tracking who was reading them. Because there was no streaming video then, most candidate pages were static, and their design left a lot to be desired.

Candidate Steve Forbes heralded the Internet age in 1999, announcing his candidacy on the Web. One observer noted: "Mr. Forbes's campaign launch was a great publicity stunt. Journalists are fascinated by the Internet, so an innovative Web campaign can be a valuable source of free press. It is also a cheap way of peddling a campaign's spin on the news, and keeps the huge media pack informed of a candidate's movements."[23]

Early pages included links to candidates' position statements and press releases. Republican candidate Bob Dole's Web site was one of the first to allow readers to customize the page.[24] Later, as the Web evolved, politicians realized that citizens could not only communicate with their representatives via e-mail but could also send a secure transaction contribution, all from the comfort of home.

In 2003–2004, the team of Democratic hopeful Howard Dean created one of the first blog sites, which not only attracted millions of loyal followers but also helped him raise money online.[25] Journalist Carl M. Cannon notes, however, "The claims of Howard Dean partisans to the contrary, Bush was also the first presidential candidate to make a digital-savvy appeal to voters. In 2000, the Bush-Cheney campaign website urged Americans to type in their annual income and estimated deductions to see how much Bush's proposed tax cut would save them."[26]

MORPHING: ALTERING THE IMAGES AND THE MESSAGE

The video altering technique known as morphing (from *metamorphosis*) became popular in 2004. Ingenious video producers, using popular software, figured out how to change an image within a video. One Web site links to more than 300 spoofs of Howard Dean's famous scream; another shows John Kerry morphed to look like comic Stan Laurel or Herman Munster (from the popular 1970s era TV show *The Munsters*). Cultural critic Henry Jenkins argues that perhaps turning politics into popular culture allows fans to become more civically engaged.[27]

New York Magazine asked several advertising agencies to design their own Bush and Kerry ads. One agency, Mother, decided a video game would appeal to voters, so it morphed the candidates to look like monkeys.

PARODY PROVES POPULAR

During the 1999 election campaign, ®™ark helped launch a Web page cloned from George W. Bush's official campaign Web site. Slight changes had been made to the content of the homepage suggesting that national politics were serving mainly corporate interests, and the rest of the site contained material from ®™ark's own Web site, http://www.rtmark.com.[28]

MAD Magazine, the long-time king of parody, jumped on the digital alteration bandwagon, creating a poster resembling the George Lucas movie *Star Wars: Episode II: Attack of the Clones* (2002). Except this movie poster parody poked fun at the George W. Bush administration's Iraq policy by changing the movie title to

MAD Magazine No. 424 © 2002 E. C. Publications, Inc. All Rights Reserved.

Gulf Wars: Clone of the Attack. And instead of the real *Star Wars* actors, the poster took some liberties, making high-ranking Bush administration officials the stars of this "movie": Obi-Wan Kenobi became President George W. Bush; Senator Amidala became Secretary of State Condoleezza Rice; and Yoda became an overweight Iraqi president Saddam Hussein. In small print, the poster said "and introducing Osama Bin Laden as the Phantom Menace."

In 2004 an animated cartoon created by two brothers hit the blogosphere and proved so popular that it became a major hit in the virtual world. The brothers called themselves "JibJab," and their political hit, a parody of Woody Guthrie's classic song "This Land Is Your Land" featured none other than Democratic presidential candidate Senator John Kerry and incumbent President George W. Bush. During the short video, both candidates claim victory and poke fun at the political process.[29]

NEW AND EMERGING TECHNIQUES

Yahoo, in a partnership with the Huffington Postblog and the online magazine *Slate,* created the first-ever online debate. Its Web page, http://debates.news .yahoo.com, featured all of the Democratic candidates and many of the top issues. Visitors were encouraged to choose one or more candidates and an issue, and then listen. The Democratic Candidate Mashup encouraged participants to vote for their favorite candidate. The participants' favorite was Barack Obama (35 percent), followed by Hillary Clinton (31 percent), John Edwards (12 percent), Dennis Kucinich (8 percent), Joe Biden and Bill Richardson (tied at 5 percent), Mike Gravel (3 percent), and Chris Dodd (1 percent).[30]

Satellite radio network XM unveiled a special radio channel devoted solely to the 2008 election: POTUS (Politics of the United States) '08. The site promotes itself as a "town-hall square" where people can get news and opinion, as well as listen to debates.[31] The XM network has more than 8.2 million listeners.

Senator Barack Obama's Web site featured social-networking-type features, allowing visitors to create their profiles and blogs, among other things.[32]

The campaign of Republican presidential candidate Rudy Giuliani began using a new tech innovation called a "widget" (a kind of computer code). Visitors to the Giuliani Web site were invited to copy and paste the code into their own blogs. Readers of the blog who clicked on the widget were then sent to Giuliani's Web site, where their e-mails could be collected for future correspondence. Meanwhile, Democratic candidate John Edwards used his Web site to appeal for volunteers who were experienced in blog creation and upkeep.[33]

Candidate Hillary Clinton used YouTube to solicit young people's opinions about which popular song should be used as her campaign theme song. In a mock-serious tone, she said: "I want to know what you're thinking on one of the most important questions of this campaign, it's something we've been struggling with, debating, agonizing over for months. So now I'm turning to you, the American people."[34] Hillary used e-mail to encourage supporters to submit questions for her September 2007 appearance on the syndicated *Ellen DeGeneres Show.*

The campaign of Republican hopeful Mitt Romney encouraged supporters to create their own "official TV ad." The campaign provided the audio, video, and photos and instructed the new ad creators to send their ads to the campaign. Supporters were invited to mash up "372 photos, 44 video clips, and 36 audio files" into a 30- or 60-second spot. "It is truly groundbreaking for amateur, grass-roots supporters to so directly assist in introducing their candidate to the American people," Alex Castellanos, Romney's media strategist and senior adviser, said in a prepared statement. "This contest demonstrates Romney for President's commitment to using unique and democratizing online tools to engage voters and harness the extraordinary enthusiasm of its growing team of supporters."[35]

Other candidates have also encouraged contributions from supporters: Senator Hillary Clinton of New York allowed supporters not only to select her campaign song but to create 30-second videos, which were shown during the July 2007 Democratic debate sponsored by CNN, YouTube, and Google. For the same debate, Senator Joseph R. Biden, Jr., of Delaware asked supporters to upload videos challenging his opponents on their plans for Iraq once U.S. troops leave. And Senator Barack Obama's campaign posted on its Web site a video of the Illinois senator eating dinner at a restaurant with low-dollar contributors.

MTV collaborated with MySpace in September 2007 to create the first-ever live series of online chats between young people and the presidential candidates. "This

Candidates seized on new media to try to gain ground against better-known (and better-funded) opponents. Former Arkansas governor Mike Huckabee was one of four candidates—two Democrats and two Republicans—who communicated via satellite with an MTV studio audience in New York City during a February 2008 forum sponsored by MTV, the Associated Press, and MySpace. (AP Photo/Frank Franklin II)

is not a debate," said MTV spokesman Ian Rowe. "Each one of these dialogues is an opportunity for young people both on a college campus—as well as millions watching via a live stream on MySpace and MTV.com—to have a one-on-one, direct, unfiltered conversation with each candidate." Questions were chosen by a moderator collaborating with political experts and an MTV news correspondent.[36]

WEB POLITICS IN THE 21ST CENTURY

What spelled success in the 2006 (off-year) elections? John Della Volpe, the director of Harvard University's Institute of Politics, cited three things:

1. Young people being integrated into the campaigns, with headquarters close to college campuses. Internships were widespread, and young people were involved in decision-making.

2. Campaigns ceded some control to the "new media." Blogs accepted critical comments, and that helped their credibility. Candidates spoke to hip-hop radio stations and student groups, all the while answering the tough questions.

3. Campaigns allowed Web users to customize and personalize candidate Web pages. User-created ads were also encouraged. The campaigns also effectively used online video and text messaging to communicate with voters and prospective voters. They created unique profiles on MySpace and Facebook. And they produced podcasts.[37]

THE ROLE OF THE BLOGS

> People say there's a lot of hostility between blogs and mainstream media, but it's really more of a symbiosis. Media often look to elite bloggers to decide if something is worth paying attention to, and vice versa.
>
> —Glenn Reynolds, InstaPundit.com (2007)

Do you read blogs? If so, you're not alone. At last count, there were more than 112 million blogs (and the number is rapidly growing) worldwide—Web logs created by ordinary people on every possible topic. Every major newspaper now has a blog, as do many news operations and television programs. Blogs are a way for people to report their own news and information, connect to one another, share information, reply to postings, provide opinions, and link to mainstream and other news sources. Blogs are very popular with those aged 18–24. A 2007 poll found 78 percent of that age group visited blogs, while 45 percent of older Americans had done so.[38]

One of the earliest and most successful blogs was created in 2003 by those working for Democratic presidential candidate Howard Dean. It was Dean's team that launched Call to Action, which later became Blog for America.[39] Dean's large campaign staffers were able to communicate with one another as well as supporters out in the field. The blog received lots of attention, not only from Dean followers, but also from those charting the future of Internet political communications. When thousands of people across the country used the site to get on board

A blogger posts from the "bloggers' lounge" at the August 2008 Democratic National Convention in Denver. The Democrats credentialed three times as many bloggers for the 2008 convention as for the 2004 event. (AP Photo/Ted S. Warren)

Dean's campaign *and* contribute money, big media, and candidates nationwide, began to take notice.

Lawyer Scott Gant sums up what some say is the blurring of lines between what is and what isn't journalism in the 21st century: "The lines distinguishing professional journalists from other people who disseminate information, ideas, and opinions to a wide audience have been blurred, perhaps beyond recognition, by forces both inside and outside the media themselves. Whatever the causes, it is harder than ever to tell who is a journalist."[40]

Those "other people" consider themselves "citizen journalists," conducting much of the legwork that traditional journalists have done. Millions of people are now producers of blogs and are providing alternative viewpoints and voices.

But those of us who consume blogs need to be just as vigilant as if we were reading a magazine or a newspaper. To recall the media literacy core concepts, each blogger has a purpose, a point of view, and uses persuasive language. Learning to critically question the blog and its content is an important 21st-century skill. Sometimes bloggers attract thousands of readers and sometimes *that* gives the blog more attention and importance than it might deserve.

Ariana Huffington, who manages the popular Huffington Post blog, says there are several reasons blogs attract large readers: "I think there really are three factors . . . First of all, the fact that technology means that more and more people get their news and opinion online. Then there is the anti-war movement; the opposition to the war fuels the blogosphere. And in 2004, when Howard Dean became the sort of darling of the blogosphere, that was very much a marginal position. Now in

2008, you had all the candidates here at Yearly Kos (convention of bloggers) in Chicago, in favor of bringing the troops home."[41]

A political science professor sums up the strength of the new media in the current political environment: "blogs and podcasts are providing the direct access to candidates that TV news, with all of its resources, refuses to do. While expensive camera crews chase fires and crime scenes and well-coiffeured former sportscasters read scripts drained of drama and controversy, bloggers and amateur videographers are on the campaign trail. Rarely do journalists follow up closely. Not even in debates are candidates closely questioned in this way on important policy matters."[42]

Political Blogs

Some of the most popular blogs on the Internet are political in nature. Here are some interesting statistics[43] about their audience:

- 9 percent of registered voters read political blogs every day.
- 75 percent of political blog readers are male.
- The median political blog reader is a 43-year-old man with a household income of $80,000.
- 37 percent of political blog readers say TV is worthless.
- 61 percent of political blog readers gave money to candidates in 2004.

SHOULD BLOGS BE REGULATED?

Should blogs and bloggers be regulated? In other words, should they be held to the same standards as journalists? Or are bloggers just blowing a lot of hot air, for anybody and everybody who will pay attention? One case demonstrates how U.S. federal regulators ruled: One conservative blogger challenged the status of a liberal blogger (Daily Kos), claiming it should comply with federal campaign finance laws because entries are free advertising and promote specific candidates. But the Federal Election Commission disagreed, ruling in September 2007 that blogs are exempt from such regulations.[44]

MEMOGATE AND THE POWER OF THE BLOGS

Some in journalism question whether today's bloggers represent qualified journalists, although most bloggers might argue that they use many of the same reporting processes as professional journalists. Professional journalists note that most bloggers have no formal training in journalism or other news gathering techniques. But that has not stopped some bloggers from engaging in conventional investigative journalism, taking on the mainstream media. In one case, among others, bloggers' journalism made national news itself.

On September 8, 2004, CBS News reporter Dan Rather, reporting for the *60 Minutes* TV news magazine, conducted an investigation into President George W. Bush's National Guard service that allegedly showed that he had evaded the draft, used influence to join the Texas Air National Guard, and later used that same influence to whitewash his service record. The news story was based on memos given to CBS by an anonymous source. The news report showed what it claimed were copies of the original 1970s-era typewritten documents. A blogger alleged the documents were forged, and the popular blog Drudge Report helped publicize the charges. Rather, who later apologized on air, admitted the documents were questionable but maintained that their content was accurate. Yet CBS's own investigation did not say whether the documents were accurate or not; however, it did criticize the network's news-gathering procedures. As a result, three CBS news employees were dismissed; another's contract was not renewed.[45]

More Questions to Consider

- How have social-networking, blogs, video-sharing and other user-generated Web sites changed the face of running for president?
- How have "citizen journalists" gotten involved in media and politics?
- How have politicians used their own Web pages to attract attention and money?

NOTES

1. Mike Shields, "New Media: Study: Social Networking Ads Take Time to Work: Report finds that becoming 'friend' to brand boosts sales," Brandweek, April 23, 2007, http://www.brandweek.com/bw/magazine/current/article_display.jsp?vnu_content_id=10 03574758.

2. "Internet Is Becoming Dominant Media Force in National Political Campaigns, Reports USC Digital Future Project," http://www.prnewswire.com/cgi-bin/stories.pl? ACCT=104&STORY=/www/story/07-31-2007/0004636112&EDATE=

3. Jim Kuhnhenn, "Presidential Hopefuls Get Some Bang from Their Ads," Associated Press, May 26, 2007.

4. Jeremy Scott-Joynt, "What MySpace Means to Murdoch," *BBC News,* July 19, 2005, http://news.bbc.co.uk/1/hi/business/4697671.stm.

5. Federal Election Commission.

6. Patrick Healy, "Clinton Steals Obama's Fund-Raising Thunder, *New York Times,* October 3, 2007, http://www.nytimes.com/2007/10/03/us/politics/03campaign.html.

7. http://online.wsj.com/article/SB119146668063148662.html?mod=googlenews_wsj.

8. "Crashing the System"; "Interview with Howard Dean: Chairman of the Democratic National Committee," *Mother Jones Magazine* (July/August 2007), 31, http://www.motherjones.com/interview/2007/07/howard_dean.html.

9. Barbara Lippert, "Barbara Lippert's Critique: The Raw and the Ugly," *Adweek,* August 27, 2007, http://www.adweek.com/aw/creative/article_display.jsp?vnu _content_id=1003627771.

10. Mark McKinnon, interviewed on CNN Special Investigation Unit documentary: *Broken Government—Campaign Killers,* January 14, 2008, http://www.cnn.com/2008/ LIVING/studentnews/01/03/cnnce.campaign.killers/index.html.

11. Katharine Q. Seelye, "CNN/YouTube Debate Ratings," *The Caucus,* http:// thecaucus.blogs.nytimes.com/2007/07/24/cnnyoutube-debate-ratings/.

12. Aman Ali, "YouTube Launches Interactive Forum for '08 Candidates," *The Hill,* April 11, 2007, http://thehill.com/campaign-2008/youtube-launches-interactive-forum-for-08-candidates-2007-04-11.html.

13. Kathleen Hall Jamieson, *Bill Moyers' Journal,* PBS, December 8, 2007.

14. Andrew Romano, "Right Place, Wrong Song," *Newsweek,* March 23, 2007, http:// www.newsweek.com/id/36024.

15. Wheaton, Ken, "Republicans Be Warned: The Hills Have Eyes; DailyKos and Readers Are Watching Closely," posted on *Advertising Age,* May 23, 2007, http:// adage.com/campaigntrail/index?sid=Busted.

16. "News Attracts Most Internet Users: One-in-Ten Voters Online for Campaign '96," Pew Research Center for the People and the Press, December 16, 1996, http:// people-press.org/reports/display.php3?ReportID=117.

17. "The Internet News Audience Goes Ordinary," Pew Research Center for the People and the Press, January 14, 1999, http://people-press.org/reports/display.php3? ReportID=72.

18. Andrew Kohut and Lee Rainie, "Internet Election News Audience Seeks Convenience, Familiar Names: Youth Vote Influenced by Online Information," Pew Internet and American Life Project, December 3, 2000, http://www.pewinternet.org/PPF/r/27/report _display.asp.

19. Andrew Kohut and Lee Rainie, "Modest Increase in Internet Use for Campaign 2002: Political Sites Gain, but Major News Sites Still Dominate," Pew Internet and American Life Project, January 5, 2003, http://www.pewinternet.org/PPF/r/82/report _display.asp.

20. "The Internet and Campaign 2004," www.pewinternet.org/ppf/r/150/report _display.asp.

21. Lee Rainie, John Horrigan, and Michael Cornfield, "The Internet and Campaign 2004," Pew Internet and American Life Project: http://www.pewinternet.org/PPF/r/150/ report_display.asp.

22. Lee Rainie and John Horrigan, "Election 2006 Online," Pew Internet and American Life Project, January 17, 2007, http://www.pewinternet.org/PPF/r/199/report _display.asp.

23. "The Battle for the White House," *The Economist (UK)* 352.8137 (September 18, 1999): S6.

24. Wayne Rash, Jr., *Politics on the Nets: Wiring the Political Process* (New York: W. H. Freeman, 1997), 36.

25. Joe Trippi, *The Revolution Will Not Be Televised: Democracy, the Internet, and the Overthrow of Everything* (New York: ReganBooks, 2004), 89.

26. Carl M. Cannon, "Surviving the Information Age," *The National Journal* 39.26 (June 30, 2007): 22.

27. Henry Jenkins, "Photoshop for Democracy," *Technology Review,* June 4, 2004, http://www.techreview.com/Biotech/13648/.

28. "Culture Jamming: Culture Jamming and Meme-based Communication," Center for Communication and Civic Engagement, http://depts.washington.edu/ccce/polcommcampaigns/CultureJamming.htm.

29. "Inanity on the Web," September 3, 2004, http://soundtracksforthem.blogspot.com/2004/09/inanity-on-web-jib-jab-emulation-and.html.

30. "Democratic Candidate Mashup," Election'08, Yahoo News, http://debates.news.yahoo.com/.

31. "XM Radio to Launch 2008 Presidential Election Channel POTUS '08 on September 24," press release, PR Newswire, May 21, 2007, http://xmradio.mediaroom.com/index.php?s=press_releases&item=1453.

32. Obama campaign Web site: http://www.barackobama.com/index.php.

33. *USA Today,* April 3, 2007.

34. "No Fleetwood Mac? Hillary's Top 10: Clinton Asks Voters to Choose among Finalists for Her Campaign Theme Song," Associated Press, May 26, 2007, http://www.cbsnews.com/stories/2007/05/26/politics/main2855312.shtml.

35. Foon Rhee and Scott Helman, "Romney Seeking Home-Grown Ads," *Boston Globe,* August 30, 2007, http://www.boston.com/news/nation/articles/2007/08/30/romney_seeking_home_grown_ads/.

36. Jake Coyle, "MySpace, MTV to Offer Candidate Chats," Associated Press, August 23, 2007, retrieved from ABC News archive, http://abcnews.go.com/Entertainment/wireStory?id=3513603.

37. Brian Goldsmith, "The 08' Vote: Teaching Generation X Why," March 12, 2007, posted by CBS News, www.cbsnews.com/blogs/2007/03/12/couricandco/printable2559542.shtml.

38. "New Study Shows Americans' Blogging Behaviour," PR Newswire, August 30, 2007, http://www.sys-con.com/read/422905.htm.

39. Joe Trippi, *The Revolution Will Not Be Televised: Democracy, the Internet, and the Overthrow of Everything* (New York: ReganBooks, 2004), 89.

40. Scott Gant, *We're All Journalists Now: The Transformation of the Press and Reshaping of the Law in the Internet Age* (New York: Free Press, 2007), 3.

41. "Blogosphere Hits Political Mainstream," *Reliable Sources,* CNN, August 5, 2007; broadcast transcript, http://transcripts.cnn.com/TRANSCRIPTS/0708/05/rs.01.html.

42. Dan Hellinger, "Political Ad-Dollar Windfall for Media: Too Bad Bloggers, Amateurs Offer Best Access to Candidates," *St. Louis Journalism Review* 36.290 (October 2006): 18(3).

43. "Crashing the System"; "Who's Plugged In?": *Mother Jones* (July/August 2007), 29, http://www.motherjones.com/news/feature/2007/07/crashing_the_system.html.

44. "FEC Shoots Down Political Blog Regulation," Bulldog Reporter's Daily' Dog, September 14, 2007, http://firmvoice.com/ME2/Audiences/dirmod.asp?sid=2436B6EB9392483ABB0A373E8B823A24&nm=&type=Publishing&mod=Publications%3A%3AArticle&mid=8F3A7027421841978F18BE895F87F791&AudID=213D92F8BE0D4A1BB62EB3DF18FCCC68&tier=4&id=0E84EC9A9E7C4D5D9CC908AAF1D01DD9.

45. Dave Eberhart, "How the Blogs Torpedoed Dan Rather," http://www.newsmax.com/archives/articles/2005/1/28/172943.shtml; NewsMax Wires, "Rather: Docs Questionable, Info Correct," http://www.newsmax.com/archives/articles/2004/9/16/111237.shtml.

10

Trying to Fix the Money Problem in Elections

The Presidency of the United States was an office neither to be sought nor declined. To pay money for securing it directly or indirectly, was in my opinion incorrect in principle.

—President John Quincy Adams (1828)

Senators and representatives, faced incessantly with the need to raise even more funds to fuel their campaigns, can scarcely avoid weighing every decision against the question, "how will this affect my fundraising prospects?" rather than "how will this affect the national interest."

—Senator Barry Goldwater

Virtually every means of communicating ideas in today's mass society requires the expenditure of money.

—U.S. Supreme Court, *Buckley* v. *Valero* (1976)

The history of campaign finance reform has been: where you put up a wall, the money will eventually find its way to flow around it.

—Mike Waldman, former aide to President Bill Clinton

Media Literacy Core Concept:
Most media messages are organized to gain profit and/or power.

Media Literacy Key Question:
Who benefits from the message?

Timeline of Campaign Finance Reform Efforts

1907	Congress bans corporate money in federal elections
1974	Congress passes Federal Election Campaign Act (FECA) in wake of Watergate abuses
1976	U.S. Supreme Court strikes down parts of FECA (*Buckley* v. *Valero*)
2001	McCain-Feingold-Cochran bill passes Senate
2002	Shays-Meehan passes Congress
2007	U.S. Supreme Court strikes down "issue ad" restrictions

What if:

- candidates for president didn't have to raise millions of dollars?
- local and network TV stations gave candidates "free air time" for ads?
- there was no need for "campaign finance reform?"
- public financing of elections worked?

According to a 2007 survey conducted by the First Amendment Center, 71 percent of Americans favor limiting the amount of money a corporation or union could contribute to a political campaign, while 64 percent said they supported such a limit on individual contributions.[1]

The role of contributions to political candidates has been an issue for many years. Both Congress and the courts have attempted to deal with various aspects of the McCain-Feingold campaign finance reform law, which has become known as the Bipartisan Campaign Reform Act (BCRA). The 2004 election was the first under BCRA; it banned unlimited "soft" money contributions to the national political parties but raised contribution limits for individuals.[2]

In 2007 the U.S. Supreme Court reversed a portion of BCRA. The high court struck down restrictions on the time limitations that had been placed on independent groups that broadcast their issue ads close to election time. The ruling was the latest in a continuing struggle by some to control campaign spending by candidates running for president.

MY, HOW TIMES HAVE CHANGED

"In 1846, Abraham Lincoln's friends raised a mere $200 to finance his race for Congress. After he won, Lincoln returned $199.25: he had canvassed the voters on his own horse and spent only 75 cents—to treat some farm hands to a barrel of cider. In 1860 Lincoln won the presidency without leaving Springfield (Illinois) or making a single speech; his entire national campaign cost $100,000—a sum now barely sufficient for one 30-minute national telecast."[3]

Today, the cost of running for office has skyrocketed. Those who run for national office, like the presidency, know that they have to raise millions of dollars. Money is used for everything from travel to salaries to postage. But the most money is spent to market the candidate on TV.

Wall Street analysts predicted television stations in the United States alone could bring in a record $2 billion to $3 billion from the 2008 election cycle.[4]

Over a span of more than 30 years, Congress has tried many times to address the issue that the millions of dollars raised by candidates, their parties, and others impacts the election process. Some say those large sums of money, raised from large wealthy donors and organizations, unduly influence voters, politicians, policies, and—eventually—laws. Efforts to block so-called "soft money" contributions have been countered by those who say such restrictions violate the U.S. Constitution's free-speech guarantees.

Presidential candidates know that they must raise huge sums of money in order to market themselves, which means soliciting funds from individuals and companies in order to produce the ads and purchase the vast amounts of advertising time on television needed to reach and influence potential voters. Some candidates who cannot raise these huge sums don't run or eventually drop out. (Republican

Days before the 2008 election, Democratic candidate Barack Obama spent millions of dollars to buy 30 minutes of "prime" television time on three major networks and four smaller channels. He used the time to air an effective infomercial, packaging his biography for the American people and showing how he planned to respond to the country's economic distress. The broadcast, which was compared by one TV critic to Ronald Reagan's "Morning in America" ad, attracted some 33.5 million viewers—more than the final game of Major League Baseball's World Series. (AP Photo/ Obama Campaign)

candidate Senator John McCain found himself faced with that dilemma in the summer of 2007, but he stayed in the race.)

Media critic Robert McChesney suggests "Many campaign-finance laws . . . focus on the supply of campaign cash. However, the solution to the ubiquity of money in politics . . . must address the demand for all that campaign cash: the need to pay for airtime on commercial media to communicate with citizens."[5] One possible solution that has been suggested is to give candidates free broadcasting air time rather than charging money for it. But efforts to expand the "free-air time initiative" have been turned back, mostly because the broadcast and cable industry generate huge profits from political advertising each year.

PUBLIC FINANCING OF ELECTIONS

In the fall of 2007, former senator John Edwards, hoping to keep pace with the large funds being raised by his Democratic opponents Hillary Clinton and Barack Obama, decided to accept public financing in his bid for the Democratic nomination for president. By his actions, Edwards's campaign became eligible to receive matching funds of as much as $250 for each contribution received from individuals. Under federal election law, a candidate is qualified to receive public money if he or she can demonstrate having raised a total of $5,000 in each of 20 states, all with contributions of $250 or less from individual people.[6] The public finance system also restricted Edwards's spending and forbade him from contributing his own money to his campaign, thus making it harder for him to compete.

Public financing of elections is not universally popular. In February 2007, after Hillary Clinton ditched the public finance system, the polling company Rasmussen Reports found that 38 percent of voters would be *more* likely to vote for a candidate who turned down public financing, compared to 25 percent who would be less likely.[7]

UPDATES ON CAMPAIGN FINANCE REFORM EFFORTS

Clean money, clean elections: in the U.S. Congress, senators Dick Durbin (D-Ill.) and Arlen Specter (R-Pa.) have introduced the Fair Elections Now Act, which would provide full public financing for Senate candidates. This proposal, Senate Bill 936, sets up a "clean" system that combines spending limits and public funding of congressional campaigns. It is based on highly successful models already working in Arizona, Maine, North Carolina, and elsewhere.[8]

Questions to Consider
- What is campaign finance reform aimed at doing?
- Has it been successful?
- Does money influence a candidate's view of an issue or law?

> • Who benefits from campaign finance reform? Who does not?
> • How does public financing of campaigns work?

NOTES

1. " '07 Survey Shows Americans' Views Mixed on Basic Freedoms," September 25, 2007, http://www.firstamendmentcenter.org/news.aspx?id=19031.

2. Alan Hall, "The Rising Price of Presidency (POP)," Market Watch, http://www.elliottwave.com/features/default.aspx?cat=mw*aid=3390*time=pm.

3. "*Time* Essay: Now Is the Time for All Good Men . . . ," *TIME Magazine,* January 5, 1968, 44: http://www.time.com/time/magazine/article/0,9171,712078,00.html.

4. "TV, Radio Look for Record Ad Money in Election," *Reuters,* August 24, 2007.

5. Robert W. McChesney, Russell Newman, and Ben Scott, eds., *The Future of Media: Resistance and Reform in the 21st Century* (New York: Seven Stories Press, 2005), 142.

6. Anne E. Kornblut and Matthew Mosk, "Edwards to Accept Public Financing," *Washington Post,* September 28, 2007, A04.

7. David Weigel, "More Money, No Problem," *Reason Magazine,* May 2007, http://www.reason.com/news/show/119233.html.

8. Public Campaign: http://www.publicampaign.org/clean123; Source: http://www.mediachannel.org/wordpress/2007/05/04/stamping-out-the-free-press-democracy-vs-zip-code-10021/.

Glossary

access.   Easily within one's reach.

ad, advertisement (aka commercial; spot).   A paid announcement, as in goods for sale, in newspapers or magazines, on radio or television, etc. (*Source:* http://www.dictionary.com)

ad watch.   A detailed analysis and breakdown of a candidate's political campaign commercial; traditionally published, broadcast, or posted online.

allegorical (from *allegory*).   The representation of abstract ideas or principles by characters, figures, or events in narrative, dramatic, or pictorial form. (*Source:* http://www.dictionary.com)

analyze.   To examine carefully.

audience.   Those to whom a particular media is designed. *See also* **demographic**

audio.   The sound portion of an event, recording, or broadcast.

bandwagon.   Type of ad which asserts that everyone is doing something, so you should too ("jump on the bandwagon").

behavioral target marketing.   Using media and technology to target or design a message for a specific demographic using the media habits of a consumer.

blog (short for Web log).   An online diary, usually posted in reverse chronological order, containing thoughts, opinion, links to sources, sometimes offering readers an opportunity to reply to entries.

bloggers.   Those who maintain, produce a blog.

blogosphere.   The world of blogs and bloggers.

campaign finance reform.   Common term for the political effort in the United States to change the involvement of money in politics, primarily in political campaigns. (*Source:* http://en.wikipedia.org/wiki/Campaign_finance_reform)

choreography.   The art of planning a production (traditionally involves dance; more recently: to lay out an event for large audience or broadcast).

codes.   Systems of signs, which create meaning. (*Source:* http://www.tki.org.nz/r/ media_studies/media_concepts/codes_and_conventions_e.php)

constructed.   The concept that all media are created, organized, and put together by someone with certain expertise.

consultant.   Wide-ranging term to describe someone hired by a candidate to perform a number of key tasks (advising, media buying, polling, etc.).

convention.   The generally accepted way of doing something. There are general conventions in any medium, such as the use of interviewee quotes in a print article, but conventions are also genre specific. (*Source:* http://www.tki.org.nz/r/media_studies/ media_concepts/codes_and_conventions_e.php)

critical inquiry.   Investigation via asking questions to gain better knowledge and/or understanding.

cut-away (a television/film production technique).   A bridging, intercut shot between two shots of the same subject. It represents a secondary activity occurring at the same time as the main action. It may be preceded by a definite look or glance out of frame by a participant, or it may show something of which those in the preceding shot are unaware. It may be used to avoid the technical ugliness of a "jump cut" where there would be uncomfortable jumps in time, place, or viewpoint. It is often used to shortcut the passing of time. (*Source:* http://www.aber.ac.uk/media/Documents/short/gramtv.html)

debate.   An event, often televised or streamed online, in which presidential candidates respond to questions.

deception.   The process of being deceived, tricked into thinking one way or another.

deconstruction.   "To take apart" in order to study, to better understand how something might be manufactured.

demographic.   A specific audience type (e.g., male, female, young, old) that media try to reach with a message.

equal time.   The equal opportunity provision of the Communications Act requires radio and television stations and cable systems that originate their own programming to treat legally qualified political candidates equally when it comes to selling or giving away air time. (*Source:* http://www.dictionary.com)

eye candy.   A visually appealing event, person, or thing.

fairness doctrine.   The policy created in 1949 (repealed in 1987) which attempted to ensure that all coverage of controversial issues by a broadcast station be balanced and fair. (*Source:* http://www.museum.tv/archives/etv/F/htmlF/fairnessdoct/fairnessdoct.htm)

fireside chat. Phrase which described the radio broadcasts of President Franklin D. Roosevelt; listeners gathered around their radios to hear him, similar to gathering around a fire for warmth.

527 committee/organization. A type of American tax-exempt organization named after a section of the U.S. tax code; created primarily to influence the nomination, election, appointment, or defeat of candidates for public office. (*Source:* http://en.wikipedia.org/wiki/527_group)

free air time. An effort to encourage broadcasters to provide presidential candidates a limited amount of ad time at no cost.

free media. Publicity (in newspapers, magazines, broadcasting) for which a candidate does not pay for.

frequency (when applied to radio ad buys). The number of times an ad runs on-air.

hard money. Individual campaign contributions that fall under FEC limits. (*Source:* Glenn H. Utter and Ruth Ann Strickland, *Campaign and Election Reform: A Reference Handbook.* Contemporary World Issues series. [Santa Barbara, CA: ABC-CLIO, 1997], 309, 318.)

infomercial. A relatively long commercial in the format of a television program. (*Source:* http://www.dictionary.com)

inoculation theory. Belief that we are inoculated (protected) against advertising (for example).

interpret. To give or provide the meaning of; explain. (*Source:* http://www.dictionary.com)

mashup. A media production in which the creator has edited together audio/video elements of different previously produced productions.

media literacy. Ability to access, analyze, interpret, and produce communication in a variety of forms.

metaphorical. Like a metaphor.

moblog (short for mobile Web log). Term given to the 2004 practice of college students who used cell phones to document happenings at the Republican National Convention.

morphing (from the word metamorphosis). The process of image manipulation, a technique in which an image is altered, changed to look like another.

MSM. Mainstream media.

MTV effect. Phrase given to any medium or effort that successfully targets to a younger audience.

MySpace. Popular social networking Web site.

narrowcast. The ability to target a message to a specific demographic using a specific medium.

neuromarketing.   A variety of brain-research techniques designed to give advertisers/ marketers more information about how the human brain, and thus people, might react to a product or service.

New Deal.   FDR's various policy initiatives designed to reinvigorate and reform the economy and put people back to work during the Depression; touted during his "fireside chat" radio addresses to the nation.

Nielsen.   The nation's major ratings service, providing service to broadcasters, print, and advertisers.

paid media.   Any media in which a politician pays money for access (purchasing ad space in a newspaper, magazine; time on radio or TV; purchase of Web space access).

parody.   Any humorous, satirical, or burlesque imitation, as of a person, event, etc. (*Source:* http://www.dictionary.com)

photo op.   Abbreviation for photographic opportunity.

plain folks.   Type of ad featuring common everyday people (e.g., farmers, housewives, businesspeople).

podcast.   A recorded audio event commonly distributed via the Internet.

political convention.   Meeting of delegates of a political party at the local, state, provincial, or national level to select candidates for office and to decide party policy. (*Source:* Political convention. *Encyclopædia Britannica,* 2007. Encyclopædia Britannica Online, July 30, 2007, http://www.britannica.com/eb/article-9060631)

poll.   A sampling or collection of opinions on a subject, taken from either a selected or a random group of persons, as for the purpose of analysis (usually communicated via broadcast, printed in newspapers, or posted online).

press conference.   Usually a scheduled event in which a candidate or politician speaks to the media.

primary.   Also called primary election. A preliminary election in which voters of each party nominate candidates for office, party officers, etc. (*Source:* http://www.dictionary.com)

produce.   To create a media work (e.g., produce a blog, podcast, Web page, digital video, etc.).

propaganda.   Information, especially of a biased or misleading nature, used to promote a political cause or point of view. (*Source:* Concise Oxford English Dictionary) *See also* **spin**; **techniques of persuasion**.

rating.   The estimate of the size of a television audience relative to the total universe, expressed as a percentage. (*Source:* http://www.nielsenmedia.com)

reach.   An advertising term that best describes the scope and composition of a target market.

reaction shot.   Any shot, usually a cut-away, in which a participant reacts to action which has just occurred. (*Source:* http://www.aber.ac.uk/media/Documents/short/ gramtv.html)

repetition.   The advertising technique that advocates repeating the name of the product or candidate in order to make sure it is ingrained in the mind of the audience.

representation.   The process by which a constructed media text stands for, symbolizes, describes, or represents people, places, events, or ideas that are real and have an existence outside the text. (*Source:* Media Awareness Network, http://www.media-awareness.ca/english/resources/educational/teaching_backgrounders/media_literacy/glossary_media _literacy.cfm#R)

script.   Words prepared in advance, usually written and delivered.

share.   The percent of the Households Using Television (HUT) or Persons Using Television (PUT) which are tuned to a specific program or station at a specified time. (*Source:* http://www.nielsenmedia.com)

soft money.   Money contributed to a political candidate or party that is not subject to federal regulations. (*Source:* http://www.dictionary.com)

soundbite.   A short, usually edited, portion of a candidate speech or interview—when used in television news broadcasts.

spin.   To provide an interpretation of (a statement or event, for example), especially in a way meant to sway public opinion. (*Source:* http://www.thefreedictionary.com/spin)

split screen.   A video production technique in which the screen is literally divided in two—allowing viewers to see two images simultaneously.

spot.   *See* **ad**.

stagecraft.   Skill in the techniques and devices of the theater. (*Source:* American Heritage Dictionary)

staged.   Not spontaneous—something planned, produced, or rehearsed in advance.

target audience.   *See* **demographic**.

techniques of persuasion.   Phrase describing a number of methods a person, or advertisement, uses to convey information or persuade a group concerning an issue, candidate, or product.

testimonial.   Type of ad in which a person gives testimony, speaks about his or her experience with a product or candidate (sometimes the person is well known).

user-generated.   Expression describing content (photos, videos, etc.) created by media producers and posted onto Web pages.

video.   The picture portion of an event, recording, or broadcast.

viral video.   A video posted on a Web page, or distributed by e-mail, so that literally millions will be exposed to it.

visual literacy.   Ability to understand, interpret and evaluate visual messages. (*Source:* Valerie J. Bristor and Suzanne V. Drake, "Linking the Language Arts and Content Areas Through Visual Technology," *THE Journal* 22 [Technological Horizons in Education], 1994, 74[4])

vlog.   Short for video weblog.

whistle stop tour.   Describes method of candidate's traveling by train and stopping periodically to speak to potential voters.

widget.   Computer code.

YouTube.   Popular Web site for posting user-made video productions.

YouTube moment.   Expression describing what happens when something or someone is captured on camera (perhaps an embarrassing moment) and then the capture is distributed via the Web and other sources (bloggers, other news sources, the mainstream media).

Resources

MEDIA LITERACY

Web Sites

Center for Media Literacy: http://www.medialit.org

Mastering the Media (Appalachian State University): http://www.ced.appstate.edu/departments/ci/programs/edmedia/medialit/index.html

Media Awareness Network: http://www.media-awareness.ca/english/index.cfm

Media Education Lab (Temple University): http://www.mediaeducationlab.com

Media Literacy Clearinghouse: http://www.frankwbaker.com

Media Literacy (KQED-San Francisco): http://www.kqed.org/topics/education/medialiteracy/

National Association for Media Literacy Education http://www.namle.net

Project LookSharp: http://www.ithaca.edu/looksharp/

Books

Beach, Richard, *teachingmedialiteracy.com: A Web-Linked Guide to Resources and Activities* (New York: Teachers College Press, 2006).

Buckingham, David, *Media Education: Literacy, Learning and Contemporary Culture* (Cambridge, UK: Polity Press, 2003).

Considine, David, and Gail E. Haley, *Visual Messages: Integrating Imagery into Instruction,* 2nd ed. (Englewood, CO: Teacher Ideas Press, 1999).

De Abreu, Belinha S., *Teaching Media Literacy: A How-to-Do-It Manual* (New York: Neal-Schuman, 2007).

Duncan, Barry, and Kathleen Tyner, eds., *Visions/Revisions: Moving Forward with Media Education* (Madison, WI: National Telemedia Council, 2004).

Hobbs, Renée, *Reading the Media: Media Literacy in High School English* (New York: Teachers College Press, 2007).

Kist, William, *New Literacies in Action: Teaching and Learning in Multiple Media* (New York: Teachers College Press, 2005).

Krueger, Ellen, and Mary T. Christel, *Seeing and Believing: How to Teach Media Literacy in the English Classroom* (Portsmouth, NH: Boynton/Cook-Heinemann, 2001).

Kubey, Robert, and Brent Ruben, eds., *Media Literacy in the Information Age: Current Perspectives,* vol. 6 of *Information and Behavior* (New Brunswick, NJ: Transaction Books, 2001).

Potter, W. James, *Media Literacy,* 4th ed. (Los Angeles: Sage, 2008).

Silverblatt, Art, *Media Literacy: Keys to Interpreting Media Messages,* 2nd ed. (Westport, CT: Praeger, 2007).

Tyner, Kathleen, *Literacy in a Digital World: Teaching and Learning in the Age of Information* (Mahwah, NJ: Erlbaum, 1998).

MEDIA AND POLITICS

Media

The Annenberg Public Policy Center at the University of Pennsylvania: http://appcpenn.org/

Campaigns & Elections Magazine: http://www.campaignline.com

Democracy in Action: P2008: Media: Covering the Campaign http://www.gwu.edu/~action/2008/media08.html. Sponsored in part by George Washington University's Institute for Politics, Democracy & the Internet, but receives no funding from the Institute and is not an official project of GWU.

The Democracy Project (PBS Kids): http://pbskids.org/democracy/

Disconnected: Politics, the Press and the Public (PBS), A Fred Friendly Seminar: http://www.pbs.org/inthebalance/archives/disconnected/about.html

ERIC Digest, The Media's Role in Political Campaigns: http://www.indiana.edu/~reading/ieo/digests/d74.html

The Influence of Media in Presidential Politics: http://www.utexas.edu/features/archive/2004/election_media.html

Joan Shorenstein Center on the Press, Politics and Public Policy Harvard University: http://www.hks.harvard.edu/presspol/index.htm

Morningside Center for Teaching Social Responsibility: http://www.teachablemoment.org/high/election2.html

NewsHour's Media Unit (PBS): http://www.pbs.org/newshour/media/resources.html

The Quill (Society of Professional Journalists), Votes & Quotes: A Guide to Understanding Election Coverage (Oct/November 2007): http://www.spj.org/quill.asp

Political Blogs

CQ Politics: http://www.cqpolitics.com/wmspage.cfm?parm1=5

The Hill (print and online newspaper): http://thehill.com/

The Pew Center on the States: http://www.stateline.org/live/

Politico: http://www.politico.com/

Politics1 (Ron Gunzburger): http://www.politics1.com/. See the Political Blog Roll (at right on the home page) for an excellent list of political blogs.

PolitifactCheck.com: http://politifact.com/truth-o-meter/ (St. Petersburg [Fla.] Times and Congressional Quarterly)

Pollster.com: http://www.pollster.com/

PressThink: The Ghost of Democracy in the Media Machine: http://journalism.nyu.edu/pubzone/weblogs/pressthink/ (Jay Rosen)

University of Virginia's Center for Politics: http://www.centerforpolitics.org/crystalball/ (Larry J. Sabato)

Wake Forest University Political Links: http://www.wfu.edu/~louden/Political%20Communication/Class%20Information/POLITICALSITES.html (Allan Louden)

Books

Bagdikian, Ben H., *The New Media Monopoly* (Boston: Beacon Press, 2004).

Barber, James D., *The Pulse of Politics: Electing Presidents in the Media Age* (New York: Norton, 1980).

Brennan, Ruth M. G., and Dan F. Hahn, *Listening for a President: A Citizen's Campaign Methodology* (New York: Praeger, 1990).

Brinkley, Alan, and Edward L. Widmer, *Campaigns: A Century of Presidential Races from the Photo Archives of the New York Times* (New York: DK Publishing, 2001).

Cavanaugh, John William, *Media Effects on Voters* (Lanham, MD: University Press of America, 1995).

Cook, Timothy E., *Governing with the News, The News Media as a Political Institution* (Chicago: University of Chicago Press, 1998).

Crouse, Timothy, *The Boys on the Bus* (New York: Random House, 1973).

Davis, Richard, *The Press and American Politics: The New Mediator,* 3rd ed. (Upper Saddle River, NJ: Prentice Hall, 2000).

Entman, Robert M., *Democracy without Citizens: Media and the Decay of American Politics* (New York: Oxford University Press, 1989).

Felknor, Bruce, *Political Mischief: Smear, Sabotage, and Reform in U.S. Elections* (New York: Praeger, 1992).

Friedenberg, Robert, *Rhetorical Studies of National Political Debate* (Westport, CT: Praeger, 1997).

Gans, Herbert J., *Democracy and the News* (New York: Oxford University Press, 2003).

Graber, Doris A., Dennis McQuail, and Pippa Norris, eds., *The Politics of News: The News of Politics,* 2nd ed. (Washington, DC: Congressional Quarterly Books, 2008).

Henggler, Paul R., *The Kennedy Persuasion: The Politics of Style since JFK* (Chicago: I. R. Dee, 1995).

Hirschbein, Ron, *Voting Rites: The Devolution of American Politics* (Westport, CT: Praeger, 1999).

Hollihan, Thomas A., *Uncivil Wars: Political Campaigns in a Media Age,* 2nd ed. (New York: Bedford/St. Martin's, 2008).

Iyengar, Shanto, and Jennifer A. McGrady, *Media Politics: A Citizen's Guide* (New York: Norton, 2007).

Iyengar, Shanto, and Richard Reeves, eds., *Do the Media Govern? Politicians, Voters, and Reporters in America* (Thousand Oaks, CA: Sage Publications, 1997).

Iyengar, Shanto, and William J. McGuire, eds., *Explorations in Political Psychology* (Durham, NC: Duke University Press, 1993).

Jackson, Brooks, and Kathleen Hall Jamieson, *UnSpun: Finding Facts in a World of Disinformation* (New York: Random House, 2007).

Jamieson, Kathleen Hall, *Dirty Politics: Deception, Distraction and Democracy* (New York: Oxford University Press, 1992).

Jamieson, Kathleen Hall, *Eloquence in an Electronic Age* (New York: Oxford University Press, 1988).

Jamieson, Kathleen Hall, *Everything You Think You Know about Politics—and Why You're Wrong* (New York: Basic Books, 2000).

Jamieson, Kathleen Hall, ed., *Electing the President, 2004: The Insiders' View* (Philadelphia: University of Pennsylvania Press, 2006).

Jamieson, Kathleen Hall, and Paul Waldman, *The Press Effect: Politicians, Journalists, and the Stories That Shape the Political World* (New York: Oxford University Press, 2003).

Jenkins, Henry, *Convergence Culture: Where Old and New Media Collide* (New York: New York University Press, 2006).

Kamber, Victor, *Poison Politics: Are Negative Campaigns Destroying Democracy?* (New York: Plenum Press, 1997).

Kendall, Kathleen, ed., *Presidential Campaign Discourse* (Albany: State University of New York Press, 1995).

Kerbel, Matthew R., *Remote & Controlled: Media Politics in a Cynical Age,* 2nd ed. (Boulder, CO: Westview, 1998).

Kurtz, Howard, *Spin Cycle: How the White House and the Media Manipulate the News* (New York: Simon & Schuster, 1998).

Lichter, S. Robert, and Richard E. Noyes, *Good Intentions Make Bad News: Why Americans Hate Campaign Journalism* (Lanham, MD: Rowman & Littlefield, 1995).

Littlewood, Thomas B., *Calling Elections: The History of Horse-Race Journalism* (Notre Dame, IN: University of Notre Dame Press, 1998).

Maltese, John Anthony, *Spin Control: The White House Office of Communications and the Management of Presidential News,* 2nd ed. (Chapel Hill: University of North Carolina Press, 1994).

McCall, Jeffrey M., *Viewer Discretion Advised: Taking Control of Mass Media Influences* (Lanham, MD: Rowman & Littlefield, 2007).

McChesney, Robert W., *Rich Media, Poor Democracy: Communication Politics in Dubious Times* (Urbana: University of Illinois Press, 1999).

McChesney, Robert W., Russell Newman, and Ben Scott, *The Future of Media: Resistance and Reform in the 21st Century* (New York: Seven Stories Press, 2005).

Nardulli, P. F., J. K. Dalager, et al., "Voter Turnout in U.S. Presidential Elections: An Historical View and Some Speculation," *PS: Political Science & Politics* 29(3): 480–90 (1996).

Newman, Bruce I., *The Mass Marketing of Politics: Democracy in an Age of Manufactured Images* (Thousand Oaks, CA: Sage Publications, 1999).

Nimmo, Dan D., *The Political Persuaders: The Techniques of Modern Election Campaigns* (1970; reprint, New Brunswick, NJ: Transaction Books, 2000 [with a new introduction by the author]).

Norris, Pippa, ed., *Politics and the Press: The News Media and Their Influences* (Boulder, CO: Lynne Rienner Publishers, 1997).

Ornstein, Norman, and Thomas E. Mann, eds., *The Permanent Campaign and Its Future* (Washington, DC: American Enterprise Institute for Public Policy Research/Brookings Institution, 2000).

Paletz, David L., *The Media in American Politics: Content and Consequences,* 2nd ed. (New York: Longman, 2002).

Patterson, Thomas E., *The Mass Media Election: How Americans Choose Their President* (New York: Praeger, 1980). [Sponsored by the Committee on Mass Communications and Political Behavior of the Social Science Research Council.]

Patterson, Thomas E., *Out of Order* (New York: Knopf, 1993).

Patterson, Thomas E., *The Vanishing Voter: Public Involvement in an Age of Uncertainty* (New York: Knopf, 2002).

Perloff, Richard M., *Political Communication: Politics, Press, and Public in America* (Mahwah, NJ: Erlbaum, 1998).

Pfau, Michael, J. Brian Houston, and Shane M. Semmler, *Mediating the Vote: The Changing Media Landscape in U.S. Presidential Campaigns* (Lanham, MD: Rowman & Littlefield, 2006).

Reinsch, J. Leonard, *Getting Elected: From Radio to Roosevelt to Television and Reagan* (New York: Hippocrene, 1988).

Rich, Frank, *The Greatest Story Ever Sold* (New York: Penguin, 2006).

Rozell, Mark J., and Jeremy D. Mayer, eds., *Media Power, Media Politics,* 2nd ed. (Lanham, MD: Rowman & Littlefield, 2008).

Ryan, Frederick J., ed., *Ronald Reagan: The Great Communicator* (New York: Harper Collins, Perennial, 1995).

Sabato, Larry J., *Feeding Frenzy: Attack Journalism in American Politics* (Baltimore, MD: Lanahan, 2000).

Sanders, Barry, *The Private Death of Public Discourse* (Boston: Beacon Press, 1998).

Schudson, Michael, *Watergate in American Memory: How We Remember, Forget and Reconstruct the Past* (New York: Basic Books, 1992).

Schultz, David A., ed., *It's Show Time! Media, Politics, and Popular Culture* (New York: Peter Lang, 2000).

Sherrow, Victoria, *Image and Substance: The Media in U.S. Elections* (Brookfield, CT: Millbrook Press, 1992).

Simon, Roger, *Show Time: The American Political Circus and the Race for the White House* (New York: Times Books, 1998).

Skewes, Elizabeth A., *Message Control: How News Is Made on the Presidential Campaign Trail* (Lanham, MD: Rowman & Littlefield, 2007).

Stempel, Guido H., *Media and Politics in America: A Reference Handbook* (Santa Barbara, CA: ABC-CLIO, 2003).

Sugarman, Sally, *If Kids Could Vote: Children, Democracy, and the Media* (Lanham, MD: Lexington Books, 2007).

Swanson, David L., and Paolo Mancini, *Politics, Media, and Modern Democracy: An International Study of Innovations in Electoral Campaigning and Their Consequences* (Westport, CT: Praeger, 1996).

Swint, Kerwin, *Dark Genius: The Influential Career of Legendary Political Operative and Fox News Founder Roger Ailes* (New York: Union Square Press [Imprint of Sterling Publishing], 2008).

Swint, Kerwin C., *Mudslingers: The Top 25 Negative Political Campaigns of All Time* (Westport, CT: Praeger, 2006).

Taylor, Paul, *See How They Run: Electing the President in an Age of Mediaocracy* (New York: Knopf, 1990).

Vermeer, Jan Pons, *In "Media" Res: Readings in Mass Media and American Politics* (New York: McGraw-Hill, 1995).

Waterman, Richard, Robert Wright, and Gilbert St. Clair, *The Image-Is-Everything Presidency: Dilemmas in American Leadership* (Boulder, CO: Westview Press, 1999).

White, Theodore H., *The Making of the President, 1972* (New York: Atheneum, 1973).

Winograd, Morley, and Michael D. Hais, *Millennial Makeover: MySpace, YouTube, and the Future of American Politics* (Piscataway, NJ: Rutgers University Press, 2008).

Woodward, Gary C., *Center Stage: Media and the Performance of American Politics* (Lanham, MD: Rowman & Littlefield, 2007).

ADVERTISING

Media

Campaign Essentials: Politics & The Media (Discovery/Times Cable Network, 2004). Note: This series is available via UnitedStreaming (Discovery): http://streaming.discoveryeducation.com/

Campaign 2008: A User-Generated Election (Ad Week) http://www.adweek.com/aw/images/pdfs/Campaign1.pdf

Democracy in Action, Interest Group and Independent Expenditure Advertising: http://www.gwu.edu/~action/2004/interestg/interestgads/igadsmain.html. Transcripts and images.

EASE History: Campaign Ads 1952–2004 (Experience Acceleration Supportive Environment, Michigan State University Cognitive Flexibility Lab): http://www.easehistory.org/index2.html

Eisenhower Political Ads. Prelinger Archives, Motion Picture, Broadcasting, and Recorded Sound Division, Library of Congress. Internet Movie Archives: http://www.archive.org/details/Eisenhow1952, http://www.archive.org/details/Eisenhow1956

How Art Made the World: The Art of Persuasion (PBS, 2006) related lesson plan: http://www.pbs.org/howartmadetheworld/resources/lesson3/

The Language of Advertising Claims: http://home.olemiss.edu/~egjbp/comp/ad-claims.html

The Living Room Candidate (Museum of the Moving Image): http://www.livingroomcandidate.org/

November Warriors, Part 4: The Modern Campaign: http://www.history.com/classroom/admin/study_guide/archives/thc_guide.0182.html

Political Literacy—Sifting thru the Spin (In the Mix, PBS): http://www.pbs.org/inthemix/. Note: Click on "Shows" at the foot of the page; select title from drop-down list at "Choose a Show Topic."

Sell & Spin: A History of Advertising (The History Channel): http://www.history.com/classroom/admin/study_guide/archives/thc_guide.0574.html

Techniques of Persuasion. Commission on Presidential Debates (2004): http://debate.uvm.edu/dcpdf/cpd2000.pdf

30-Second Candidate (PBS): http://www.pbs.org/30secondcandidate/

University of Iowa: Online Communications Studies Resources, Political Advertising:
    http://www.uiowa.edu/~commstud/resources/pol_ads.html
University of Wisconsin at Madison: Wisconsin Advertising Project: http://polisci.wisc
    .edu/tvadvertising/Political%20Advertising%20in%20the%202002%20Elections
    .htm
View Smart to Vote Smart (Cable in the Classroom): http://www.ciconline.org/viewsmart
Walter Cronkite Remembers the 20th Century: Television, Politics & JFK (videorecord-
    ing); Reader's Digest Association, Inc., in association with CBS, Inc., and Cronkite,
    Ward, and Company, 1997.

Books and Articles

Ansolabehere, Stephen, and Shanto Iyengar, *Going Negative: How Political Advertise-
    ments Shrink and Polarize the Electorate* (New York: Free Press, 1995).
Benoit, William L., *Seeing Spots: A Functional Analysis of Presidential Television Adver-
    tisements, 1952–1996* (Westport, CT: Praeger, 1999).
Biocca, Frank, *Television and Political Advertising,* 2 vols. (Hillsdale, NJ: Erlbaum,
    1991).
Brader, Ted, *Campaigning for Hearts and Minds: How Emotional Appeals in Political Ads
    Work* (Chicago: University of Chicago Press, 2006).
Dover, E. D., *Images, Issues, and Attacks: Television Advertising by Incumbents and
    Challengers in Presidential Elections* (Lanham, MD: Rowman & Littlefield, 2006).
Goldstein, K., and P. Freedman, "Campaign Advertising and Voter Turnout: New Evi-
    dence for a Stimulation Effect," *Journal of Politics* 64(3): 721–40 (2002).
Jamieson, Kathleen Hall, *Packaging the Presidency: A History and Criticism of Presiden-
    tial Campaign Advertising,* 3rd ed. (New York: Oxford University Press, 1996).
Kaid, Lynda L., and Anne Johnston, *Videostyle in Presidential Campaigns: Style and Con-
    tent of Televised Political Advertising* (Westport, CT: Praeger, 2001).
Kern, Montague, *30-Second Politics: Political Advertising in the Eighties* (New York:
    Praeger, 1989).
McGinniss, Joe, *The Selling of the President 1968* (1969; reprint, New York: Penguin,
    1988).
Meirick, Patrick, "Cognitive Responses to Negative and Comparative Political Advertis-
    ing," *Journal of Advertising* 31 (2002).
Packard, Vance, *The Hidden Persuaders* (1957; reprint, New York: Pocket Books, 1980;
    with a new afterword).
Pinkleton, Bruce E., Nam-Hyun Um, and Erica Weintraub Austin, "An Exploration of the
    Effects of Negative Political Advertising on Political Decision Making," *Journal of
    Advertising* 31 (2002).
Plissner, Martin, *The Control Room: How Television Calls the Shots in Presidential Elec-
    tions* (New York: Free Press, 1999).
Pratkanis, Anthony R., and Elliot Aronson, *Age of Propaganda: The Everyday Use and
    Abuse of Persuasion,* rev. ed. (New York: W. H. Freeman & Co., 2001).
Richardson, Glenn W., Jr., *Pulp Politics: How Political Advertising Tells the Stories of
    American Politics,* 2nd ed. (Lanham, MD: Rowman & Littlefield, 2008).
Rutherford, Paul, *Endless Propaganda: The Advertising of Public Goods* (Toronto, Buf-
    falo: University of Toronto Press, 2000).

Schultz, David A., ed., *Lights, Camera, Campaign!: Media, Politics, and Political Adver-
tising* (New York: Peter Lang, 2004).
Schwartz, Tony, *The Responsive Chord* (Garden City, NY: Anchor Books, 1973).
Thurber, James A., Candice J. Nelson, and David A. Dulio, eds., *Crowded Airwaves:
Campaign Advertising in Elections* (Washington, DC: Brookings Institution Press,
2000).
West, Darrell M., *Air Wars: Television Advertising in Election Campaigns, 1952–2004,*
4th ed. (Washington, DC: Congressional Quarterly Press, 2005).

THE PRESS

Media

Columbia Journalism Review: http://www.cjr.org/
The Joan Shorenstein Center on The Press, Politics and Public Policy (Harvard Univer-
sity): http://www.hks.harvard.edu/presspol/index.htm
The New York Times: Past Convention Coverage: http://www.nytimes.com/library/
politics/camp/whouse/convention-ra.html
Poynter Online. The Poynter Institute: http://www.poynter.org/
Project for Excellence in Journalism (PEJ). Understanding News in the Information Age:
http://www.journalism.org/

Books and Articles

Hess, Stephen, and Sandy Northrop, *Drawn & Quartered: The History of American Politi-
cal Cartoons* (Montgomery, AL: Elliott & Clark, 1996).
Kuhn, Raymond, and Erik Neveu, *Political Journalism* (New York: Routledge, 2002).
Leonard, Thomas C., *The Power of the Press: The Birth of American Political Reporting*
(New York: Oxford University Press, 1986).
Liebovich, Louis, *The Press and the Modern Presidency* (Westport, CT: Praeger, 2001).
Mears, Walter R., *Deadlines Past: Forty Years of Presidential Campaigning: A Reporter's
Story* (Kansas City, MO: Andrews McMeel, 2003).
Merzer, Martin, *The Miami Herald Report: Democracy Held Hostage* (New York:
St. Martin's, 2000).
Pinkleton, Bruce E., "Effects of Print Comparative Political Advertising on Political
Decision-Making and Participation," *Journal of Communication* 48 (1998).
Ritchie, Donald A., *Press Gallery: Congress and the Washington Correspondents* (Cam-
bridge, MA: Harvard University Press, 1991).
Rozell, Mark J., *The Press and the Bush Presidency* (Westport, CT: Praeger, 1996).
Shogan, Robert, *Bad News: Where the Press Goes Wrong in the Making of the President*
(Chicago: I. R. Dee, 2001).
Tebbel, John, and Sara Miles Watts, *The Press and the Presidency: From George Wash-
ington to Ronald Reagan* (New York: Oxford University Press, 1985).
Vermeer, Jan P., *The View from the States: National Politics in Local Newspaper Editori-
als* (Lanham, MD: Rowman & Littlefield, 2002).
Walsh, Kenneth T., *Feeding the Beast: The White House versus the Press* (New York:
Random House, 1996).

RADIO

Media

Empire of the Air: The Men Who Made Radio, a Florentine Films production produced in association with WETA-TV, Washington. Director and executive producer, Ken Burns; produced by Ken Burns, Morgan Wesson, Tom Lewis ; written by Geoffrey C. Ward ; additional writing, Tom Lewis, Ken Burns (PBS, 1992-01-29).

The 1924 Radio Election: http://web.archive.org/web/20040224221424/http://www.swl.net/patepluma/genbroad/elec1924.html

Books

Douglas, Susan J., *Listening in: Radio and American Imagination* (Minneapolis: University of Minnesota Press, 2004).

Lewis, Tom, *Empire of the Air: The Men Who Made Radio* (New York: HarperCollins, 1991).

Reinsch, J. Leonard, *Getting Elected: From Radio to Roosevelt to Television and Reagan* (New York: Hippocrene, 1988).

TELEVISION

Media

MTV's Rock the Vote: http://www.rockthevote.com/home.html

Political Spot Advertising (Wake Forest University) [Bibliography page includes video of the famed Daisy Spot ad]: http://www.wfu.edu/~louden/Political%20Communication/Bibs/SPOTBIB.html

Reliable Resources for Broadcast Political Coverage: http://reliableresources.org/. Hosts the annual Walter Cronkite Award for Excellence in Television Political Journalism.

The Rise and Fall of the Televised Political Convention, by Zachary Karabell, Discussion Paper, Joan Shorenstein Center for Press, Politics, and Public Policy, Harvard University John F. Kennedy School of Government, 1998: http://www.hks.harvard.edu/presspol/research_publications/papers/discussion_papers/D33.pdf

Books and Articles

Adatto, Kiku, *Picture Perfect: Life in the Age of the Photo Op,* new ed. (Prinseton, NJ: Princeton University Press, 2008). [Original edition published as *Picture Perfect: The Art and Artifice of Public Image Making.*]

Ansolabehere, Stephen, Roy Behr, and Shanto Iyengar, *The Media Game: American Politics in the Age of Television* (New York: Macmillan, 1992).

Barbatsis, Gretchen, " 'Look, and I Will Show You Something You Will Want to See': Pictorial Engagement in Negative Political Campaign Commercials," *Argumentation and Advocacy* 33 (1996).

Collins, Scott, *Crazy Like a Fox: The Inside Story of How Fox News Beat CNN* (New York: Portfolio, 2004).

Diamond, Edwin, and Stephen Bates, *The Spot: The Rise of Political Advertising on Television,* 3rd ed. (Cambridge, MA: MIT Press, 1992).

Farnsworth, Stephen J., and S. Robert Lichter, *The Nightly News Nightmare: Television's Coverage of U.S. Presidential Elections, 1988–2004,* 2nd ed. (Lanham, MD: Rowman & Littlefield, 2006).

Foote, Joe S., *Television Access and Political Power: The Networks, the Presidency, and the "Loyal Opposition"* (New York: Praeger, 1990).

Graber, Doris A., *Processing Politics: Learning from Television in the Internet Age* (Chicago: University of Chicago Press, 2001).

Harris, Jay S., comp., *TV Guide: The First 25 Years* (1978; reprint, New York: New American Library, 1980).

Iyengar, Shanto, *Is Anyone Responsible?: How Television Frames Political Issues* (1991; reprint, Chicago: University of Chicago Press, 1994).

Iyengar, Shanto, and Donald R. Kinder, *News That Matters: Television and American Opinion* (Chicago: University of Chicago Press, 1987).

Jamieson, Kathleen Hall, and David S. Birdsell, *Presidential Debates: The Challenge of Creating an Informed Electorate* (New York: Oxford University Press, 1988).

Kellner, Douglas, *Television and the Crisis of Democracy* (Boulder, CO: Westview, 1990).

Mickelson, Sig, *From Whistle Stop to Sound Bite: Four Decades of Politics and Television* (New York: Praeger, 1989).

Minow, Newton N., and Craig LaMay, *Inside the Presidential Debates: Their Improbable Past and Promising Future* (Chicago: University of Chicago Press, 2008).

Minow, Newton N., John Bartlow Martin, and Lee M. Mitchell, *Presidential Television* (New York: Basic Books, 1973).

Patterson, Thomas E., and Robert D. McClure, *The Unseeing Eye: The Myth of Television Power in National Elections* (New York: Putnam, 1976).

Plissner, Martin, *Control Room: How Television Calls the Shots in Presidential Elections* (New York: Free Press, 1999).

Reinsch, J. Leonard, *Getting Elected: From Radio to Roosevelt to Television and Reagan* (New York: Hippocrene, 1988).

Rosenstiel, Tom, *Strange Bedfellows: How TV and the Presidential Candidates Changed American Politics, 1992* (New York: Hyperion, 1993).

Scheuer, Jeffrey, *The Sound Bite Society: How Television Helps the Right and Hurts the Left* (1999; reprint, New York: Routledge, 2001). [Original edition entitled *The Sound Bite Society: Television and the American Mind.*]

Schram, Martin, *Great American Video Game: Presidential Politics in the Television Age* (New York: Morrow, 1987).

Schroeder, Alan, *Presidential Debates: Forty Years of High-Risk TV* (New York: Columbia University Press, 2000).

Smoller, Fredric T., *The Six O'Clock Presidency: A Theory of Presidential Press Relations in the Age of Television* (New York: Praeger, 1990).

Sterling, Christopher H., and John M. Kittross, *Stay Tuned: A Concise History of American Broadcasting,* 2nd ed. (Belmont, CA: Wadsworth Publishing, 1990).

Swerdlow, Joel L., ed., *Media Technology and the Vote: A Source Book* (Washington, DC: Annenberg Washington Program in Communications Policy Studies of Northwestern University, 1989 [dist. by Westview Press]).

Swerdlow, Joel L., ed., *Presidential Debates 1988 and Beyond* (Washington, DC: Congressional Quarterly Books, 1987 [in cooperation with the League of Women Voters]).

Tedesco, John C., Lynda Lee Kaid, and Lori Melton McKinnon, "1998 Network
    Adwatches: Policing the 1996 Primary and General Election Presidential Ads,"
    Journal of Broadcasting & Electronic Media 44 (2000).
Watson, Mary Ann, *The Expanding Vista: American Television in the Kennedy Years*
    (1990; reprint, Durham, NC: Duke University Press, 1994).
West, Darrell M., *Air Wars: Television Advertising in Election Campaigns, 1952–2004,*
    4th ed. (Washington, DC: Congressional Quarterly Press, 2005).

THE INTERNET

Media

By the People: Election 2004 (PBS): http://www.pbs.org/elections/. Includes lesson plans.
Haridakis, Paul, "Social Media and Presidential Election: Kent State Professor Examines
    Impact of YouTube, MySpace."http://www.eurekalert.org/pub_releases/2008-10/
    ksu-sm103108.ph (accessed December 2, 2008).
Mother Jones. July/August 2007 issue Politics 2.0 Smackdown. http://www.motherjones
    .com/toc/2007/07/index.html.

Books

Anderson, David M, and Michael Cornfield, eds., *The Civic Web: Online Politics and
    Democratic Values* (Lanham, MD: Rowman & Littlefield, 2003).
Davis, Richard, *The Web of Politics: The Internet's Impact on the American Political Sys-
    tem* (New York: Oxford University Press, 1999).
Davis, Richard, and Diana Owen, *New Media and American Politics* (New York: Oxford
    University Press, 1998).
Diamond, Edwin, and Robert A. Silverman, *White House to Your House: Media and Poli-
    tics in Virtual America* (Cambridge, MA: MIT Press, 1997).
Kaid, Lynda Lee, and Dianne Bystrom, eds., *The Electronic Election: Perspectives on the
    1996 Campaign Communication* (Mahwah, NJ: Erlbaum, 1998).
Margolis, Michael, *Politics as Usual: The Cyberspace "Revolution"* (Thousand Oaks,
    CA: Sage Publications, 2000).
Trippi, Joe, *The Revolution Will Not Be Televised: Democracy, the Internet, and the Over-
    throw of Everything* (New York: ReganBooks, 2004).

CONSULTANTS

Media

Ailes, Roger, with Jon Kraushar, *You Are the Message: Secrets of the Master Communica-
    tors* (New York: Doubleday, 1989).
Center for Public Integrity: Campaign Consultants: The Price of Democracy: http://
    projects.publicintegrity.org/consultants/

Books

Dulio, David A., *For Better or Worse: How Political Consultants Are Changing Elections
    in the United States* (Albany: State University of New York Press, 2004).

Institute of Politics, John F. Kennedy School of Government, Harvard University, *Campaign for President: The Managers Look at 2004* (Lanham, MD: Rowman & Littlefield, 2006).

Johnson, Dennis W., *No Place for Amateurs: How Political Consultants Are Reshaping American Democracy,* 2nd ed. (New York: Routledge, 2007).

Lathrop, Douglas A., *The Campaign Continues: How Political Consultants and Campaign Tactics Affect Public Policy* (Westport, CT: Praeger, 1992).

Sabato, Larry J., *The Rise of Political Consultants: New Ways of Winning Elections* (New York: Basic Books, 1981).

Thurber, James A., ed., *The Battle for Congress: Consultants, Candidates, and Voters* (Washington, DC: Brookings Institution Press, 2001).

Thurber, James A., and Candice J. Nelson, eds., *Campaign Warriors: The Role of Political Consultants in Elections* (Washington, DC: Brookings Institution Press, 2000).

CAMPAIGN FINANCE REFORM

Media

The American Conservative Union: http://www.conservative.org/

Brookings Institute: http://www.brookings.edu/topics/campaign-finance.aspx

Campaign Finance Information Center: www.campaignfinance.org. "Calculating influence: How it all adds up."

Center for Public Integrity: http://www.buyingofthepresident.org/. Studies the impact of money on public policy.

Center for Responsive Politics: http://www.opensecrets.org/. Nonpartisan, nonprofit research group that tracks money in politics and its effect on elections and public policy.

Common Cause: http://www.commoncause.org/site/pp.asp?c=dkLNK1MQIwG&b=186966. Publishes investigative studies on the effects of money in politics and reports on a variety of ethics and integrity-in-government issues; site offers an extensive section on campaign finance reform.

Congressional Quarterly: http://www.cqmoneyline.com/pml/home.do

Data on campaign contributions in both the presidential and the House and Senate campaigns.

Federal Election Commission: http://www.fec.gov/

Hoover Institution: http://www.campaignfinancesite.org/

Money and Politics: http://www.cato.org/researcharea.php?display=5. Cato Institute papers promoting limited government, individual liberty, free markets and peace; views extensive new regulations on campaign finance as both flawed and unconstitutional.

Pew Charitable Trusts: http://www.pewtrusts.org/our_work_detail.aspx?id=492. Supports as a signature issue nonpartisan efforts to help reform the role money plays in political campaigns; page presents numerous reports and papers on campaign finance reform.

Public Campaign: www.publiccampaign.org. Nonprofit, nonpartisan organization dedicated to dramatically reducing the role of special interest money in America's elections.

Western Knight Center for Specialized Journalism (now the Knight Digital Media Center):

The Idiot's Guide to Money in Politics (the history and context of campaign finance law and regulation): http://www.wkconline.org/index.php/seminar_showcase/cc_story/an_idiots_guide_to_money_in_politics/

Understanding the New Federal Commission Finance Laws (the impact of the Bipartisan Campaign Reform Act of 2002): http://www.wkconline.org/index.php/seminar_showcase/cc_story/so_much_for_campaign_finance_reform/

Understanding the State and Local Campaign Finance Laws (how local laws differ in various states): http://www.wkconline.org/index.php/seminar_showcase/cc_story/group_urges_standardized_reporting_requirements/

What You Are Up Against: Political Consultants Take Aim at the '04 Elections ("insider" tips from political consultants): http://www.wkconline.org/index.php/seminar_showcase/cc_story/journalists_looked_on_to_keep_campaigns_honest/

Books

Corrado, Anthony, *Campaign Finance Reform: Beyond the Basics* (New York: Century Foundation Press, 2000).

Corrado, Anthony, et al., eds., *New Campaign Finance Reform: A Sourcebook* (Washington, DC: Brookings Institution Press, 2005).

Moss, Alan L., *Selling Out America's Democracy: How Lobbyists, Special Interests, and Campaign Financing Undermine the Will of the People* (Westport, CT: Praeger, 2008).

Samples, John, *The Fallacy of Campaign Finance Reform* (Chicago: University of Chicago Press, 2006).

Urofsky, Melvin I., *Money and Free Speech: Campaign Finance Reform and the Courts* (Lawrence: University Press of Kansas, 2005).

POLITICAL INFORMATION

Annenberg Political Fact Check Sheet: http://www.factcheck.org

Commission on Presidential Debates: http://www.debates.org. Transcripts and video clips of presidential debates from 1960 to the present.

Council on Foreign Relations: U.S. Strategy and Politics: http://www.cfr.org/issue/136/us_strategy_and_politics.html

CSPAN Historic Ads and Campaign Speeches: http://www.c-span.org/classroom/govt/video.asp

DemocracyNet: http://www.dnet.org/. Elections and issues, from the League of Women Voters.

FairVote: Voting and Democracy Research Center: http://www.fairvote.org/. Promotes "equally protected right to vote in secure and fairly administered elections."

National Political Index: http://www.politicalindex.com/. Links to varied political and government sites and services.

Political Money Line: http://moneyline.cq.com/pml/home.do. From Congressional Quarterly, Federal Election Commission data.

Poynter Institute, Republican & Democratic Convention History (1856–2008): http://
      poynter.org/column.asp?id=49&aid=68171. The Poynter Institute is a school for
      journalists, future journalists, and teachers of journalism.
Project Vote Smart: http://www.vote-smart.org/. Tracks candidates, officials, and issues in
      order to empower voters.
Public Agenda: http://www.publicagenda.org/. Research on major issues presented in a
      nonpartisan manner.
U.S. Bureau of the Census, Voter and Registration Demographics: http://www.census.gov/
      population/www/socdemo/voting.html. Information on reported voting and registra-
      tion, sorted according to various demographic and socioeconomic characteristics

Index

About the Author

FRANK W. BAKER is a nationally recognized media literacy consultant and the webmaster of Media Literacy Clearinghouse, a respected media literacy resource Web site. He has worked in television news and as an administrator for instructional television and distance learning in the Orange County (Orlando), Florida, public school system. He is the author of *Coming Distractions: Questioning Movies* (2007), an introduction to media literacy for elementary school students.